D0655606

JOHN PAUL II

JOHN PAUL II

CHRONICLE *of a* REMARKABLE LIFE

FOREWORD BY FATHER MICHAEL COLLINS

A Dorling Kindersley Book

Dorling Kindersley

LONDON, NEW YORK, SYDNEY, DELHI,
PARIS, MUNICH, JOHANNESBURG

Created and produced by Catherine and Jacques Legrand,
who would like particularly to thank Yves Trestournel and Emile H. Ouaknine

© 1998 Jacques Legrand SA – Editions Chronique for the original French edition

© 2000 Dorling Kindersley, London, for the English-language edition

First published in Great Britain in 2000 by
Dorling Kindersley Limited, 9 Henrietta Street, London WC2E 8PS

2 4 6 8 10 9 7 5 3 1

All rights reserved. No part of this book may be reproduced, stored in a
retrieval system, or transmitted in any form or by any means, electronic,
mechanical, photocopying, recording or otherwise, without the prior
written permission of the copyright owner.

A CIP catalogue record for this book is available from the British Library

ISBN 0 7513 0853 6

Printed and bound by L. Rex Printing Company Limited, China

see our complete
catalogue at
www.dk.com

Contents

The model school student
1933

First pope to enter a synagogue
1986

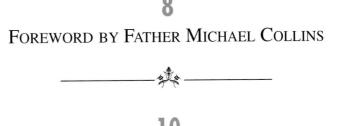

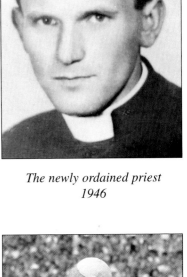

The newly ordained priest
1946

A message of hope for Poland
1979

Making his mark at Vatican II
1965

Renewing his mission at age 75
1995

Poland's youngest ever bishop
1958

Solidarity with AIDS sufferers
1987

Foreword

*O*N THE NIGHT OF HIS ELECTION *as pope in 1978 John Paul II appeared on the balcony of St Peter's Basilica to give his blessing to the vast crowd gathered in the square below. In a voice trembling with emotion, the new pope introduced himself – the first non-Italian pope since 1523 and the first ever Polish pope – as 'a man from afar'. Speaking in halting Italian, he asked his listeners to forgive him if he made mistakes 'in your – no, in* our *– language'. The crowd roared its approval.*

As a younger man Karol Wojtyla reveled in the outdoor life in his beloved Poland. His expeditions always involved not only enjoyment of the countryside but, even more importantly, his continuing quest for spiritual development.

AND SO IT WAS THAT KAROL WOJTYLA stepped onto the stage of world history to begin the longest pontificate in the 2,000-year history of the papacy. During the course of the years since that October evening the 'man from afar' has become a familiar figure, capturing the world's imagination with his mischievous smile, the dynamic energy of his personality, and his many and varied interests. Certainly no previous pope had ever been seen skiing!

Karol Wojtyla's vocation to the priesthood was forged in the horrific crucible of World War II Poland. His beloved country was invaded by Nazi Germany when Karol was just nineteen, and he witnessed the attempted annihilation of Poland's Jews, some of whom he numbered among his schoolmates and close friends. During these formative years he developed a burning respect for human rights and justice, values that he would carry into his pontificate.

After ordination he served briefly in parochial work before embarking on postgraduate studies in theology and philosophy. The academic world fascinated him, and eventually he became professor of philosophy in Lublin University. He caught the imagination of the students by organizing skiing and canoeing trips for them, joining with evident glee in cooking and the other chores of camping. When he was appointed auxiliary bishop of Cracow in 1958 at the age of thirty-eight he was the youngest bishop in the world; five years later he was named archbishop of the diocese. Pope John XXIII convened a meeting of the world's bishops that met at the Vatican between 1962 and 1963: Karol Wojtyla's enthusiastic participation in the sessions introduced him to a wider audience outside Poland. With his phenomenal capacity for hard work he was soon busy helping prepare some of the decrees of the Council. He admits how important these meetings with the world's bishops were in broadening his horizons. Meanwhile in Poland he continued to engage in the seemingly endless conflict between the Church and the country's Communist government, and frequently had cause to denounce what he saw as the curtailing of religious freedom.

Soon after his election as the 261st successor to St Peter, John Paul threw himself into a hectic whirl of visits to every part of the world, addressing his ministry not only to his fellow Catholics but to all people of good will. From the very start of his pontificate he aimed to prepare the Catholic Church to enter the third Christian millennium. His deep sense of history has led him to search for means of uniting the Christian churches by overcoming centuries of division caused by bigotry and intolerance. This same sense of history has informed his attempts at reconciliation between Catholics and Jews. He has also dedicated his energy to encouraging Catholics in Africa and Latin America.

To be a cardinal in 1970s Poland was to be at the center of unending conflict between the Church and the Communist government. Mgr Wojtyla worked closely with his primate, Stefan Wyszinski, to defend Polish religious freedom.

In May 1981, while the pope was entering St Peter's Square to meet pilgrims, he was shot by a Turkish assassin. John Paul was rushed to the hospital, where a team of doctors performed a long operation to save his life. Despite this brush with death, within a remarkably short time he had resumed his frenetic schedule both at the Vatican and abroad.

This pope has not been without his critics, especially when, by unashamedly restating the Church's traditional teaching on such subjects as contraception and abortion, he swims against the tide of modern secular culture. He has also not been afraid to denounce, as crimes against humanity, avoidable evils like famine and third-world debt. Even among his critics, however, few have doubted his extraordinary sincerity. He is above all a man of deep prayer. Each morning, after he rises he spends an hour in prayer in his chapel before celebrating Mass at 7.30, and the intensity and depth of his devotion invariably impress those who are privileged to participate with him in the liturgy. As he kneels in silence, his head buried in his hands, praying on behalf of a world so full of joy and sadness, who can imagine what thoughts pass through his mind? Often those near him hear him sigh as he continues his quiet colloquy with God.

John Paul, for all his learning and deep intelligence, delights people with his simplicity and impish sense of humor. Shortly after his election following the sudden death of John Paul I – who had been in office for only a month – he was given money by Polish-American benefactors to build a swimming pool at the papal summer residence at Castel Gandolfo. When he was criticized for accepting the gift he remarked whimsically, 'It is cheaper than another conclave'!

At the beginning of his pontificate Pope John Paul II urged all who heard him to open their hearts to Christ, the Light of the World. As this book, with its many intimate photographs, so clearly shows, John Paul has dedicated his entire life to following his own precept, faithfully and humbly walking in the path of the Gospel.

Michael Collins

Karol and Emilia Wojtyla, newly-wed, are posted to Wadowice

Wadowice, 1904
Karol Wojtyla originally wanted to be a tailor. Concerned for his future family's security, he decided to join the army four years ago. Now a non-commissioned officer with the 56th Infantry Regiment of the Austrian army, he has just been posted to Wadowice. Between 1831 and 1847, a third of the town's population died of typhoid. But, by the time of Emilia and Karol's arrival, Wadowice was undergoing full expansion, thanks to the presence of the Austrian army. A monastery of Discalced (ie barefoot) Carmelite friars (followers of the teachings of Saint John of the Cross), built in 1892, was proof of the strength of faith in this part of Poland. Karol was put in charge of administrative tasks, and as such could live outside the barracks. This came as a great blessing for Emilia, who had grown up in the midst of a noisy family of nine children, of which she was the fifth. She was grateful to get some peace, at least while preparing to start her own family.

Emilia, daughter of a saddler from Cracow, marries a military man.

Cardinal of Cracow uses political vote

Rome, August 4, 1903
Two weeks after Leo XIII's death in Rome on July 20 (born March 2, 1810), the cardinals have agreed on the name of his successor. He is Cardinal Giuseppe Sarto, the Patriarch of Venice. It was Cardinal Rampolla, secretary of the Vatican State since 1887, who had been tipped as the favorite. However, his election had been vetoed by none less than the emperor of Austria himself, Franz Jozef, who had asked Cardinal Jan Puzyna, archbishop of Cracow, to block Rampolla's appointment. The new pope, aged 68, is, unusually, from a modest background, having only managed to pursue his studies thanks to a scholarship. He is both exacting and diplomatic, and is admirably active; and he has never ceased to work toward improving the lot of the poor. He who has chosen the name of Pius X has now to face up to the challenge of dealing with the modernist crisis currently shaking the Church, as well as the general increase in anticlerical sentiment.

Edmund weeps at loss of his sister, Olga

Wadowice, Spring 1914
Eight long years after the birth of their son, Karol and Emilia Wojtyla have at last had a daughter. Emilia was keen to call her Olga, after one of her own elder sisters who had died young. But baby Olga's life, too, has been tragically brief. She died when only a few days old, carried off by an illness that no doctor had been able to diagnose, let alone find a cure for. Karol and Emilia can draw some comfort from the certainty that their little one is now in the kingdom of heaven; Edmund is too young to do other than cry.

1908: Edmund is Infantry Lieutenant Wojtyla's only son and heir.

'Poland' becomes little more than a battlefield

Poland, August 6, 1914

Polish families are being torn apart. The powers who together own Poland have just declared war on each other: on the one hand, Russia, and on the other, the German and Austro-Hungarian Empires. As a result, all young men of fighting age are being conscripted, wearing different uniforms. They will soon find themselves being ordered to shoot at their brothers and cousins, in the interests of foreigners. Russia started moving her troops westwards yesterday. Meanwhile, Grand Duke Nicholas, commander-in-chief of the czar's armies, has said that if the Poles join the Russian ranks, they will be given sovereignty of their own country once victory is achieved. Few dare believe him. In fact most Poles hold out more hope with the Austrians whose presence, to date, has been less oppressive than the Russians. Jozef Pilsudski, renowned socialist agitator and patriot, today created a Polish Legion to fight against the Russians.

The First World War cleared the countryside: Russia's scorched earth policy provoked a mass exodus in 1915.

Benedict XV is to succeed Pius X

Rome, September 3, 1914

Pope Pius X (b. June 2, 1835) died on August 20, conscious of his failure to avert war. Cardinal Giacomo della Chiesa, archbishop of Bologna, has been elected his successor on the third day of the conclave. An Italian diplomat and aristocrat, he has chosen the name of Benedict XV. The transition may prove difficult, since although Cardinal della Chiesa has instigated far-reaching reforms such as the idea of a Code of Canon Law, he is also opposed to "modernism," which he sees as "the meeting point for all heresies."

German troops take control of Warsaw

Warsaw, August 8, 1915

The czar's troops have been forced to flee in the face of the combined forces of Austria and Germany. A parade of German might today marched through the streets of Warsaw, in the wake of the Russian 10th army's departure. Russia has fallen back on all fronts. Credit must mainly go to the German general, Paul von Hindenburg who, called out of retirement at the start of the conflict, succeeded at Tannenberg in blocking the Russians in northern Poland, in August 1914. Next in Germany's sights is Lithuania.

Giacomo della Chiesa, the new Italian pope, mounts the papal throne.

Lieutenant Wojtyla (center) served with an Austrian infantry regiment.

Age 0		Age 1

Europe, January 10, 1920.
The Treaty of Versailles comes into effect.

Munich, February 24, 1920.
The German Workers' Party (DAP) is renamed the National Socialist German Workers' Party (NSDAP).

Rome, May 16, 1920.
Canonization of Joan of Arc (1412-1431), beatified in 1909.

Riga, October 6, 1920.
Signature of armistice between Poland and Russia.

Crimea, November 16, 1920.
General Wrangel orders the dissolution of the White Russian Army, marking the end of the counter-revolution in Russia.

Geneva, November 17, 1920.
The League of Nations confirms the status of Danzig as a Free City.

Tours, December 30, 1920.
Split within the *Section française de l'Internationale ouvrière* (SFIO) gives birth to the Communist party, the *Section française de l'Internationale communiste (SFIC),* in line with Moscow.

Paris, May 16, 1921.
Resumption of diplomatic relations between France and the Holy See, broken off in July 1904 due to the anti-clerical views of Emile Combes, theologian and head of government.

Moscow, May 21, 1921.
Birth of Andrei Sakharov.

Munich, July 29, 1921.
Adolf Hitler becomes president of the NSDAP.

Second son for the Wojtyla household

The child's birth was registered in the official records of the Church of Our Lady of Eternal Hope in Wadowice.

Wadowice, May 18, 1920
As the midwife opened the window, Emilia's bedroom was filled with the sound of singing: Latin canticles to the glory of the Virgin Mary rising up from the church opposite. It was time for Vespers in the month of May, the month of Our Lady. Karol Jozef was the name given to the Wojtylas' second son: Karol after his father, and Jozef because Emilia wanted him to have the name of Christ's father, and because Karol wanted to give thanks to General Jozef Pilsudski for his victory over the Reds in Kiev ten days before. That very morning in Warsaw, an immense crowd was giving the general a standing ovation, and a *Te Deum* was being celebrated in his honor in the cathedral. Although the Wojtyla apartment in Rynek Square only had three rooms including a kitchen, it was easily big enough to accommodate the four of them. Many of the town's inhabitants lived in considerably more cramped conditions. Access to the apartment was through the kitchen, luckily the warmest room to be in anyway in winter; but this inconvenience was offset by the fact that they were on the second floor of the building, overlooking an interior courtyard where neighbors could chat and children could play. In the grim post-war period this kind of solidarity was reassuring.

Emilia was 36 years old when she had Karol, younger brother to Edmund.

Young Wojtyla is welcomed into the arms of the Catholic church

Wadowice, June 20, 1920
A little more than a month after his birth, the time has come for the most recent addition to the Wojtyla family to be baptised. The status of young Karol's father as a lieutenant in the Polish army gives him the right to ask the army chaplain, Father Franciszek Zak, to perform the baptism. The ceremony took place today over the carved stone baptismal font in the Church of Our Lady in Wadowice. Both godparents have been selected from among Emilia's immediate family, and have been carefully chosen to ensure that the child benefits from a Christian upbringing even if he should be so unfortunate as to lose both his parents. Karol's godmother is Maria Anna Wiadrowska, the only one of his mother's three elder sisters still living. His godfather is Jozef Kuczmierczyk, his maternal uncle, who has been twice widowed by the deaths of Olga and Helena, the two elder sisters of Karol's mother. On the certificate of baptism, written in Latin – and no doubt in haste – one of the names is wrongly spelled: *Carolus Josephus*'s paternal grandmother is given as Anna Przeczka rather than the correct Przeczek. No matter: the main object of the ceremony – Karol receiving the Holy Spirit – has been accomplished.

The Church of Our Lady is just across the road from the Wojtyla apartment.

De Gaulle's mission comes to an end

Warsaw, January 10, 1921
Sent to Poland in April 1919, Captain de Gaulle has completed his mission there, to the general acclaim of his superiors. Despite his "rather haughty appearance," he seems to have been greatly appreciated as an "officer of the very first rank." He spent a year instructing Polish officers, and was then attached to the general staff. Although a fervent admirer of the "extraordinary" marching endurance of the Polish soldiers, he is not so complimentary about their superior officers' "lack of method," which particularly struck him on the northern front, when faced with Tukhachevsky's troops. He fears the day is not far off when "we will once again see Germans and Muscovites seeking to join forces against the Poles."

Karol at nearly one. His 14-year-old brother, Edmund, is his great hero.

Maxime Weygand to the rescue

Warsaw, July 21, 1920
After early Polish successes, Russian counterattacks – together with fears of a Communist uprising in Germany – have made the Poles desperate for outside assistance. Where better to turn than France, with whom Poland has had friendly ties since 1830? Although France has responded by sending one of her war heroes, General Maxime Weygand's entry into Warsaw today was far from glorious. A soldier of his rank can hardly be proud of heading a French delegation which must refer all important matters back to Paris for decision. Alexandre Millerand, French prime minister and foreign minister (and sole decision-maker since President Paul Deschanel's fall from a train in May) does not want to involve France directly in the struggle against the Red Army. Weygand is aware, nevertheless, that he has an important, if unofficial, role as a military adviser to the Poles. As one of Marshal Foch's main aides during the Great War he made no secret of his esteem for Pilsudski, whom he has described as a "pillar of Christian civilization in the West." His association with Foch is likely to stand Weygand in good stead.

Father Kolbe's new Catholic journal

Cracow, December 31, 1921
What a curious person Maximilian Kolbe is. His detractors call him a fanatic and consider his evangelical faith exaggerated. The Franciscan priest doesn't seem to mind. Indeed, he's just named his new monthly journal *Knight of the Immaculate*, as a sign of "total and irrevocable submission" to the Virgin Mary. The first issue is due to appear in a few days, and is expected to be a paper with a purpose, namely to spread the gospels and the cult of Mary. Father Kolbe is convinced that some time in the future we will be able to see "a statue of the Virgin looking down over Moscow from the top of the Kremlin!" The Virgin said as much in her apparition to the three young children in Fatima, and that is good enough for him.

Age 1   Age 5

Rome, January 22, 1922.
Death of Pope Benedict XV
(b. November 21, 1854).

Brussels, May 25, 1922.
Death of the Belgian
industrialist Ernest Solvay
(b. April 16, 1838).

Warsaw, December 16, 1922.
Gabriel Narutowicz, president
of the Polish Republic, is
assassinated one week after
taking office.

Moscow, December 30, 1922.
Creation of the Union of Soviet
Socialist Republics (USSR).

Kornik, July 2, 1923.
Birth of Wislawa Szymborska.

Kurow, July 6, 1923.
Birth of Wojciech Jaruzelski.

Gorky, January 21, 1924.
Death of Lenin (b. April 22,
1870).

Wadowice, June 1924. Edmund
Wojtyla passes his school
leaving examinations.

Belgium, July 20, 1924.
Abbot Joseph Cardijn founds
the Young Christian Workers.

Stockholm, November 13, 1924.
The Nobel prize for literature is
awarded to the Polish writer
Wladyslaw Stanislaw Reymont.

Rome, January 3, 1925.
Pope Pius XI inaugurates the
Holy Year.

Rome, March 15, 1925.
Start of the beatification
proceedings of Frédéric
Ozanam (1813-1853), founder,
at the age of 21, of the
Society of St. Vincent
de Paul.

Warsaw, December 5, 1925.
Death of Wladyslaw Stanislaw
Reymont (b. May 7, 1867).

Cardinal Achille Ratti to be new pope under name of Pius XI

Rome, February 6, 1922
At half past twelve on Friday, the first black smoke was sighted, to announce the failure of the first round of papal elections. This morning at 11.42 precisely, white smoke was seen, this time to signal the successful election of Cardinal Achille Ratti as the new pope. At 64, he is not the youngest of the cardinals, but he is their newest member, having only joined their ranks last June, when Pope Benedict XV made him archbishop of Milan. Despite total secrecy, there is little doubt that Cardinal Edmund Dalbor, primate of the Polish church, voted in favor of the man who was the pope's representative in Poland in difficult times, when the Red Army was poised to take Warsaw. It is also known that the German cardinals did not vote for him. Mgr. Ratti, henceforth known as Pius XI, grew up in a middle-class Milanese family. He is a man of great culture: a former professor of Hebrew, he was in charge of the Ambrosiana Library and curator of the Vatican Library. But his great passion is mountain climbing, about which he wrote in 1890 in his work *On Monte Rosa*. No sooner was he elected than Pope Pius XI appeared on the balcony of St. Peter's to give his blessing – a highly political gesture, indicating that it was time to begin discussions with Italy. Not since the fall of Rome in 1870 has any pontiff done this.

The new pope was the apostolic nuncio to Poland from 1919 to 1921.

Jozef Pilsudski opts for resignation

Warsaw, December 9, 1922
Marshal Pilsudski has had enough of Polish politics. Named head of State by the Council of Regency in 1918, he was elected president of the Republic by the Diet in 1919. Today he stood down in favor of one of his ex-ministers, the scholarly, Swiss-educated Gabriel Narutowicz. Even as a national hero, Pilsudski never sought the presidency, claiming to be out of sympathy with the direction in which Polish politics was moving. While complaining of being held back by what he described as his limited presidential powers, he nonetheless failed to convey his conviction of the need for reform.

Karol loses his grandfather Maciej

Lipnik, September 23, 1923
Maciej Wojtyla died today, aged 71. His funeral is fixed for next Tuesday, when he will be buried alongside his second wife, Maria Zalewska, who died in 1917, and by whom he had one daughter, Stefania Adelayda. It was by his first marriage, to Anna Przeczek, that he was related to Karol. He was the only grandparent the child ever knew, as his three other grandparents all died before his birth. Sadly, Karol will never be able to commemorate Maciej's birthday with any certainty, as the old man himself was not sure whether he was born on January 1 or February 1, 1852!

Concordat signed with Polish state

Rome, February 10, 1925
Pius XI and President Stanislaw Wojciechowski have found some common ground, no doubt helped by the pope's years in Poland, as papal representative and then papal nuncio. The new Polish republic, which owes much to the church for keeping alive national fervor, has agreed to make religious instruction obligatory in schools. For their part, the clergy have undertaken not to oppose the regime, and even to pray for it. The pope must restructure the clerical hierarchy in Poland, subject to frontier changes. It is no secret that Cracow's bishop will be her next archbishop.

Holy Year honors for French

French priest chosen for canonization

Rome, May 1925

By a strange twist of fate, Jean-Marie Vianney, the country priest who was turned down by the Lyon seminary on grounds of unsuitability, has just been canonized. Born in Dardilly, near Lyon, in 1786, the man whom the world knows as the priest of Ars, grew up in the wake of the French Revolution, scarcely an easy time for entering the priesthood. His faith was stronger than him, and at the age of 30 he became assistant to Father Balley at Ecully and then, in 1817, priest of Ars-sur-Formans, a small village in the department of Ain. He spent the rest of his life there, trying to rekindle the faith of his parishioners, whose souls had been lost to the Cult of Reason. By the time of his death in 1859, his church had been a place of pilgrimage for many years. In 1845 alone, 45,000 visitors were recorded. People flocked to see the exemplary priest who was said to work miracles, and whose reassuring words detained him at the confessional box for up to twenty hours a day! He was single-handedly responsible for the revival of the cult of Saint Philomena. Revered as a saint within his lifetime, his recent canonization is timely.

Sister Theresa is made a saint, twenty-eight years after her premature death at the Carmelite convent in Lisieux.

Theresa of Lisieux is made a saint

Rome, May 23, 1925

Not since 1870 has St. Peter's seen so splendid a spectacle. Over half a million people flocked to fill the square in front of the basilica, backing right up the Quirinale and the Pincio, to see the magnificent sight of St. Peter's illuminated by hundreds of flaming torches. Not even the canonization of Joan of Arc saw such a display. It is the first time the pope has used amplification: modern contrivances called megaphones projected his voice out from the altar, pronouncing the new saint's name. This ceremony is undoubtedly the most beautiful way in which the Church could have paid tribute to this most humble of people. Thérèse Martin entered the order of the Carmelites at the age of 15, giving up her name to become Sister Theresa of the Infant Jesus and the Holy Face. If it had not been for her fight against tuberculosis, which led to her premature death in 1897, age 24, nothing would have set her apart from her Carmelite sisters. Her illness and suffering made her doubt her own beliefs and better understand the doubt that racks certain souls. It ultimately strengthened her own faith and led to her writing *The Story of a Soul*, at the request of the mother superior of the convent, who was none other than her sister. Her book describes the "little way" she chose to follow, full of humility and submission, which led to her sainthood.

Bernadette Soubirous is beatified in Rome

Rome, June 14, 1925

"Blessed are the poor in spirit for theirs is the kingdom of heaven." Thus spoke the Lord. The beatification of poor Bernadette Soubirous (1844-1879), so maligned during her own lifetime, proves the importance the Church accords to grace and visions. Bernadette was only fourteen when "somebody" appeared to her on February 11, 1858, at Massabielle, near the Gave de Pau in Lourdes. Bernadette said that it was a "beautiful lady" who asked her to come near. The miller's daughter was too frightened to obey her. However, at the lady's request, Bernadette returned to the place seventeen times. On February 25, following the lady's instructions, she swallowed some mud from the cave where she had had her vision. The next day there was a natural spring in place of the mud. On March 2, Bernadette went to see the priest and told him, in Béarnais, that this "aquero" wished a chapel to be built there and that it should be a place of pilgrimage. Unsurprisingly, the priest did not believe Bernadette and refused her request. It was not until March 25 that Bernadette asked the lady her name. She replied: "I am the Immaculate Conception." It was only four years previously that this dogma of the Immaculate Conception had been defined. There was no way that an uneducated girl like Bernadette could have known about it.

Brussels, January 23.
Death of Cardinal Désiré Mercier (born November 22, 1851), symbol of the Belgian Resistance during the First World War, and architect of the reconciliation between Catholics and Anglicans.

Brazil, February 2.
Recovery of Fernando Luis Benedicto Ottoni, a baby afflicted with a seemingly incurable kind of diphtheria. He had been commended in prayer to Frédéric Ozanam.

Suwalki, March 6.
Birth of Andrzej Wajda.

Poland, June 2.
Ignacy Moscicki becomes president of the Republic, but most powers remain with Marshal Pilsudski, officially the minister for military affairs and head of the armed forces.

Paris, September 17.
Birth of Aaron Lustiger. His family were recently naturalised French citizens, of Polish origin and of Jewish faith, and he was named in memory of his maternal grandmother, a rabbi.

Rome, November 13.
Publication of Pope Pius XI's *Letter to Cardinal Bertram,* in which he outlined the objectives of the secular branches of *Action Catholique.*

Rome, December 29.
Publication of the Decree of the Holy Office, condemning Charles Maurras' movement *Action Française,* and inscribing its journal in the Index of forbidden books.

The Good Friday processions make a deep impression on Karol

Kalwaria Zebrzydowska, Easter
Karol had never seen anything like it before. Thousands of penitents reliving Christ's Passion with an exuberance and fervor welling up from the innermost soul of Poland. The site was just over nine miles from Wadowice and had been a place of pilgrimage since about 1600, when the governor of Cracow province, Mikolaj Zebrzydowski, had had a chapel built there, in honor of its uncanny resemblance to Jerusalem. Karol's father was keen for his son to hear the Good Friday Stations of the Cross in this place, where Christ's suffering was not only celebrated but relived as if it were happening then and there. Karol saw just how vibrantly living the Christian faith could be.

The sanctuary of Kalwaria Zebrzydowska where Karol celebrated Easter.

Marshal Jozef Pilsudski's coup d'état

Warsaw, May 14
After two days of constant fighting in the capital, the death toll now stands at nearly four hundred. The armed forces loyal to President Stanislaw Wojciechowski and his recently elected prime minister, Wincenty Witos, were no match for the fourteen regiments who supported Jozef Pilsudski. The main political parties on the left, and a large proportion of the population, worn down by the chronic political instability, have come out in support of Pilsudski's coup d'état. The "hero of the Vistula," now that he is back in power, has expressed his clear determination to "clean up" his country. Neither the creation of the zloty, index-linked to the Swiss franc, which replaced the Polish mark in April 1924, nor the founding of the Bank of Poland, have sufficed to stem rising inflation and ever-growing unemployment. The real catalyst, however, for the coup d'état was the government's failure to bring about necessary agrarian reforms. The Diet was left with little option but to resign.

Strategic buildings throughout Warsaw are seized by forces supporting Marshal Pilsudski's coup d'état.

Society of Mary recognized

Cracow, June 20

Monsignor Adam Stefan Sapieha, archbishop of Cracow, recently welcomed the Society of Mary into the Catholic Church. It was Father Kazimierz Praznowski, the catechism teacher at the Marcin Wadowita High School in Wadowice, who set up the organization last year, placing it under the patronage of the Virgin Mary, mother of Poland, and Saint Stanislas, the country's patron saint. The Society aims to help deepen the religious knowledge of its members, to strengthen their character, and to encourage them to become involved with humanitarian activities. Its very name speaks of solidarity.

Daily dose of religious education

Wadowice, Christmas

Father Franciszek Baranczyk, the catechism teacher at the Marcin Wadowita School, is most pleased with Karol's religious education. At six years old, his knowledge already outstrips most of his seniors, and his observance of the faith is intense. From a very early age, Karol has seen his family dipping their fingers in the holy-water stoop by the front door and making the sign of the cross every time they go in or out of their apartment. There is also a *prie-dieu* in the living room to encourage prayer. Every morning before going to school, Karol also attends mass, except on those rare occasions when he is late. This time of contemplation is not too onerous, as his school is just behind the church, which is itself just opposite his parents' apartment. Every evening after school, his mother reads passages from the Holy Scriptures to him. They study Jesus' life, so full of vivid images for a small child. Karol has understood that the life of a Catholic is primarily founded on principles which need to be respected. Looked at from this point of view, freedom is not the right to do whatever one wants, but rather the opportunity given to man by God to do God's will. Karol retained an understanding of the need for humility from this most important lesson.

Karol has Jozef Koman as his teacher for his first school term

Karol's first school was named after a local boy who prospered in Rome.

Wadowice, September 15

The start of the school term has been delayed by an epidemic of scarlet fever. The headmaster of the Marcin Wadowita School, where Karol is enrolled, along with 67 other boys of his age, took the decision to start the term late rather than risk the outbreak spreading. His teacher will be Jozef Koman, and his role model is the successful and generous Marcin Wadowita, for whom the school is named. Born in Wadowice in 1567, Wadowita left to study in Cracow and then Rome, where he acquired a doctorate in theology. A scholar, whose advice was often sought by popes, he bequeathed his fortune to his home town, prior to his death, to build a hospital and a school there.

Nicknamed Lolek by his mother, Karol had an excellent relationship with his father, proud to have a model child.

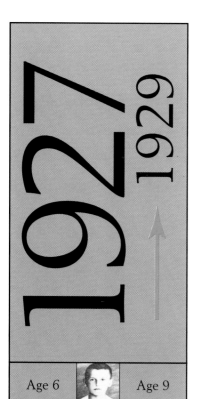

Age 6 | Age 9

Marktl, April 16, 1927.
Birth of Joseph Ratzinger in Bavaria.

Plock, April 18, 1927.
Birth of Tadeusz Mazowiecki.

Moscow, November 15, 1927.
Stalin expels Leon Trotsky and Grigori Zinoviev from the Communist party.

France, March 25, 1928.
The ban on *Action Française* comes into operation.

Vatican, May 14, 1929.
Pius XI replies to those who reproached him for dealing with Mussolini: "When it is a question of saving souls, we summon up the courage to deal with the devil himself."

Vatican, June 7, 1929.
Pius XI proclaims the fundamental law (Constitution) of the Vatican.

Fatima, June 13, 1929.
The Virgin appears in a vision before Sister Lucia at the Carmelite convent. She tells her the time has come to consecrate Russia to her Immaculate Heart.

Lille, September 21, 1929.
Marcel Lefebvre is ordained priest.

New York, October 24, 1929.
"Black Thursday" at the Wall Street Stock Exchange. The crash bankrupts thousands of investors.

Inowroclaw, December 18, 1929.
Birth of Jozef Glemp.

Vatican, December 31, 1929.
Publication of Pius XI's encyclical *Divini Illius Magistri*, reminding families of their duty to teach the Christian faith.

Karol's father takes retirement

Wadowice, 1927
At 48, Karol Wojtyla has decided to take early retirement in order to dedicate himself to his two major interests: his younger son, Karol, and the history of Poland. Having started his military career wearing an Austrian uniform, he is proud to have ended it as a captain in the Polish army. His superiors accepted with reluctance his request to retire: they will undoubtedly miss his "highly developed sense of duty," his "thoroughness" for whatever administrative task he was given, and his ability to "type at great speed." He was decorated for the part he played in the Polish Legion during the First World War.

On June 26, 1927, the ashes of the poet Juliusz Slowacki arrived back in Warsaw, on board the steamship *Mickiewicz*, named in memory of Poland's great poet. Slowacki was originally buried in the Montmartre cemetery in Paris, but will now find peace in Wawel Castle in Cracow.

Karol's first school report shows him to be an excellent pupil.

Nine 'very goods' on school report

Wadowice, June 1927
Karol is a remarkable little boy, with a rare sense of perseverence for a seven year old. At the end of his first scholastic year he has received very good mentions in every subject. "A healthy mind in a healthy body" is the common verdict. He even did well in mathematics and Polish, the two subjects where he had no more than a "good" mention at the start of the year. It is the same for religious instruction, drawing, singing, and gymnastics. With no apparent weak point, he is following in the footsteps of his brother Edmund, a top athlete with a sharp intellect.

Jurek and Lolek, inseparable friends

Wadowice, February 1928
If Karol is Lolek, Jerzy is Jurek. The first is Catholic, the second Jewish; indeed he is the son of Wilhelm Kluger, the influential lawyer and president of the town's Jewish community. The two children are the best of friends. This winter the frozen lakes have provided ideal hockey pitches for them. In spring, they will splash about in the Skawa, a tributary of the Vistula, which flows through the surrounding area and is neither deep nor dangerous.

Vatican City State comes into being

Church condemns anti-Semitism

Rome, March 25, 1928
Chosen race or destroyers of the faith? Pius XI made his view quite clear in a decree issued by the Holy Office concerned with the doctrine of the faith. In it, he tells Catholics that anti-Semitism is not compatible with the teachings of the Church. The text is totally unambiguous: "Because he deeply disapproves of all hatred and ill-feeling between peoples, his Holiness wholeheartedly condemns all hatred of God's former chosen people, that hatred most commonly described as anti-Semitism." In Europe today, where hostility towards the Jewish people is on the increase, one wonders if the pope's voice will be heard.

Escriva de Balaguer founds Opus Dei

Madrid, October 2, 1928
Josemaria Escriva de Balaguer is a fervent believer in the mysteries of grace. Which is just as well since the young priest was spoken to today by God. He was meditating in the home of the Society of St. Vincent de Paul, in Garcia de Paredes Street, when God told him he had been chosen to undertake His work. Hence the name he has chosen for his organization: Opus Dei (Work of God), which must exist for "as long as there is man on earth." The aim of this organization is to bring together lay Christians to help them to lead a more saintly existence through their everyday actions: in their work, their family or wherever they may be. Although he is only 26 now, Father Josemaria was barely 16 when he became aware of his vocation. One bitterly cold winter evening, upon seeing the footsteps of a Discalced Carmelite friar in the snow, he realized the degree of sacrifice required in the total giving of oneself to God. An indefatigable worker, Father Josemaria nearly trained as an architect, but turned his attention to law instead. All those dreams of building will now have to be focused in another direction. The Lord chose to enlighten Father Josemaria today, on the feast of the Guardian Angels. May it be a good omen.

Mussolini and Cardinal Gasparri (center) after signing the accord that reconciled the Church and the Italian State.

On ceremonial occasions, the pope is still carried on the sedia gestatoria.

Rome, February 11, 1929
At midday today, the Vatican City State came into being, over a hundred acres in size. The accord was signed in the Lateran Palace by Benito Mussolini, head of the Italian government, and Cardinal Gasparri, secretary of the Vatican State, and brings to an end the long-running conflict which dates back to the capture of Rome in 1870, and the annexation of the Papal States by the Kingdom of Italy. Both a treaty and a concordat were signed. The first, and most important, states that "the Vatican City shall be accepted [by Italy] as neutral and inviolable territory, under all circumstances." All of the Holy See's property is recognized, as is its total sovereignty over all its possessions. Apart from the Vatican itself, the new state is now the proprietor of twelve other buildings in Rome, as well as the Palace of Castel Gandolfo. Financial compensation has also been granted. For his part, the pope agrees to recognize the existence of the Kingdom of Italy with Rome as its capital, on the understanding that Catholicism is the sole state religion. The concordat goes on to state that religious education shall become obligatory for all Italian children. The Duce has nonetheless retained a right of veto over the nomination of Italian bishops by the pope.

Karol's mother, Emilia, dies of kidney disease

Wadowice, April 13, 1929
Emilia Wojtyla finally succumbed to the kidney disease which had haunted her since her childhood. Karol had just returned from school and was looking forward to seeing his parents, when Zofia Bernhardt, a neighbor and teacher in his school, stopped him in the courtyard and told him the dreadful news of his mother's death. She had died that afternoon, while being taken to hospital. At times, Emilia had been forced to retire to bed for weeks on end, where she refused to allow Karol to see her, for fear that she could not hide her pain. She had been suffering increasingly from dizzy spells, often without warning, which made dissimulation difficult. She had become noticeably weaker, avoiding climbing the stairs to their apartment any more than necessary. Her morale was also low, and she had never managed to get over the loss of her daughter Olga. Her sole comfort was the Catholic faith, and the assurance that both her sons abided by its teachings. Thanks to his mother Karol had learned to make the sign of the cross and had read whole passages from the Bible, for she loved to sit and read to him. As a baby she had called him Lolus, a diminutive of Carolus, and then as he grew older, she had referred to him as Lolek. Ever calm and gentle, she sometimes appeared distant, but never tired of praising her children. Her dearest wish was for Edmund to become a doctor –which he might well do by next year if he gets his diploma – and for Karol to dedicate his life to God, either becoming a priest or taking orders as a monk. After receiving extreme unction Emilia passed away, at peace with herself. She was 45 years of age (born March 26, 1884).

Edmund, Emilia's elder son, had always tried to please his mother. Sadly, she did not live to see him become a doctor.

Pilgrimage to the Virgin's sanctuary

Kalwaria Zebr., April 17, 1929
A funeral service was held yesterday for the repose of Emilia's soul, in the nearby Church of Our Lady in Wadowice. After the burial, Karol, Edmund and their father all went to the sanctuary of Our Lady in order to commend their beloved one's soul to the Holy Virgin. They knelt and prayed in front of the image of the Virgin and child for some while. The sanctuary has been venerated by Polish Catholics since 1641, when the Virgin was said to have shed tears. Other miracles had taken place, which scientists had failed to explain. United in their thoughts, all three prayed to the Mother of God to give them comfort and strength in this their hour of need.

She wanted him to be top of the class

Wadowice, June 1929
Karol has only missed twenty-four lessons throughout the entire school year. It would appear that the death of his mother has made him even more diligent and hard-working, if such a thing were possible. He has been rewarded with coming top of the class, ahead of all the other 67 boys who have just finished their third year at the Marcin Wadowita Primary School. His marks are very good in every subject. Next year he should have Jozef Koman as his teacher again – he was taught by him in his first year. It is Koman who is tipped to succeed the man who was headmaster for the previous seventeen years, Kazimierz Romanski, who died in April.

May 25, 1929: Karol Wojtyla takes his First Communion in Wadowice, without his mother. Just previously, he had been given zero in his catechism test; he was the only one who had not cheated. "Don't worry, it's not as if you wanted to be pope," a classmate said to comfort the tearful Karol.

Vatican, February 8.
Outright condemnation by Pius XI of the persecution of Christians in the USSR.

Vatican, February.
Cardinal Eugenio Pacelli is named secretary of State for the Vatican.

Wadowice, June 30.
Karol Wojtyla is in church, when his friend Jerzy Kluger arrives with the good news that they have got into high school. This intrusion by the son of the head of the town's Jewish community upset some parishioners.

Mainz, June 30.
Departure of the last of the French troops occupying the Rhineland, five years prior to the date fixed by the Treaty of Versailles.

Lower Silesia, July 10.
A firedamp explosion in a mine in Neurode, near Breslau, kills 162 people.

Rome, August 2.
Signature of an accord between the Vatican and the Italian State, allowing the Vatican to print its own money.

Germany, September 14.
The National-Socialists win 18.3% of the vote in the parliamentary elections, increasing their deputies from 12 to 107.

China, October 24.
President Chiang Kai-shek's conversion to Christianity.

Vatican, December 31.
Publication of *Casti Connubii*, Pius XI's encyclical, reminding married couples of their sacred duties and of the permanence of their vows.

Karol finishes with primary school

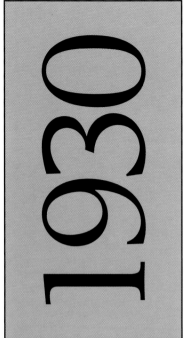

This last class photo at Karol's primary school was taken upon return from an outing to the salt mine at Wieliczka. Karol's father (right of center) accompanied the children on their expedition, now he has plenty of time on his hands.

A sporty class representative

Wadowice, May 18
Only a few more weeks and Karol will have finished primary school. His classmates have chosen him to be their class representative because of his maturity, his kindness and his devotion. His duty is to act as their spokesman before Jozef Koman, the director, as well as with the teachers such as Marian Zmuda, Zofia Bernhardt and Jan Skopinski, not forgetting their catechism teacher, Father Jan Pawela – Father John Paul. Today is Karol's tenth birthday, and as usual on a Sunday, he is out playing sport with his friends. His father has asked him to take great care, for it is not so long since that dreadful Sunday when Karol returned with his face covered in blood, having been wounded in a game of hockey. His fellow players, including Jurek, had been extremely worried about him. Luckily, the wound looked worse than the actual damage, which only affected Karol's eyebrow.

Lolek to follow his brother's footsteps

Wadowice, June 27
For the past two days Lolek has been studying hard in order to be able to pursue his secondary studies. His previous four years of excellent reports do not grant him automatic entry to high school: he has to pass an entrance exam. If successful, he will go to the state high school in September. Even if his father could afford it, he would not wish his son to go to one of the religious schools in Wadowice. Karol will follow the same route as his brother Edmund, who has just finished his medical studies at Cracow, and is now a qualified doctor. In fact Karol and his father attended Edmund's graduation ceremony a few days ago at Jagiellonian University in Cracow. Edmund, who will be 24 in August, has recently obtained a post at the children's hospital in Cracow. If he shows the same kindness to his young patients as toward his younger brother, he will undoubtedly be a great success.

Emilia's absence is still sorely felt

Wadowice, Summer
Karol's father is still finding it hard to cope with the loss of his wife. His hair has turned white and his fervor has gone. Sometimes when Karol wakes at night he finds his father on his knees, absorbed in prayer. A life of constant prayer seems to be the only way in which Karol's father can cope with the void left by his wife's death. Karol himself refers to their current set-up as "a sort of domestic seminary." He no longer gets up to pranks in the way that had once so delighted both his parents. He feels it is out of place in their rather too austere existence. From time to time, nonetheless, cries of joy are still heard in the Wojtyla apartment. The neighbors smile knowingly: the Captain, as he is still referred to in spite of his retirement, and his son are playing their special game of football with a rag ball. There is no need to go outside, as their apartment, with one room leading off the next, makes a perfect football pitch.

Tough regime at home and school

Wadowice, September

Karol Wojtyla has started at high school. The only continuity with his previous school is the actual name of its benefactor, Marcin Wadowita, whose statue is given pride of place above the entrance in Mickiewicz Street. Like all his other 49 new classmates, Karol has to wear a school uniform: dark blue, with his school number on it, 374. It is obligatory to wear it at all times, both within and without the school walls. Even though Karol is not a boarder, he is not allowed to walk about in the town by himself after 9 at night, in the summer, and 8 in the winter. This quasi-military rule is a legacy from the time of the Austrian occupation, and applies for all eight years of his time here. During this first year Karol's studies include several new subjects, some of which he will later be allowed to drop, with permission from his main teacher, Adam Romanowski. In Wadowice, the high school is not mixed; the girls have a separate high school not far away. While some of his classmates find acceptance of these constraints difficult, Karol does not. But then his father already imposes a very rigorous routine on him at home. Karol is woken at 6 o'clock every morning by his father, who has retained his military habit of rising early. He quickly washes, in cold water, and has breakfast, and then goes to mass. Then it is straight to school, where Karol sees the Latin motto, taken from Tibullus, which he knows by heart: "That which is pure pleases the gods: he who comes here, may his dress be clean and his hands spotless, in order to draw water from the spring." Pagan verses perfectly integrated by Catholicism. Once his classes have finished early in the afternoon, Karol is free to relax. He is often found playing football against the walls of the Church of Our Lady, much to the annoyance of Father Zacher. But all is usually forgiven at the end of each day, when Karol goes to mass again. He then goes home to do his homework, with his attentive father ready to help him if need be. After dinner, Karol and his father often go for a stroll, hand in hand, Karol always looking smart in his school uniform.

After last year's crisis, Poland is sinking ever-deeper into misery. Begging is common among the unemployed, whose numbers are continuing to rise despite Marshal Jozef Pilsudski's efforts to set his country back on course.

Caucasus, March 2, 1931.
Birth of Mikhail Gorbachev.

Spain, April 14, 1931.
The Republic is proclaimed.

Madrid, May 10, 1931.
Anticlerical riots. Several religious buildings are burned down. Cardinal Pedro Segura, primate of Spain, is forced to seek refuge in France.

Vatican, May 15, 1931.
40 years after the encyclical *Rerum Novarum*, Pius XI publishes his encyclical *Quadragesimo Anno* which recommends "restoring social order" by means of "just distribution," and calls upon the laity to carry out the social doctrine of the Church.

Vatican, June 29, 1931.
Pius XI publishes the encyclical *Non Abbiamo Bisogno*, denouncing the "pagan idolization of the state" that constitutes Fascism.

Moscow, December 5, 1931.
The Church of the Redemption is blown up to build a Soviet palace.

Spain, January 23, 1932.
The government dissolves the Society of Jesus.

Vatican, February 11, 1932.
Mussolini has an audience with Pius XI.

Germany, July 31, 1932.
The National Socialists come top in the parliamentary elections, with 37.4% of the vote.

Mexico, October 6, 1932.
After Pius XI's encyclical condemning the anti-Catholic scheming by the Mexican government, the papal legate is expelled.

Karol takes his new role as a choirboy extremely seriously

Father Kazimierz Figlewicz can now count on the help of a new acolyte during mass: Karol, seen here on his right.

Wadowice, 1931
Karol looks like the very image of piety, clad in his red vestment and white surplice, with short hair and fixed gaze, totally wrapped up in his task. Father Edward Zacher can only be thankful for this new recruit that Father Figlewicz has sent him. It is not unusual for Karol Wojtyla to serve at mass several times a day. His favorite place is off to one side of the church, the chapel dedicated to Our Lady of Everlasting Help. He feels particularly comfortable there. The celebration of mass, which for many children is long and repetitive is, on the contrary, a source of great joy for Karol. He has discovered the nature of holiness and he fully intends to explore its mysteries more deeply.

Father Figlewicz is his spiritual guide

Wadowice, 1931
Whenever Karol mentions Father Figlewicz, he refers to him as "my confessor and my spiritual leader." Father Kazimierz Figlewicz is in charge of religious instruction at the town's high school, and is also the assistant parish priest, under Father Zacher. Although Karol only met him last September, he instantly felt an affinity for this man who could easily have been his brother. For his part, the young priest immediately noticed the "shadow of an early sadness" hovering over Karol – no doubt that of the loss of his mother, which he never referred to. They spend hours together discussing the meaning of life and God's reason for imposing his ordeals.

Karol goes to monastery to pray

Wadowice, 1931
The Carmelite monastery which overlooks the town from its wooded heights was only built at the end of the last century. This was largely thanks to Raphael Kalinowski, an ex-army officer, who decided to re-establish the Order of Saint John of the Cross in Poland. At first, Father Jozef Prus, the abbot, was rather surprised to find such a young boy praying all alone in the chapel. Then he got used to it. Karol always prayed in the same spot, in front of the image of the Virgin. One day, Father Prus left a scapular for Karol – an exact replica, in miniature, of the cowl worn by monks. Karol tied it around his neck and from then on the holy garment never left his body.

Lolek and Jurek raid the orchard

Wadowice, 1931
The two inseparable schoolmates are forever plotting what they grandly call their "big expeditions." These usually turn out to be stealthy visits to the large garden of Jurek's grandmother, Madame Huppert. For her part, she pretends not to see them, while they devour as much fruit as possible from her orchard – apples, cherries, and strawberries. Sometimes the little scoundrels come back home with such stomach aches that one wonders how they manage to explain them away at dinner time ... Lolek is always the one to put an end to their adventures. He invariably announces "it's time to study," and off they go, for Jerzy knows it is pointless to argue.

Marconi meets Pius XI for the inauguration of Radio Vatican

The Vatican, February 12, 1931
For those who happen to tune into it by chance, there will be no mistaking Radio Vatican, for its theme music is none other than the early Christian canticle "Christus vincit, Christus regnat, Christus imperat." The new radio station will transmit its programs in as many languages as possible. Its creation is in large part due to Pope Pius XI's desire to make maximum use of the most modern means of communication available, and in particular to use the technical knowledge of one man, Guglielmo Marconi, the inventor of the wireless. Having been rejected as a madman in Italy, Marconi had been forced to turn to England for support in completing his research, for which he was given the Nobel prize for physics, in 1909. This joint venture is proof that progress is not the enemy of faith.

Guglielmo Marconi (right) being presented to Pius XI and Cardinal Pacelli.

Soviet-Polish pact of friendship

Poland, January 25, 1932
Poland and the USSR promise not to fight one another. That is the essence of the pact which has just been signed by both countries. Representing the Soviet camp was Vyacheslav Molotov, chairman of the Council of People's Commissars, and on the Polish side was August Zaleski, minister of foreign affairs, and his deputy, Jozef Beck. Former head of Cabinet under Jozef Pilsudski, Jozef Beck is forging himself a name as Poland's leading peacemaker. Much still remains to be done however in this domain. Relations with both Czechoslovakia and Lithuania are still strained, and indeed the USSR's acceptance of this accord is purely self-serving. It will give Stalin more time to be able to establish his new regime.

Edmund dies suddenly from scarlet fever

Bielsko-Biala, December 5, 1932
Aged 26, the young and brilliant Doctor Edmund Wojtyla's future seemed assured. He was one of the most respected practitioners at the Bielsko-Biala hospital. But in just four short days, he was carried away by scarlet fever – four days of pain and suffering. What had he done to deserve such a fate? His only fault had been to try so hard to save a young woman already suffering from the disease, that he ended up catching it himself and then dying from pulmonary complications. Karol is completely devastated by his brother's death (b. August 27, 1906), even more than he was by his mother's. In both cases, to his eternal regret, he had not been able to share their last moments with them. Mundek, as Edmund was called by his close family and friends, was Karol's icon of success. Karol had never been as happy as the day he attended his brother's degree ceremony at the Jagiellonian University in Cracow with his father. That was barely two years ago. As for their poor father, he is overwhelmed by this tragic turn of events. Karol is now the only person left to him.

A chest expert himself, Edmund died of lung complications.

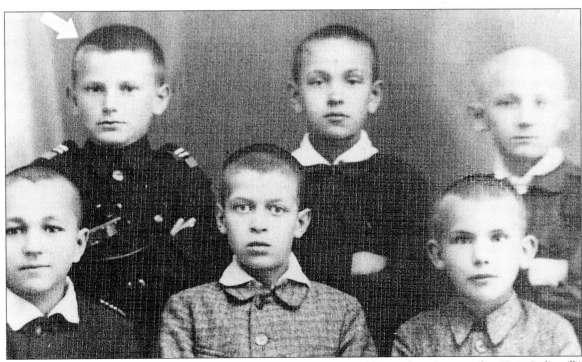
Lolek was grief-stricken by his brother's death but nonetheless told a neighbor, Helena Szczepanska, "It is God's will".

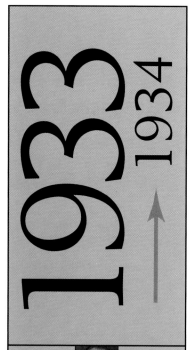

| Age 12 | | Age 14 |

Berlin, January 30, 1933.
Adolf Hitler becomes chancellor of Germany.

Wadowice, June 14, 1933.
Karol Wojtyla completes his third year at high school, with particularly brilliant results, as witnessed by the *satisfecit* written in his school report by his Polish teacher, Bronislaw Babinski.

Vatican, July 9, 1933.
Signature of a concordat with Germany.

Wadowice, September 1933.
Karol Wojtyla starts to learn Latin.

Cologne, October 13, 1933.
Edith Stein joins the Carmelite Order.

Vatican, December 8, 1933.
Canonization of Bernadette Soubirous.

Moscow, January 26, 1934.
The XVII Congress of the Communist party endorses the putting into place of the 2nd Five-Year Plan, recommending the eradication of all religion.

Europe, January 26, 1934.
Signature of a treaty of nonaggression between Poland and Germany, valid for six years.

Warsaw, June 9, 1934.
Poland recognizes the USSR. The two countries exchange ambassadors.

Sallanches, France, July 4, 1934.
Death of the French scientist of Polish origin, Marie Curie, née Sklodowska (born November 7, 1867), Nobel prizewinner for physics (1903) and chemistry (1911).

Karol longs to be the next Columbus

Wadowice, March 15, 1933
Today it is 440 years to the day since Christopher Columbus returned triumphantly to the port of Palos, on the southeast coast of Spain, from where he had set sail the previous August. Meanwhile, he had discovered what was to become America. "The cannon was fired, the church bells were rung, to welcome him back." Two years later, the Holy See divided up these colonies between Spain and Portugal, who thereby promised to convert the idol-worshipping peoples living there. Karol is fascinated by this tale, as he has never yet been beyond the boundaries of his native region. He studies the names of all these faraway countries in his atlas, not to mention the names of their so-called primitive inhabitants. He even tells a friend "later on, I will travel around the world." And as if to check the truth of what he is reading, he asks: "Does India really exist?" Fact and fiction are mixed up in his head in a wonderful world of make-believe, fuelled by reading Jules Verne.

Lolek forms band of abstainers

Wadowice, June 1933
Another school year is coming to an end for Karol, with excellent marks as usual. However, it has also seen the emergence of young Lolek as a leader. During the course of the year, his class seems to have divided into two distinct camps. One side, led by the cheerful Piotrowski twins, have formed a Revellers' Club which, as the name suggests, groups together those whose primary aim is to turn every possible occasion into a party. The other side, led by Karol, has pitched itself in total opposition, forming a Circle of Abstinents. They have sworn abstinence from smoking and drinking alcohol. While not against parties, which they are not at all averse to organizing themselves, they consider that neither tobacco nor alcohol increases their enjoyment of just simply being together. On the contrary, they have chosen to remain in total control of their physical and intellectual capabilities.

"When I grow up I shall travel the world as an explorer. ..."

Moving homage by 'President' Lolus

Wadowice, August 1933
The article is right up front in *The Little Chimes*, Wadowice's parish newspaper, alongside a picture of its author. The caption refers to him as the "President of the Choirboys' Circle." His name: Lolus Wojtyla. It is not by chance that Karol has chosen to sign this, his first article, with the diminutive of his first name in Latin, Carolus. For him, it is yet one more way of showing his affection for the person about whom the article is written: Father Kazimierz Figlewicz. The priest is leaving Wadowice for higher office. Karol is determined that all the parishioners realize just how much he is loved by his young flock.

Karol develops taste for poetry

Wadowice, 1934
Karol is one of the pillars of the small literary salons which usually take place in the stationmaster's house. There are rarely more than a dozen children, taking it in turns to read out poems which have particularly moved them. They tend to read from works of the two great 19th-century Polish Romantics, Adam Mickiewicz and Juliusz Slowacki. Nicknamed "the satan of poetry" while exiled in France, Juliusz Slowacki is the author of the verse which many Poles see as a premonition: "When dangers mount up, the all powerful God/Pulls a large bell on the end of a rope /And he offers his throne/To a new Slav pope ..."

Curtain rises to reveal the magical world of theater for Karol

Wadowice, 1934
On several occasions Edmund had told his younger brother about his visits to a certain Kotlarczyk, the Polish teacher at the girls' high school. Karol had never found the time to go with him, nor ever shown any particular interest in so doing. Recently seized by curiosity, Karol braved the entrance of Mieczyslaw Kotlarczyk's home. It was as if he had stepped into another world. In front of him were people dressed in costumes, stage sets, props and all the paraphernalia of the theater. Despite a less than popular entry – he managed to step on part of the stage set – he was allowed to come and sit in on rehearsals, and before long he became a member of the youth theater group itself.

The parish hall where most of the theater performances took place.

Goebbels' Warsaw visit turns sour

Warsaw, June 15, 1934
The minister of propaganda for the Third Reich, Joseph Goebbels, is on a visit to Poland. The trip began two days ago in a "frank and cordial" atmosphere, according to official sources. Goebbels was seen smiling alongside Bronislaw Pieracki, the Polish minister of the interior. Not long afterwards, Mr. Pieracki was found dead. Investigations are at present centered around the Ukrainian nationalists but have not yet ruled out various pro-German factions. A shadow has certainly been cast over the tail end of this visit which was supposed to strengthen both political and economic links between Germany and Poland.

Karol and his father (center) still manage to surround themselves with friends and members of the family for the all important Sunday walk.

The Feast of Corpus Christi is celebrated in Poland ten days after Pentecost, occasioning outbursts of popular piety, as here in Warsaw.

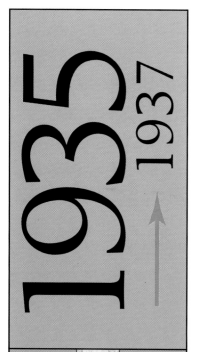

1935 1937

Age 14 Age 17

Poland, April 23, 1935.
Promulgation of a new
constitution giving
Poland an authoritarian
regime.

Laeken, August 25, 1935.
First world congress of the
International Young
Christian Workers (JOCI),
held in Belgium. Twenty-
five countries are
represented.

Wadowice, December 14, 1935.
Karol Wojtyla enrols in the
Society of Mary.

France, August 1936.
The French Confederation
of Christian Workers
(CFTC), founded in 1919,
is recognized as a
representative union. Its
work is based on the social
doctrine of the Church.

Spain, September 30, 1936.
The archbishop of Salamanca,
Mgr. Enrique Pla y Deniel,
gives the church's support
to the military revolt started
by General Francisco
Franco on July 18. Since
the start of the Civil War,
nearly 16,000 members of
the religious community
have been killed and
hundreds of churches
burned.

Germany, March 21, 1937.
On Palm Sunday, the encyclical
Mit Brennender Sorge is
read out in every Catholic
church across the country, to
the surprise and fury of
the National Socialist
leaders.

Rome, November 6, 1937.
Fascist Italy joins Germany and
Japan in the Anti-Comintern
Pact.

Poland loses her hero, Pilsudski

Cracow, May 18, 1935
Marshal Pilsudski's coffin was today brought to Cracow. Poland's hero, who died on Sunday May 12, aged 67 (b. Dec. 5, 1867), will be buried in the crypt of Wawel Cathedral, alongside the kings of Poland, in a ceremony led by Archbishop Adam Sapieha. Jozef Pilsudski's requests concerning the disposal of his organs have been carried out: that his heart should be taken to Vilnius, near his mother's remains, and that his brain should be sent to the Warsaw Institute of Anatomy, "for scientific research." Yesterday morning a funeral service was held in St. John's Cathedral in Warsaw. His body was borne there on a gun carriage, amidst a large and emotional crowd, who shared the sentiment expressed by Ignacy Moscicki, president of the Republic: "This man, the greatest in the history of our country, has used up the very forces which drove him to greatness. We must take up the legacy he has left to us." Marshal Pétain and Pierre Laval, minister for foreign affairs, were there to represent France. Although Pilsudski never wished to be anything other than minister of war and head of the armed forces for his nine long years in power, there is now no doubt that he was really master of all Poland.

With both cancer of the liver and stomach, Pilsudski's last days were painful.

Close shave with bullet

Wadowice, 1935
"Hands up or I'll shoot," said young Boguslaw Banas, brandishing a gun. Karol smiled when he saw the fake sinister look on his friend's face, two years younger than him. Boguslaw had sneaked the pistol from the cash register of his parents' restaurant. It belonged to a policeman who came in for a few too many drinks every evening, and wisely left it with them until the next morning. Boguslaw's brother was sitting opposite Karol, laughing too. Not for long, however. Boguslaw pulled the trigger ... the bullet brushed past Karol and out through a windowpane. The safety catch had not been on. Karol only came to his senses when Mr. Banas appeared, fuming. He ensured that poor Boguslaw was not punished.

Theatrical couple hailed a success

Bielsko-Biala, March 1936
The review in Wadowice's *The Voice of the Young* was glowing. The play in question was *Virgins' Vows* (1833) by Aleksander Fredro, performed by the town's youth theater company. "The play was an absolute success. Gustaw (Mr. Wojtyla) and Aniela (Halina Krolikiewicz) were most convincing as young lovers." The other actors received equal praise, especially Pomezanski who, as Albin, had "brought the house down." The text's wit was exploited to the full, showing the extent to which the author was influenced by the works of Molière. The company have just completed a small tour, with several performances first in Wadowice, and then in Andrychow, on the road to Bielsko-Biala.

Goalkeeper for the Catholics

Wadowice, Spring 1936
As the weather begins to thaw, the high school children have started to play football again on their makeshift pitch near the railway line. To simplify the question of choosing teams, they simply divided themselves into Jews and Catholics. Karol is the goalkeeper for the "Cathos." And what a goalkeeper! His skill and energy have earned him the nickname of Martyna, the name of a Polish footballer. However, Karol is not as good as his *alter ego* in the Jewish team, Poldeck Goldberger. He is a big fellow, the son of a dentist, and indisputably the best goalie in town. Courtesy being the rule, Karol is always asked to play in goal by the Jewish team when Goldberger is unavailable.

Society of Mary led by Karol

Wadowice, April 26, 1936
Karol certainly does not seem to shun responsibility. As if he did not have a busy enough timetable, with his studies, his hours of prayer and serving at mass, his sport, his Band of Abstainers, and his theater, he has now accepted the presidency of the Society of Mary within the high school itself. He has only been a member of the Society for six months, but the seventy other members nonetheless all voted him the most suitable to lead them in their devotion of Our Lady, for Karol's dedication to the Virgin Mother is close to mysticism. It is with her, and only with her, that Karol finds the comfort, peace, and strength he needs.

Marx does not have all the answers

Wadowice, 1937
Karol is at the age of questioning, of searching and reflecting. He devours any books which tackle the meaning of life. In fact, he has just read Karl Marx's *Das Kapital* (1867), in German, much to the surprise of Jozef Prus, the superior of the Carmelite monastery, who has been following Karol's spiritual quest with close interest. He reckons the Socialist manifesto is justified in its criticism of the capitalist system, but inherently at fault in its purely materialist and economic vision of society. Karol believes above all in the spiritual – a notion which Marx challenges – and he also refuses to condone class struggle, believing it can only lead to yet more hatred.

Karol and Halina make good competitors

Karol and Halina (on the right) as lovers in Fredro's play "Virgins' Vows."

Wadowice, early 1937
The cooperation that obviously exists between Karol and Halina does not rule out a sense of competitiveness. Having played together as lovers both in Sophocles' *Antigone* and in Fredro's *Virgins' Vows*, they found themselves competing against each other in their high school recitation competition. They both went to ask the actress Kazimiera Rychter, in repertory in Wadowice at the time, to preside over the jury for the competition. She accepted. Halina chose to recite *Autumn Rain*, a beautiful poem written by the contemporary poet Leopold Staff, and full of onomatopoeia. As for Karol, he chose *Promethidion* (1851), by the great Polish poet Cyprian Kamil Norwid. It is based on the myth of Prometheus, who is punished by the god Zeus for having stolen the holy fire in order to try to create mortals with mere clay ... the ultimate pagan myth. Halina herself described Karol's poem as "extremely difficult, both in words and ideas." The jury may well have agreed, for they gave Halina the first prize; but they nonetheless still gave the second prize to Karol.

High school teachers laugh and shout

Wadowice, May 1, 1936
Every year on this date, Professor Gebhardt, Karol's history teacher, proudly sports a bright red cravat to proclaim his Socialist views. Those with different political opinions say that he is not a very personable teacher. He certainly won't take any joking or laughing in his class. Unlike Szeliski, one of the Greek teachers, whom the students have nicknamed *Krupa*, which as Jurek explains, is "the name of a rather tasteless barley broth." In fact, Szeliski is "a good sort." So much so that the students make fun of him all the time. Even Karol, normally so well behaved, can't resist mimicking him in class, says Jurek. They all find him a breath of fresh air after Damasiewicz, the previous Greek teacher, who treated any vaguely lively students as "stinking brats," telling them that they had nothing but "straw in their stupid little heads..."

Lolek has now been at the Marcin Wadowita High School for six years.

Acting careers are not on the cards

Wadowice, 1937
It is out of the question! Despite their acclaimed performances, there is no chance that either Karol or Halina will be allowed to become professional actors. No chance of drama school for them; just serious studies. That is what has been decided for them by both their fathers. Halina's father is hardly the kind of person to take kindly to opposition. Jan Krolikiewicz is headmaster of the Marcin Wadowita High School and teacher of Latin and Greek, and is, in the words of his own daughter, who admits to being "frightened of him," a "very severe man" and "an extremely exacting father." Karol's is equally intransigent. It's no!

Rydz-Smigly follows Pilsudski's lead

Poland, February 21, 1937
A Camp of National Unity is born. Colonel Adam Koc announced as much on the radio, in his presentation of the new party. It aims to merge all the other parties into one political group, both as a buffer against Communism, and as a tool to fight for improved social rights for the workers and peasants. The Colonel was spokesman for Marshal Edward Rydz-Smigly, the country's real leader since Jozef Pilsudski's demise. Alongside President Ignacy Moscicki and Jozef Beck, minister for foreign affairs, it is Marshal Rydz-Smigly who has been the true inspiration behind all the major measures and reforms.

The Church starts to smell trouble in the air

Pius XI spent a long time preparing the text of his two encyclicals denouncing the two anti-Christian ideologies, National Socialism and Communism.

'Mit brennender Sorge' targets Adolf Hitler

Vatican, March 14, 1937
Pope Pius XI was determined that his encyclical should be published in German instead of Latin, and he has given it a most explicit title: *Mit brennender Sorge*, which roughly translated means *With a Burning Doubt*. The archbishop of Munich, Cardinal Michael von Faulhaber, helped the pope with his German. The encyclical clearly denounces the National Socialist ideology of the government in Germany, where a number of Catholic Action officials have been physically eliminated, and where the *Zentrum*, the Catholic party, has already been dismantled. "Whoever exalts race, or the people, or the State distorts and perverts an order of the world planned and created by God." Pantheism, which substitutes "a dark and impersonal destiny for the personal God, denies the Wisdom and Providence of God." This "aberration" should be rejected.

'Divini Redemptoris' hits at Communism

Vatican, March 18, 1937
Just four days after his outspoken denunciation of National Socialism, Pius XI has launched an attack on Communism in his latest encyclical. He calls it "intrinsically wrong, and no one who would save Christian civilization may collaborate with it in any undertaking whatsoever." *Divini Redemptoris* condemns the very foundations of Communism. It also acts as a warning for French Catholics to ignore the appeals for help thrown their way in the past year by Maurice Thorez, secretary general of the French Communist party, following the victory of the Popular Front. The pope says that "those who permit themselves to be deceived into lending their aid toward the triumph of Communism in their own country, will be the first to fall victims of their error." The persecution of Catholics in the USSR stands witness to the timeliness of the pope's warning.

Karol marries Halina in Juliusz Slowacki's play *The Balladyna*

Wadowice, May 14, 1937
Karol Wojtyla, not yet seventeen, and Halina Krolikiewicz, the same age, were united for better or for worse in front of a packed audience attending the premiere of Juliusz Slowacki's play *The Balladyna*. And to think that the performance was nearly cancelled! Yesterday, the student playing the second male role had had a confrontation with the headmaster of the high school, Halina's father. He had threatened to kill Mr. Krolikiewicz if he did not give him good marks at the end of the year! Jan Krolikiewicz had punished him on the spot and forbidden him to perform in the play. Halina had been unable to sway her father, who seemed to be insensitive to the bitter disappointment his daughter would feel if she could not play out her lead role. It was Karol who came up with a solution. The character he was playing, Kirkor, was never on stage at the same time as the second male role, so he could replace the missing actor himself. In a single day Karol learned his lines. Thus this evening, Karol appeared on stage in two different costumes, totally at ease with the two very different roles he was playing. His performance was impeccable: no stammering or forgetting his lines. Even Halina, who already knows just how talented Karol is, was impressed by his self-assured performance.

Lolek (second from left) is often the life and soul of the party when in the midst of his friends, many of whom are actors with him in Wadowice.

Germany plays the friendly neighbor

Berlin, 5 November 1937
Nothing must be allowed to upset the Poles. This appears to be the current instruction to his officials from Hitler, Chancellor of the Third Reich. Hermann Goering, who has been negotiating with the influential Polish marshal, Edward Rydz-Smigly, has given him his firm assurance that the Reich accepts "the present territorial arrangements" that exist between their two countries. He also says that "Germany will not attack Poland," and that she has no intention of annexing the Danzig corridor. The Fuhrer has reiterated the same assurances himself to the Polish ambassador in Berlin. In the light of these promises, Poland has just concluded a treaty of friendship with the Reich which, in the first instance, will annoy the Soviets, not least because they will see it as an act of allegiance by Warsaw to the Germans. Poland's other neighbors are no happier: Czechoslovakia is well aware of the threat this new friendship poses with regard to carving up her territory. Indeed, with the treaty barely signed, Hitler called a meeting of his most senior military personnel in order to show them his plan of invasion! Alongside Austria, Czechoslovakia is seen to be the first of the Reich's military objectives.

Re-elected to lead the Society of Mary

Wadowice, May 18, 1937
Today Karol was unanimously re-elected to lead the high school branch of the Society of Mary, for a further term of one year. The excellent results of his previous term in office speak for themselves: with one in four high school children now belonging to their particular branch of the Society, Karol's dynamism and proselytizing are clearly paying off. The students' readiness to help the ever-increasing numbers of needy and to spread the cult of Mary, go way beyond all expectations. Karol's exceptional ardor is due to his belief that while Poland is undoubtedly a Catholic country, it still remains a land wide open to missionary effort.

More good reports for every subject

Wadowice, June 1937
Karol Wojtyla has just completed his seventh year at high school. It was much like previous years, with yet more excellent reports all round – no less than "eminent" according to some. His father certainly has no regrets about spending part of his rather meagre pension on educating Karol. The school fees this year will have cost his father 120 zlotys, which is considerably less than the standard rate of 220 zlotys, because he is entitled to a reduction having served the state for so many years. Armed with his glowing reports, Karol is off to join a youth camp this summer in Hermanice, near Ustron. He is just the right age to receive some military training.

Unfruitful visit of French minister

Warsaw, December 1937
Yvon Delbos, the French minister for foreign affairs, has just ended his visit to Poland. A well known radical, Yvon Delbos is seeking to create "reverse alliances" with the Eastern European countries, in the hope of countering "German expansion" and ensuring France's security. However, his reception by his Polish counterpart, Jozef Beck, did not live up to his expectations. Jozef Beck was instrumental in the recent rapprochement between Poland and Germany. He is therefore unlikely to change camps. However, in a private meeting they did discuss a delicate issue, Poland's desire to be rid of her Jews. Madagascar was mooted as a possibility.

An urgent need to be alone

Wadowice, end 1937
Behind the Carmelite monastery is what all the high school children like to refer to as Lovers' Lane. For it is here, in this out-of-the-way spot, away from prying eyes, that young couples come to be alone together. Not so Karol, for he is not interested in fooling around, even though many girls find him "good-looking." At seventeen and a half he feels quite "ready to live his life without committing mortal sin." He likes to be alone in God's company. He is happy to spend hours kneeling in the church or the monastery chapel, or even sitting in the grass, just meditating, deep in contemplation, worshipping and praying to the Creator of all things.

31

Wadowice, February 1.
To celebrate the feast of the patron saint of the president of the Polish Republic, Ignacy Moscicki, Karol's drama group give a performance. Karol is the author of the play.

Wadowice, February 17.
Karol Wojtyla gives a talk at a meeting of the Marine and Colonial League, on the theme of the alliance between Poland and the sea.

Vienna, March 14.
Adolf Hitler proclaims the annexation of Austria by the German Reich.

Wadowice, April 12.
Karol Wojtyla's school career is at an end, with glowing reports in every subject.

Cracow, May 22.
Karol Wojtyla enrols in a course of Polish philology at Jagiellonian University.

Wadowice, May 27.
School leaving party at the Marcin Wadowita High School. Karol Wojtyla gives a speech on behalf of all the graduates.

Cracow, September 27.
Karol Wojtyla enrols in the Academic Legion of Jagiellonian University.

Munich, September 30.
Signature of an accord between France, Britain, Italy and Germany: Adolf Hitler can now oust Czechoslovakia from the Sudetenland. Peace appears to have been secured in Europe.

Cracow, Autumn.
Karol Wojtyla starts to write *The Ballad of the Wawel Gate.*

Poland's economic and social profile looks set for hard times

Too many farm workers and not enough land leaves the peasants little choice but to try their luck in the towns.

Poland, January

Four hundred thousand births per year. If figures could speak, then this would shout disaster. It is quite clearly excessive for a country of 34 million inhabitants, which is no longer capable of providing food for its people. Six Poles out of ten live in the countryside. A recent study stated that the number of agricultural workers per two hundred and fifty acres of cultivated land, should not exceed thirty. In Poland the current figure is forty-eight. This means that there are nearly ten million peasants too many for the size of Poland. It is not surprising that their income is diminishing every year. Last December, it was less than half what it had been ten years before. Such poverty among the peasantry is hardly encouraging for industry. People who can barely feed themselves are not likely to have money to spare to buy industrial products. And so the sinister cycle is set in motion, whereby the peasants come looking for work in the towns, while the industries in those towns lay off yet more workers. The official number of unemployed is now at 466,000, as opposed to 126,000 just seven years ago. During that same period, the workers themselves have seen their spending power reduced by half. Bitter feelings are on the rise. Many hold the Jews responsible for much, if not all, of this.

Polish industry is in a totally archaic state. The coal mines and oil wells do not generate sufficient wealth.

Tension mounts between the Jews and much of the population

Lolek lets Jurek copy his work

Wadowice, Spring
Gebhardt took his history class as usual, with a very serious expression. One by one he looked each of his pupils straight in the eye, and then said, angrily: "I sincerely hope that none of you were among last night's thugs." As the tension around the classroom lessened, he continued: "I am not speaking to you as your teacher, but as a fellow Pole. Such behavior is totally out of keeping with Poland's beliefs." That night, the shop fronts of the town's Jewish shops had been smashed. Earlier the same day, tough-looking young men wearing the insignia of the Radical National Organization had demonstrated along the Rynek, rallying the inhabitants to boycott Jewish-owned shops. Wadowice's 722 Jews (out of a total population of 5,374), are clearly in danger.

Poland's three million Jews are being used as scapegoats by many people.

Wadowice, April 25
All the candidates were aware of the importance of today's exam, and the tension was palpable. The result of their end-of-school exams depends to a large extent on this Latin paper. So it is no small thing to say that Jerzy Kluger, Karol's Jewish friend, is unlikely to pass. Showing no sign of nerves, he sat in the place behind Karol. As soon as the exam papers had been distributed, Karol started translating. Not so Jurek, who whispered to Karol. In all his eight years at high school, Lolek had never allowed anyone to copy his work. Nevertheless, he moved very slightly to one side, so that Jurek could see his paper. After the exam, Jurek wanted to thank him. Karol said nothing. He just smiled.

A rather out-of-the-ordinary Confirmation

Karol sails through Certificate of Maturity

Wadowice, May 6
In the space of just four days, Karol Wojtyla has met Monsignor Adam Stefan Sapieha, the archbishop of Cracow, on two separate occasions. He is known as "the prince," due to his dignified profile, a reminder of his aristocratic forebears, descendants of a grand duke of Lithuania. On May 3, it was the archbishop himself who gave the Confirmation sacrament to Karol, welcoming him "to the adult years of spiritual life," to use Thomas Aquinas' definition. Then today, Karol himself had the honor of welcoming the prince to the high school, giving a speech in Latin. Monsignor Sapieha was most impressed and asked Father Zacher what higher studies the brilliant young orator had chosen to pursue. Upon learning that Karol Wojtyla had opted for philology – the study of language – he was heard to say: "What a pity he has not chosen to study theology."

Wadowice, May 14
Just this morning Karol received the excellent news that he had passed his Certificate of Maturity – the Polish end-of-school exams. He had a *bardzo dobry* mention, ("very good") in almost every subject: Greek, Latin, Polish, German, with its oral exam ... Unsurprisingly in the circumstances, Jurek also got his Certificate. The graduates all met up this evening for a party given in the sumptuous surroundings of Wadowice's Civil Servants' Club. Everybody was soon whirling to the rhythm of mazurkas, polkas, and waltzes. While Karol danced a slow number with Halina, Jurek looked on amused, as one of their friends giggled at the prospect of a burgeoning flirtation. Their close friendship has certainly got jealous tongues wagging. And there are quite a few of those, as the girls all reckon that Karol is really rather good-looking.

Karol welcomes Archbishop Sapieha, who recently confirmed him.

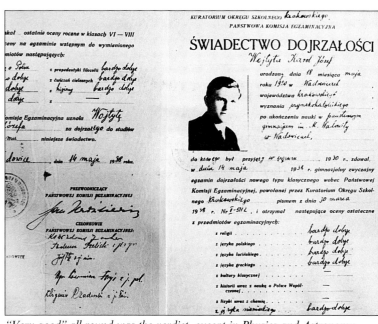
"Very good" all round was the verdict, except in Physics and Astronomy.

Shifting earth and peeling potatoes are all part of camp life

Zubrzyca Gorna, July 17

Nobody knows quite how Karol fell into the well-known trap of being volunteered for potato peeling duty at the youth camp. Like all the other boys of his age, he was called up to spend a month here. Having arrived on June 20, he is leaving tonight, armed with a certificate proving that he has done his time with the 7th Battalion of the 9th Company of youth works, based at Zubrzyca Gorna. However, Karol has not only been doing chores. He has been developing his muscles while helping to build a road from Zubrzyca to Krowiarki, as part of the badly-needed improvements to infrastructure. Since 1918, Poland has built 1,240 miles of railroad, and ten times as much road. Karol has also made a new friend, Jerzy Bober who, like him, is enrolled at university and mad about the theater.

Karol always wears around his neck the scapular given him by Father Prus.

Speechless in face of Jewish issue

Wadowice, late July

When Ginka Beer appeared on their doorstep, Karol and his father knew at once that something was wrong. Although a long-standing neighbor and a close friend of Karol's, the young woman had never previously dared set foot in their apartment. Ginka entered and announced her departure for Palestine, along with her father. "You've seen what's happening to the Jews in Germany? The same thing is starting here. My country is now over there." Karol was stunned. Had the fate of the Jews reached the point at which their safety was ensured only by taking flight? Deeply shocked, he was incapable of uttering a word. But when she kissed him goodbye, Ginka could sense that he was not far from tears.

Karol's studies take the Wojtylas to Cracow

Cracow, August

Karol's father did not want him to go off to Cracow by himself. Not that he did not trust his son, but that quite simply Karol is all he has left in life. So they have both moved to a house in the Debnicki district, belonging to Karol's uncle Robert, and his maternal aunts, Anna and Rudolfina (known as Guillemina).

The front of the house overlooks the Vistula, with a small garden out the back. Karol and his father share two rather dark rooms which lie between the lower ground floor and the first floor, with a view barely above ground level. The two aunts live above them, and the top floor is rented to Bogumila Gradowska, mother of eight children.

The aunts' house, at 10 Tyniecka Street, where the two Karols lodged.

In September, Karol finishes his preparatory military training with the university Legion, and has his induction deferred. He can stay in Cracow, where he enjoys his walks with his aunt and godmother, Maria Anna.

Anti-Semitism is anti-Christian

Vatican, September 6
The Belgian pilgrims to whom Pius XI had granted an audience, had no idea their visit would provoke such a reaction. The Holy Father had barely started leafing through the missal which they had just given him, when he stopped to read a prayer on the sacrifices of Abraham and Abel. Suddenly he launched into a violent tirade against anti-Semitism, calling it a "repugnant movement in which we Christians can have no part." With steady voice he continued: "Through Christ and in Christ, we are the spiritual descendants of Abraham. It is not possible for Christians to participate in anti-Semitism." And he concluded with the following words, which struck everyone: "Spiritually we are Semites!"

No respite for budding actor

Cracow, December
Despite his philology studies, undertaken at the request of his father, Karol is determined to pursue his love of the theater and poetry. Jerzy Bober, whom he had met at the youth camp, had the brilliant idea of introducing him to another young man, Juliusz Kydrynski. The two of them immediately hit it off, sharing a love of dramatic art and of pure and clear diction. To complete the troupe, Halina Krolikiewicz, also studying philology at Jagiellonian University, has joined them, as has Tadeusz Kwiatkowski, twelve days older than Karol. Kwiatkowski has become acquainted with Jadwiga Lewaj, who has started to give him private French tuition, as she does already for Kydrynski. The core of the troupe's artistic activity consists of evening recitals, where each of them recites some verses from an author chosen from the pantheon of Polish poets. All except Karol, that is, who declaims verses of his own poetry with "a most beautiful voice and faultless articulation," according to Halina. The real mastermind behind these sessions is Tadeusz Kudlinski, whose efforts are entirely dedicated to developing the beauty of language.

Following in Copernicus' footsteps at Jagiellonian University

Jagiellonian University is one of the oldest and most important in Europe.

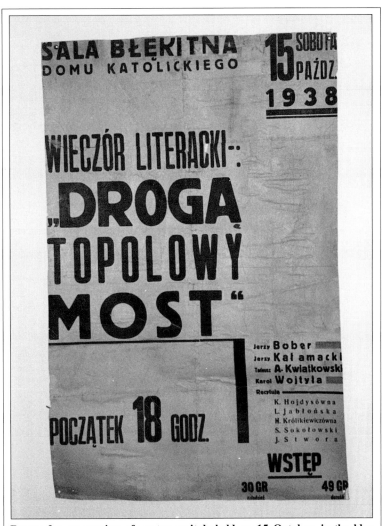

Poster for an evening of poetry recitals held on 15 October, in the blue room of the Catholic club in Cracow. Karol and Halina both participated.

Cracow, October
When Karol first set foot in his new university, he was quite naturally full of awe. Jagiellonian University, along with that of Prague, is the oldest university in Central Europe – it was built in 1364. It owes its name to the Jagiellonian dynasty which, in the 15th century, made Poland into the largest European State, including Lithuania (from whence the kings were themselves descended), and much of Prussia. The country was also prosperous and intellectually active at that time. Nicolaus Copernicus was a student at the university from 1491 to 1495, before becoming a canon, and then going on to make the discovery, in 1543, that the Earth revolves around the Sun. Although dedicated to Pope Paul III, this discovery led to the inscription of all Copernicus' writings in the Index.

A student not quite like others

Cracow, December
First Karol's fellow students tried to drag him along on their roisterings. But his repeated refusals rather put them off. He certainly is a strange young man. With his old shoes ever on the point of falling apart, his threadbare, rustic trousers, lovingly patched by a father who has not forgotten that he is the son of a tailor, and his obvious need to be alone. All of this sets him apart, as does his aura of quiet intelligence, goodness and infinite tolerance. Soon the history of Polish literature, and the etymology and phonetics of his language, will no longer hold any secrets for him. He recently gave a talk on *Mme de Staël as Theoretician of Romanticism*, for one of his courses with Professor Stanislaw Pigon. It examined the influence of her work *On Germany*, as well as that of the *Genius of Christianity* by François-René de Chateaubriand, on the Polish pre-Romantics. Both works had first been translated around 1815. Karol returns to be with his father every evening, and they discuss much of Karol's work, his father helping him where possible. At the rate at which Karol is absorbing knowledge, he will soon have outstripped his father.

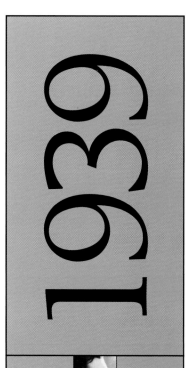

Age 18   Age 19

Cracow, January 26.
Karol Wojtyla joins the Society of Lovers of the Polish Language. Subscription: 4 zlotys.

Cracow, February 6.
Karol Wojtyla joins the university's student branch of the Society of Mary.

London, April 6.
Signature of a mutual defense agreement between Great Britain and Poland.

Raba Wyzna, April 27.
Birth of Stanislaw Dziwisz.

Berlin, April 28.
Adolf Hitler revokes the nonaggression pact between Germany and Poland.

Europe, September 3.
Germany refuses to withdraw her troops from Poland, so Great Britain and France declare war on her.

Cracow, September 6.
German troops occupy the city.

Warsaw, September 27.
The city surrenders in the face of the German army.

Poland, October 26.
Hans Frank, governor of Poland under German control, decrees forced labor for all Poles between 18 and 60 who are not able to provide proof of "a proper, stable job."

Wadowice, November.
The Germans destroy the town's synagogue.

Warsaw, December 1.
Creation of the first ghettoes for Jews expelled from Germany and the territories occupied by the Reich.

Unanimous vote for Pius XII

Vatican, March 2
Twenty-two hours sufficed for the sixty-two cardinals to agree on a successor to Pius XI, who died at dawn on February 10 (b. May 31, 1857), after a seventeen-year reign. By the third round of voting, a two-thirds majority had been reached in favor of Cardinal Eugenio Pacelli, the man who, in 1930, had succeeded Mgr. Pietro Gasparri as secretary of the Vatican State. Brought up in a family of senior lay Vatican officials, the new pope has chosen the name of Pius XII, a fine homage to the work of his predecessor. It may be chance, or even providence, that his election should fall on the same day as his 63rd birthday.

World War looms over Danzig

Europe, July 30
The Free City of Danzig is at stake in a grave European crisis. Adolf Hitler has publicly demanded that it be given to West Prussia and that Poland's corridor to the sea, where a port has been created at the old fishing village of Gdynia, be crossed by another corridor, under German control. The demand is unacceptable to Poland, which would thus find herself cut off from the sea. Having already seized Czechoslovakia in March, the Reich has been severely warned against any further action, by Great Britain and France, where the notion of dying for Danzig is becoming an increasingly likely prospect.

USSR and Germany against Poland

Berlin, August 24
"Henceforth, I hold Poland." These were the words used by the Reich's chancellor to describe the signing of a nonaggression pact in Moscow last night between the German and Soviet foreign ministers. Hitler is well aware of the secret protocol, an annexe to the accord, which recognizes the right of both parties to extend their "sphere of interest." Poland is effectively partitioned.

In June, Cracow's Theater Society, better known as Studio 39, to which Karol belongs, puts on a musical comedy based on a Polish legend, *The Knight of the Moon*, by Nizynski. Karol plays the part of a bull.

In July, Karol participates in military training at a camp in Ozomla, near Lvov. For the past year he has been with the University Legion.

Blitzkrieg removes Poland from the map

Stukas strike during confession

Cracow, September 1

Just as on every other first Friday of the month, Karol went to confession in Wawel Cathedral. His confessor was Father Figlewicz, his spiritual guide since childhood, with whom he had renewed contact since his move to Cracow. The sudden noise of engines followed by explosions made them jump. There could be no doubt: the Germans had started their attack. At 4.15 this morning, the first bomber planes had crossed the frontier. Germany was invading Poland without even declaring war. Father Figlewicz asked Karol to help him say mass. Then the young man rushed home to find his father. They decided to leave immediately and head east.

Powerful neighbors partition Poland

Poland, September 30

Poland's twenty-one years of freedom and independence are at an end. Today she lies humiliated and occupied by her two powerful neighbors. Despite heroic resistance she was quite simply unable to fend off her German and Soviet invaders. Warsaw is in ruins and is now part of the German occupied zone, as is Cracow. The Soviets have taken the whole of the eastern part of the country. The division follows the course of the San, Zegr and Pissa Rivers. Although the chief political figures fled to Romania as early as September 17, the resistance lives on in an organization called "To the Service of Victory in Poland" (SZP), created after the appeal by Marshal Rydz-Smigly. It also lives on in Paris, where earlier today a Polish government in exile was formed by General Sikorski, former prime minister and companion in arms of Pilsudski (with whom he subsequently quarrelled). The Wojtylas have returned to Cracow, after their long and tiring journey. With no possibility of leaving the country, and with no money to travel anyway, they are better off at home.

The partition of Poland as agreed between Germany and the USSR

Pius XII aims to help save the Catholics

Vatican, October 20

Pope Pius XII finds himself in an awkward situation. If he condemns outright the acts of aggression committed by the USSR and the Third Reich, he automatically exposes the Catholics in those countries and the occupied territories to reprisals and possible death. On the other hand, if he chooses to act as mediator, he risks being accused of weakness. His encyclical *Summi Pontificatus* takes the second option. In it, he calls for international peace.

Soviets block exodus to the east

Poland, September 17

Karol Wojtyla and his father took flight on September 1 with just one suitcase full of a few personal effects and their own two feet to walk on. With the invasion in the west, they had decided to head as far east as possible, to seek a haven of peace untouched by the Germans. They had covered one hundred and twenty five miles. Near Rzeszow they narrowly escaped death when an airplane fired at their long column of refugees. It was only when they reached the river San that they realized the futility of their flight: the Soviets had themselves deployed their troops in the east. Poland was squeezed from both sides. Karol and his father decided to turn back.

Courses come to a halt: no professors

Cracow, November 6

Having got through his first year at university without any real problem, Karol was all set to start his second year of Polish philology studies, in spite of the war. It was only when he arrived at the university that he learned the terrible news about his professors. All one hundred and eighty-three of them had been invited by the Germans to a meeting at Jagiellonian University, under the pretext of examining the content of their courses in detail and, no doubt, adapting them to bring them in line with the ideological demands of National Socialism. But it proved to be a trap. When they arrived, they were all immediately arrested and taken off to concentration camps at Sachsenhausen and Oranienburg. Nobody knows what has become of them. Karol is stunned, but has not given up all hope. In a recent letter to his former drama professor, Mieczyslaw Kotlarczyk, who had stayed in Wadowice, he wrote that he believed that "our liberation awaits us at Christ's door. ... I see an Athenian Poland, but more perfect even than Athens thanks to the immensity of Christianity."

1940 → 1941

Auschwitz, March 27, 1940.
Heinrich Himmler decides to construct a concentration camp at Auschwitz, to the east of Cracow.

Paris, June 14, 1940.
The occupation of Paris by German troops is a disaster for the Poles, who had been relying on French support to rid them of their common enemy.

Taizé, August 20, 1940.
Arrival of Roger Schutz, a young protestant pastor.

Orléans, August 25, 1940.
Baptism of Aaron Lustiger, who chooses John and Mary as his Christian names.

Warsaw, November 15, 1940.
300,000 Jews are walled up in the ghetto.

Soviet Union, June 22, 1941.
Germany invades the Soviet Union. Eastern Poland becomes a battlefield.

Cracow, August 22, 1941.
Creation of the Rhapsodic Theater, led by Mieczyslaw Kotlarczyk.

Cracow, November 1, 1941.
The Rhapsodic Theater's first performance of *The King Spirit* by Juliusz Slowacki, held in an apartment at 7 Komorowski Street, with Karol in the lead role.

Moscow, December 6, 1941.
For four days the Germans have been in sight of Moscow but unable to reach it because of bad weather. Now they must face up to a counteroffensive by the Red Army.

Mystic Tyranowski crosses Karol's path

Cracow, February 1940
The first room in Jan Tyranowski's apartment contains a bed, a sewing machine and odd bits of material; the second room contains a piano, burgundy in color: most surprising; as was Jan's approach to Karol after mass outside his local parish church in Debnicki. Having worked as an accountant, Tyranowski chose to become a tailor, in order to have more time to pray. Self-educated, he even taught himself Latin. It was in 1935 that he discovered the faith, during a sermon in which the priest was explaining that anybody could become a saint. He is slowly getting Karol involved in a prayer movement, the Living Rosary, composed of groups of 15 people, each saying one of the mysteries every day.

Jan Tyranowski put his rosary before his career in order to pray more.

Extremely harsh working conditions

Cracow, February 1941
This winter, the thermometer has been down to -40° Fahrenheit. Just to look at Karol one feels frozen, unused as he is to hard labor in the snow, with his wooden clogs and his outsize red overalls which hamper his movements. Luckily he is quite hardy. His tasks vary from day to day. As he wrote to Mieczyslaw Kotlarczyk, in an effort to reassure him: sometimes he helps place the explosives, other times he lays "the rails which take the little train from the quarry to the Solvay factory in Borek Falecki." Karol has even managed to draw some merit from all this labor, despite working eight-hour days in extremely difficult conditions, eating little and badly, and losing weight. Several university colleagues are with him, including Juliusz Kydrynski, who also works at the quarry. "Don't be worried," Karol continues to Kotlarczyk, "the hard work kills the time. And it is through work that man more fully becomes man." This very Christian vision of his situation enabled him to put up with what is no more than the lot of most workers, about which he was totally ignorant. Even if most workers do not share Karol's view of work, which for them is merely necessity, at least it has given Karol an understanding of real working conditions.

Karol works as explosives helper

Cracow, September 1940
Karol Wojtyla had no choice: he had to justify "a proper, stable job," in order to avoid being drafted for obligatory work duty (similar to forced labor, and, what is more, in Germany). He got a job in a quarry as an explosives helper working for the Solvay chemical factory, half an hour's walk from his home, in the Zakrzowek district of Cracow. His employer, a man called Franciszek Labus, straightaway spotted Karol's spiritual quest in life. Indeed he went so far as to tell Karol: "You should become a priest. You could sing well, as you have a fine voice, and you could certainly make a good living. ..."

He weeps for his father

Cracow, February 22, 1941
Since the beginning of winter, Karol's father's health had steadily declined. In December, a medical examination revealed a heart problem which confined him to his bed much of the time. Karol made sure he had everything he needed. On the evening of February 18, after work, he and Maria Kydrynski, Juliusz's sister, were bringing Karol's father his supper, when they found him dead (b. July 18, 1879). Karol wept, all the more upset because of the guilt he felt at not having been present at the moment of his father's death, just as had been the case with the death of his mother and of his brother Edmund. The past four days and nights Karol has spent alone, close to his father, deep in prayer. Today, his father was buried alongside his wife, whose remains had been transported to Cracow.

Karol had become even closer to his father after his brother's death.

Raid leaves parish without priests

Cracow, May 23, 1941

The Germans arrived at great speed, surrounded the Church of Saint Stanislaw Kostka, rounded up all the Salesian monks and novices (followers of St. Francis of Sales), and took them away, nobody knows where. Karol continued to frequent this parish church in Debnicki, even though he had moved away from the district after his father's death, and even though his new lodgings with his friend Juliusz Kydrynski, were right beside the Church of Sister Felicienne. Few priests escaped the raid, but this did little to persuade Karol to join the ranks of resistance fighters. "Prayer is the sole arm which counts," he insisted.

Cramped living is fine among friends

Mieczyslaw Kotlarczyk, fellow actor from Karol's youth in Wadowice.

Cracow, early August 1941

Karol is back living in his two-room lodgings in Tyniecka Street, but not alone. Mieczyslaw Kotlarczyk and his wife, hunted by the Germans, have been forced to leave Wadowice and have come to Cracow. Without asking any questions, Karol has agreed to let them live with him. Kotlarczyk is obsessed with one overriding idea, that of forming another theater company. Thanks to Halina Krolikiewicz and her family who are still in Wadowice, he and Karol have been able to correspond about this plan. He wants to set up what he calls a rhapsodic theater – a name taken from the *Rhapsodies* of Juliusz Slowacki. The word describes both part of a poem and the very greatest kind of poetry itself.

Maximilian Kolbe dies for another

Auschwitz, August 14, 1941

Father Kolbe is dead (b. January 8, 1894). He died voluntarily, in a manner of speaking, even though physically his death was caused by an injection of poison. Following the escape of a prisoner from Block 14 on July 30, the commandant of the camp selected ten prisoners in reprisal, intending to shut them up in a cave, without food, and leave them to die. Father Kolbe persuaded the Germans to send him in the place of one of the young men on the list, Franciszek Gajowniczek, a father of young children, whose life was spared. Today, along with the other three starving survivors, number 16,670 was executed.

Karol's reading is helped by the workers

Cracow, October 1941

At the beginning of the month, Karol Wojtyla was transferred from the quarry, where he had spent the past year, to the Solvay chemical factory in Borek Falecki, a suburb of Cracow. He works at the water purification plant of the factory, which produces bicarbonate. The work here is less taxing, all the more so because the other workers have taken Karol to heart and often take on some of his work so that he can read, particularly during the night shifts. Following Jan Tyranowski's advice, he devours endless books, such as those of St. John of the Cross. But the one which has most moved him is *The Treatise of True Devotion to the Blessed Virgin*, by Louis-Marie Grignion de Montfort, which he now always carries about with him, its cover stained with lime. Even if some of his reading is rather arduous, it makes him think about what path to follow in life.

Working conditions at the Solvay chemical factory are considerably better.

Both Karol and Halina belonged to Kotlarczyk's Rhapsodic Theater from the start. In November, Karol had the title role in *The King Spirit*, the company's first play. In it, he orders the murder of a bishop!

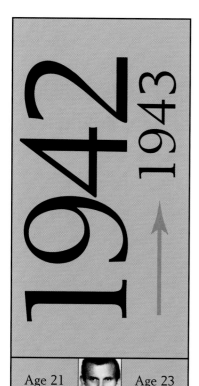

| Age 21 | | Age 23 |

Vatican, July 27, 1942.
Pius XII creates the Institute of Religious Works, a Vatican bank whose foundations were laid by Leo XIII in 1887. It is open to all Catholic organizations, from the Holy See to parishes, as well as to Vatican employees.

Auschwitz, August 9, 1942.
Death of Edith Stein (born October 12, 1891), a Jew who converted to Catholicism and became a Carmelite nun under the name of Theresa Benedict of the Cross. She was arrested on August 2, in Echt, in the Netherlands.

Vatican, December 24, 1942.
Pius XII pays tribute to the "hundreds of thousands of people who, through no fault of their own, and solely because of their nationality or their ethnic origin, have been condemned to death or progressive extinction."

Vatican, June 29, 1943.
Publication of Pius XII's encyclical *Mystici Corporis*, dedicated to relations with the Mystical Body of Christ.

Popowa, September 29, 1943.
Birth of Lech Walesa.

Tehran, November 28, 1943.
Joseph Stalin obtains agreement of Winston Churchill and Franklin Delano Roosevelt that, once victory has been won, Soviet frontiers will be extended westwards, to the detriment of Poland.

The theater as a tool of resistance

Cracow, early 1942
All performances by the Rhapsodic Theater follow the same pattern: the spectators arrive one by one at the pre-arranged spot, which is rarely the same twice, and then they leave again one by one, so as not to attract attention. Karol was recently acting the part of a priest saying confession before dying when, outside, loudspeakers started broadcasting harsh German messages. Karol kept going as if nothing had happened. After the performance he explained to the actor Juliusz Osterwa, who said he himself would have stopped: "No, one cannot allow oneself to be dominated by the invader."

Metaphysics gives Karol some doubts

Cracow, December 1942
Karol Wojtyla certainly never thought his first few weeks in the seminary would be so difficult. He has just spent "two months fighting with [his] manual," and only just managed to emerge the victor. He said that "at first it was a hindrance because my literary training, based on humanities, had not prepared me for the academic formulas and the theses which the manual contained from cover to cover." Finally he had succeeded in "clearing a path ... through the thick undergrowth of concepts, analysis and axioms," to "cut a way through this vegetation [to reach] the clearing!"

Karol for the priesthood

The clandestine courses of the seminary took place at the church in Debnicki.

Cracow, October 1942
Karol's apartment will no longer be available for rehearsals. The core members of the theater troupe – Danuta Michalowska, also a native of Wadowice, Juliusz Kydrynski, and Halina Krolikiewicz – must wonder why. Karol is giving up the theater to become a priest. When Karol recently spent an evening with Mieczyslaw Kotlarczyk, he told him that he had taken his decision. Mieczyslaw tried, in vain, to dissuade him, despite being a good Catholic himself. His friend Tadeusz Kudlinski said that Karol had told him that he did not wish to cut himself off from the world by becoming a monk, but rather he wanted to get even more involved, by becoming a priest. Karol has already contacted Jan Piwowarczyk, the rector-priest at the seminary. It has been agreed that Karol will continue to work at the factory and will follow his training in secret.

Discovery of mass grave at Katyn horrifies all of Poland

In April 1940, 4,131 Polish officers were unceremoniously piled into this pit.

Poland, April 15, 1943
4,131 bodies have been discovered in a forest near Katyn, west of Smolensk, piled one on top of the other in at least twelve layers, in a vast pit. The corpses were all Polish officers who had been shot through the head, with their hands and feet bound. The German authorities who made this macabre discovery two days ago, have attributed responsibility for the massacre to the Soviets. After 48-hours' silence, they have denied any involvement and in return have denounced this as an act of "Germano-Fascist bandits."

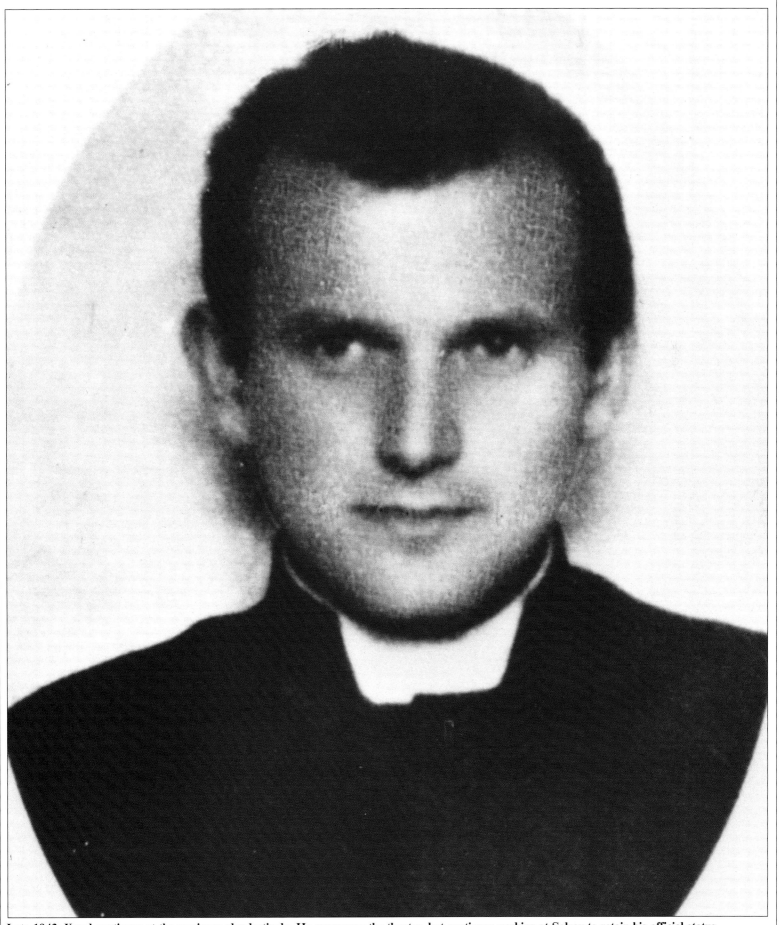

Late 1943: Karol continues at the seminary clandestinely. He renounces the theater, but continues working at Solvay to retain his official status.

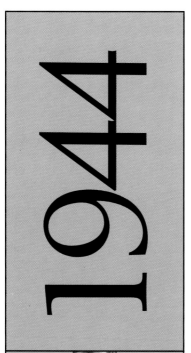

1944

Poland, April 11.
Death of Jozef Kuczmierczyk (b. September 12, 1868), Karol's godfather and uncle by marriage. Married to Olga Marianna Kaczorowska, he married, after her death in 1902, her elder sister.

France, June 6.
Operation *Overlord* is launched: the Allied troops land in Normandy. At 6 pm, General de Gaulle declares on BBC radio: "The supreme battle has been joined."

Majdanek, July 23.
The Red Army enters the concentration camp.

Warsaw, August 1.
Insurrection of the Home Army (AK) against the German occupiers.

Paris, August 25.
The French capital is liberated from its German occupiers.

Bulgaria, September 8.
After Romania on August 25, Bulgaria turns against Germany.

Poland, September 11.
On Moscow's orders, the Polish National Council adopts a law transforming itself into a parliament. Henceforth, Boleslaw Bierut wields all the power, as both president of Parliament and head of State.

Moscow, December 10.
France, represented by General de Gaulle, head of the Provisional Government of the French Republic (GPRF), signs a treaty of alliance and bilateral assistance with Joseph Stalin's USSR.

Karol is knocked down by a truck

Cracow, March 12
Karol Wojtyla was lucky. Two weeks ago he suffered an accident that could have cost him his life, but today he is being allowed to leave hospital. On February 29, Karol was on his way home after a day's work, when he was knocked over by a German truck. The driver did not stop to help him, no doubt for fear of his superiors' wrath; he just left Karol unconscious on the road. When he reached hospital, he was suffering from bloody head wounds and from concussion. Rather than go home today, he is going to Irena Szkocka's house to convalesce, for she is like a grandmother to him. She also lives in the Debnicki area, at 12 Szwedzka Street. Passionately interested in Romantic literature, it was she who introduced Karol to the poems of Norwid, and has often lent her apartment to the Rhapsodic Theater for rehearsals. Karols sees his convalescence as "time for a spiritual retreat, a gift from God."

He is convalescing with the Szkockis, whom he has known since late 1938.

A government awaiting Stalin's orders

Chelm, July 22
With the German army retreating on all fronts, the Soviets are losing no time: in east Poland, at Chelm, they have already set up a Polish Committee for National Liberation. Surprisingly, given its name, this organization is largely made up of politicians faithful to Moscow. In fact they are all still in Moscow, awaiting orders from Stalin and news of the Red Army's advance, so that they can move to Chelm or to Lublin, 31 miles to the east, as soon as the German troops have left the town. This tactic is aimed at preventing Stanislaw Mikolajczyk, head of the Polish government still in exile in London, from claiming to be the legitimate government.

Boleslaw Bierut, apparatchik par excellence, *is the new man in power.*

Karol's name is on the wanted list

Cracow, August 6
Karol was alone in his apartment, praying, when the Germans burst into his aunts' house. By chance, or maybe by a miracle, as they climbed the staircase to the upper floors, they failed to notice the doorway tucked in behind the stairs, leading to his rooms. His friends referred to them as his "catacombs", because of their position half underground and because of the clandestine meetings which took place there, reminiscent of early Christianity. Karol's catacombs now lived up to their name. The Germans were seeking thousands of men, aged between 15 and 50: anyone likely to take up arms against them or to help the Resistance. On this "Black Sunday", as the Poles had already named it, over 7,000 people were arrested in Cracow alone. The raid followed the recent insurrection of a large part of the population in Warsaw, in support of the uprising set in motion by the armed resistance. Karol will have to watch out because his name is on the Germans' wanted list.

Archbishop Sapieha takes Karol into hiding in his own seminary

Cracow, August 10
Irena Skzocka went ahead to ensure that there were no German roadblocks on the route between her house and Franciszkanska Street, on the opposite bank of the Vistula, where the archbishop lives. Three days ago, Mgr. Adam Sapieha, the archbishop of Cracow, gave word to all of his seminarists spread throughout the town, that he was expecting them in his episcopal palace as soon as possible. Karol bade farewell to his "grandmother" and hurried away. That morning, Mgr. Sapieha had contacted one of the directors at the Solvay factory to ask him to remove Karol's name from his register. This he did, so that Karol would not be reported absent. The Germans had again been round to his house looking for him.

Hidden in the seminary, Karol "disappeared" from Solvay and the Germans.

Warsaw rising comes to an end

Warsaw, October 2
200,000 civilian dead, about 25,000 military dead, a city totally in ruins – this is the toll from the Warsaw uprising against the occupying power. It started on August 1 and ended today, with the surrender of the insurgents after 63 days of terrible fighting. Their mistake was to believe that the Soviets, who were drawing nearer the capital, would come to their aid against the common enemy. Stalin had decided otherwise, preferring to leave the Germans to wipe out these Poles who, for him, represented the old order. He deliberately condemned them to death, Communists as well, because they had refused to toe the line of his Lublin government.

Wojtyla receives his first two minor orders

Cracow, December 17
After two years as a seminarist, Karol Wojtyla, aged 24, received the first two minor orders today. He was also tonsured, according to the medieval rite. Accession to the priesthood entails a long apprenticeship. The Code of Canon Law states that all four minor orders cannot be conferred on the same day. (The four degrees of minor order are porter, exorcist, lector, and acolyte.) Once one reaches the sub-diaconate, the first of the three major orders, "clerics are compelled to continence and to the recital of the breviary." Next is the diaconate, nomination as a deacon, and then the ministry, itself subdivided into the priesthood and the episcopate. Archbishops and cardinals are dignitaries. To complete his training, Monsignor Sapieha has sent Karol to spend a few weeks in Raciborowice, a parish a few miles northeast of Cracow. The seminarists so rarely get out of the Archbishop's Palace, for fear of German raids, that Karol is treating this sojourn as a "holiday." This in no way prevents him from feeling extremely grateful toward Father Jozef Jamroz, the parish priest, and toward the assistant priests, including Father Franciszek Szymonek and Father Adam Biela, a native of Wadowice, from whom he has learned a lot.

Karol cannot yet wear a cassock officially, but Mgr. Sapieha sometimes dresses his seminarists thus to protect them.

Age 24	Age 25

Warsaw, January 18.
Boleslaw Bierut takes control in the capital.

Cracow, March 24.
Publication of the first issue of *Tygodnik Powszechny*, a weekly newspaper edited by Jerzy Turowicz.

Cracow, April 9.
Karol Wojtyla is elected vice president of *Bratniak Pomoc*, an inter-student aid organization.

Cracow, April 22.
The Rhapsodic Theater comes out of hiding.

Berlin, April 30.
Adolf Hitler (b. April 20, 1889) kills himself in his bunker, along with Eva Braun (b. February 6, 1912), whom he had married the day before.

Berlin, May 8.
Marshal Wilhelm Keitel signs the Act of Capitulation of the Third Reich.

Poland, July 20.
Cardinal August Hlond, primate of Poland since 1926, returns to his country. He had been exiled in France, arrested in Hautecombe, in Savoie, and imprisoned in Germany.

Potsdam, August 2.
The British, Americans and Soviets come to an agreement over the western frontier of Poland, fixed along the Oder-Neisse Line. The southern frontier still remains to be fixed.

Poland, August 15.
Cardinal Primate August Hlond nominates temporary administrators for the dioceses in the territories regained from the Germans (63,400 square miles).

Poland sheds one yoke for another

Cracow is taken by the Soviets

Cracow, January 18
A violent explosion shattered the windows in the Archbishop's Palace: Debnicki bridge had just been blown up by the Germans in an effort to slow down the advance of the Red Army. Cracow is on the point of being liberated by the Soviets. Yesterday, the troops of the Third Reich deserted Warsaw in the face of the Soviet grand offensive, begun on January 13. This afternoon, loud knocking at the door of the Archbishop's Palace had the residents worried. Karol Wojtyla opened the door and found himself face to face with a Soviet soldier. He let him in. The soldier began talking, asking if he could become a seminarist!

At Auschwitz, the survivors are scarcely more than walking cadavers.

End of nightmare for camp detainees

Auschwitz, January 27
The sight that met the Soviets when they arrived at Auschwitz was quite indescribable: human beings little more than skin and bones. At least they were still alive. The unlucky ones, hundreds of thousands of men, women and even children, had quite simply perished in this camp as in many others set up on Polish soil by the Germans. Reduced to slavery, they had succumbed to epidemics or died of exhaustion, when not exterminated because of their race (Jews, Gypsies) or their known or presumed opposition to the Third Reich. Never has anything like this been seen before.

Yalta endorses USSR appropriation

Yalta, February 11
After a week of negotiations, Joseph Stalin has emerged the victor at this conference being held near the spa town of Yalta in the Crimea. His conditions were met by Franklin Roosevelt, the American president, and by Winston Churchill, the British prime minister. Poland's eastern frontier is fixed along the Curzon Line; the Lublin Government is recognized as legitimate; and the forthcoming elections will take place with no outside control.

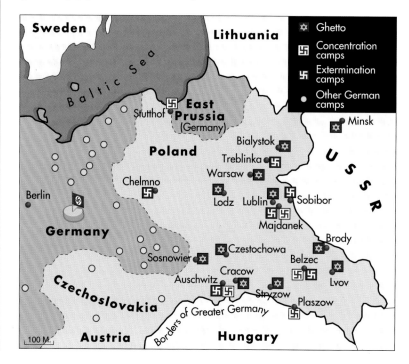

Chart of Polish losses during the Second World War	
Total number of dead approximately 7.7 million of which :	
• *Jews*	*3 000 000*
• *Other victims of German troops*	*2 400 000*
• *Civilian victims of the Soviet Army*	*1 600 000*
• *Military victims of the Soviet Army*	*700 000*
Within the Catholic clergy	
Bishops	*4*
Priests and seminarists	*2700*
Monks	*200*
Nuns	*190*

Political Police already in action

Poland, May

The Lublin Government has not wasted time in putting in place two police forces, both created in the past year: the Civic Militia (MO) and the Political Police (UBP), run by Stanislaw Radkiewicz, a Moscow-trained Communist. They track down "enemies of democracy," or, rather, enemies of the regime, and prevent actions "directed against the State." The militia is 50,000 strong, while the police is 23,000. Experts from the Soviet NKVD are supervising their deployment.

Karol signs a one-year contract with Jagiellonian University

L.384/45

U M O W A

o pracę, zawarta w Krakowie dnia 15 października 194 5 r.
między Dziekanem Wydziału **Teologicznego** Uniwersytetu Jagiellońskiego działającym w imieniu Skarbu Państwa, jako pracodawcy a Pan **em**
W O J T Y Ł A Karolem jako pracownikiem.-
1).Pan W O J T Y Ł A Karol zwany w dalszej treści niniejszej umowy pracownikiem, przyjmuje na siebie od dnia 1 listopada
1945 r.do dnia 31 sierpnia 1946 r.obowiązki **kontr.**
młodszego asystenta przy Seminarium dogmatyki szczegółowej i hist.dogmatów Uniw.Jagiell.w wymiarze 15 godzin tygodniowo.
2).Pracownik otrzymywać będzie wynagrodzenie ustalone rozporządzeniem Ministra W.R.i O.P.z dnia 15 grudnia 1936 r.o wynagrodzeniu zastępców profesorów, kontraktowych pomocniczych sił naukowych i za godziny zlecone w państwowych szkołach akademickich, oraz przewidziany dodatek naukowy po myśli dekretu z dnia 6.VI.1945 (Dz.U.Nr 25 poz. 152),, które to wynagrodzenie wypłacane mu będzie do miesiąc z góry.-

Cracow, October 15

Karol Wojtyla has enrolled again at Jagiellonian University, which has just reopened, but this time to read theology. However, he will be no ordinary student. As well as being a seminarist, he has just signed a contract with the university to work as an assistant professor within the theology faculty, teaching "detailed systematic theology and the history of dogmas." Between November 1 and August 31, 1946, Karol will therefore be required to teach 15 hours per week. It has obviously been decided that Karol is now ready to transmit knowledge.

Excellent marks all round: just like school

Cracow, May 26

Karol Wojtyla's professors should certainly be proud of his marks. Most columns of his report have the number 1 alongside his name, which signifies *eminente*, the Latin term for excellent. He received this mark for Church history, Greek, apologetics, metaphysics (despite the terrible difficulty he had had with this at the start of the year), moral principles and General Introduction to the Bible. His worst subject is psychology, but even for that he managed to get a *bene* (good); and as for his knowledge of cosmology, he was given a *valbe bene*, which means very good.

Wykaz not egzaminacyjnych w tajnym nauczaniu w latach 1941-1945.

I. rok studiów.

	Logika II	Meta fizyka I	teoria poznania I	Kosmo logia II	Histori Kościoła cz. I	Apolo getyka cz. I	Wstęp ogólny do Pisma św.	Język grecki	Herme neutyka
Baziński Andrzej	1	2	3	2	3	2	1.natch 2.kzn.tabt		1
Borowy Kazimierz	2	1	1	2	2	2	1 natch 3 kzn. 2	1	1
Majda Władysław	1	1	2	1	1	2	1	2	1
Sidełko Jan	2	3	4	3	3	4	2.natch 3.kzn.dekt	2	3
Suder Kazimierz	2	1	1	3	3	2	2.kzn.tabt 2.natch	3	2
Targosz Karol	2	1	1	2	1	2	2.kzn.tabt	2	2
Wojtyła Karol	2	1	2	2	2	1	2 natch 1 kzn	1	1
Konieczny Franciszek		3		2	2	3	3.natch 3.kzn.tab	3	3
Kościelny Stanisław	4	2	3	3 4	2	2	2.natch 3	2	3
Wilczyński Ryszard	3	2	3	3	2	1	2	1	2
Starowieyski Stanisław				2					

II. rok studiów.

	Psycholog	Historia filozofii	Je princ.osp Morał.ona Mina	Wstęp do Hist. teologi provi.idyd	Historia Kościoła	Apologety. cz.it. O Kościele
Baziński Andrzej	3	3	3	4	3	2 2
Borowy Kazimierz	2	2	2	1	2	2
Majda Władysław	2	2	1	1	1	3
Sidełko Jan	3		2		2	3
Suder Kazimierz	3	3	2	2	3	3
Targosz Karol	2	1	1	2	1	2
Wojtyła Karol	3	2	1		1	1
Konieczny Franciszek					1	3
Kościelny Stanisław						
Wilczyński Ryszard	2					

Qualification for cassock rewards efforts

The archbishop's private chapel, where he received the other two orders.

Cracow, December 12

Karol Wojtyla has received his two other minor orders as well as his cassock. Lively praise is forthcoming from Father Karol Kozlowski, the rector of the seminary, only in the job since the summer, having previously been in Wadowice, and from Father Jozef Matlak, one of the parish priests from Debnicki, to where Karol still returns regularly. Father Matlak said: "Karol Wojtyla is a boy with many qualities, clearly enthusiastic about his work and about the Holy Faith. Devoted to God, he is heading unerringly towards the priesthood. On the moral level, a great certitude and a deep knowledge." Far from any pride, Karol gives thanks to his teachers.

1946

| Age 25 | | Age 26 |

Fulton, March 5.
During a conference in Missouri, Winston Churchill, the former British prime minister, states that "an iron curtain has descended across the Continent."

Cracow, May 3.
On the anniversary of the promulgation of the Polish Constitution of 1791, an important demonstration confirms Cracow as the most hostile town in Poland to the Communist regime.

Poland, June 30.
A referendum is held on constitutional and economic issues. The rigged results gave an overwhelming majority to the regime.

Poland, July 5.
Official censor established for all publications.

Cracow, October 13.
Karol Wojtyla becomes a sub-deacon.

Nuremberg, October 16.
After receiving the death sentence on October 1, Hans Frank, the governor of occupied Poland, is executed (born May 23, 1900).

Cracow, October 20.
Karol Wojtyla becomes a deacon.

Poland, November 15.
Karol Wojtyla leaves for Rome, with Brother Stanislaw Starowieyski. It is his first time abroad.

Rome, end November.
After a stop in Paris, at the Polish seminary at 5, rue des Irlandais, Father Wojtyla reaches Rome.

Song of the Hidden God is published

Cracow, early 1946
Only the editors of the review *Glos Karmelu* (Voice of the Carmelites) are aware that Karol Wojtyla is the real author of the anonymous poem entitled *Song of the Hidden God*. Karol is seeking neither publicity nor praise; he quite simply reckons that some of his poems deserve to be better known because their very nature is uplifting to the reader. He is forever searching, not for perfection, which he knows does not exist in this life, but for the most noble poetic form possible. However, he has clearly specified that some of his work, such as a piece called *Job*, should not be published. The same goes for *David*, which he wrote in 1939 for his mother.

The Polish Church affirms its identity

Poland, March
"Poland cannot be atheist, Poland cannot be Communist, Poland must remain Christian." These were the words used in a letter read in every church throughout Poland to inform the faithful of the frank, clear and unequivocal position adopted by the Polish bishops. And the country is less than three months away from a referendum aimed at giving an appearance of popular support to the Communist regime. Since political opposition has been extinguished, the Church is the last, and so far impregnable, bastion for opponents of collectivization.

Karol keen to join Czerna Monastery

Czerna, September
Yet again Mgr. Sapieha was obliged to say no to Karol Wojtyla. Karol had been to Czerna again to visit the Carmelite monastery there, as he is still tempted to withdraw from the world to dedicate his life entirely to the adoration of God. Last year, he went to see the superior, Father Leonard Kowalowka, to inform him of his desire to become a monk. Sapieha reckons: "We have great need of Wojtyla in the diocese."

Karol becomes a priest

Cracow, November 1
"You must first finish that which has been commenced." These were the words of Mgr. Sapieha, archbishop of Cracow, to Karol Wojtyla when the young seminarist asked permission to train to become a monk. After four years, his time in the seminary is nearing an end, as he has just been ordained priest. The ceremony took place in the private chapel of the Archbishop's Palace. Karol received the blessing of Mgr. Sapieha, alone, after six days of spiritual retreat. The dank grey day outside contrasted strongly with the joy and light which filled his whole being. At the very moment when, at long last, he received the laying on of hands, a strong memory came to mind. It was the image of Jerzy Zachuta, a young man who, like him, had pursued his studies at the seminary clandestinely, under the Occupation, and who one day disappeared. It was upon reading the list of names of Poles arrested by the Germans, the following day, that he learned of his friend's fate. He had fallen into enemy hands and was due to be executed. It was towards him, for him, that Karol Wojtyla said his first prayer as a priest, on this feast of All Souls, which the Church normally takes to be a day of happiness.

Karol says first mass for his family

Father Wojtyla baptizes Monika

Wadowice, November 10

Father Edward Zacher, Karol's old catechism teacher, looked even happier than Karol, if such a thing were possible. Back in his home town, Father Wojtyla had just celebrated mass in the church he could almost claim as his, so many hours had he spent there in prayer, in meditation and in serving at mass for Father Zacher. What was said between the two men concerns only them, and God. But everyone knows that they hold each other in mutual respect and affection. Karol's first masses in Cracow were in memory of his family. On November 2, the day when the dead are celebrated, Karol had dedicated his first mass to his brother and his parents, in the Crypt of St. Leonard in Wawel Cathedral. Having finished this inaugural mass, he celebrated a second one in another place dear to him, the Church of St. Stanislaw Kostka, in his once-familiar district of Debnicki, where, during the war, the Salesian fathers had taken him in, risking their own lives, in order to guide him on his path through the seminary. At Wawel, he was assisted at mass by Father Kazimierz Figlewicz, and Mieczyslaw Malinski helped serve. At Debnicki, as soon as the mass was over, everybody who had come to support Karol was invited to a celebratory luncheon given by Irena Szkocka, his "grandmother." The only sad note was the absence of Jan Tyranowski, the venerated founder of the Living Rosary. He had been taken to hospital.

Wawel Cathedral (above) in Cracow and its Crypt of St. Leonard (below).

Cracow, November 11

The first baptism administered by Father Wojtyla since his ordination was to none other than the daughter of Halina Krolikiewicz, his childhood friend. She had married one of the young actors of their theater group, Tadeusz Kwiatowski. Halina Kwiatowska had asked Karol to baptize their daughter, Monika, in their home. One of the godfathers was the famous writer Wojciech Zukrowski. During the ceremony, the child cried so much that Karol got slightly flustered. Ever in a hurry, he left without realizing that he had forgotten his frugal snack in the hallway: two slices of black bread spread with bacon fat.

Karol pursues his studies in Rome

Rome, Christmas

Father Wojtyla is living abroad, having never before left Poland. But being in Rome, the Eternal City, is a little bit like being at home anyway for a priest. He is accompanied by Brother Stanislaw Starowiecki who was with him at the seminary. Karol spent his first three weeks here in lodgings in the Via Pettinari, but he is now living in the Belgian College at 26 Via Quirinale, run by Mgr. Maximilien de Furstenberg. He is enrolled at Angelicum University. At St. Peter's, he has already had a glimpse of Pope Pius XII.

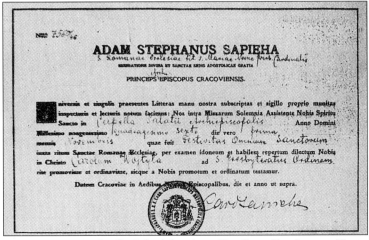

On November 1, Cardinal Sapieha signs Karol's ordination certificate. Eight years earlier, he had predicted Karol's vocation.

Karol (top left) spent his time in the company of other priests at the Belgian Pontifical College in Rome, while studying at Angelicum University.

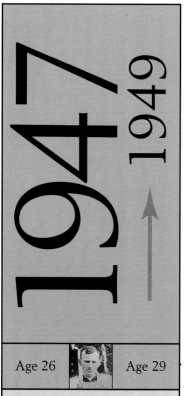

1947 1949

Age 26 | Age 29

Poland, February 3, 1947.
Creation of the Pax Association.

Rome, July 2, 1947.
Karol Wojtyla obtains his theology degree.

Vatican, July 20, 1947.
Father Louis-Marie Grignion de Montfort (1673-1716) is canonized by Pius XII.

Ars, end October 1947.
Karol Wojtyla visits the Ain to pay homage to St. Jean-Marie Vianney.

Belgium, Christmas 1947.
Father Werenfried van Straaten founds Aid to the Church in Need, to give material and moral support to the Church in Eastern Europe.

Tel Aviv, May 14, 1948.
David Ben Gurion proclaims the creation of the State of Israel.

Poland, June 30, 1948.
Death of Rudolfina Kaczorowska (b. March 31, 1889), Karol Wojtyla's maternal aunt.

Amsterdam, August 23, 1948.
First meeting of the Assembly of the World Council of Churches, made up of 147 Protestant and Orthodox Churches. The Roman Catholic Church is not a member.

Cracow, October 24, 1948.
Karol Wojtyla receives his theology doctorate.

Warsaw, September 5, 1948.
Wladyslaw Gomulka, secretary general of the central committee of the Communist party, is dismissed.

France, November 25, 1949.
Abbé Pierre founds the Emmaüs organization.

Wojtyla's thirst for foreign languages

Rome, January 1947
Father Wojtyla is keen to learn at least three European languages at present. Italian, because he will be in Rome for at least two years. French, because all the intellectuals in Cracow speak it anyway, and he has already had a taste of it with Jadwiga Lewaj, Irena Szkocka's neighbor. And Spanish, because it would be helpful for reading the original versions of the works of St. John of the Cross. In between, he tries to find time to visit Rome itself. Here, as he wrote to a friend, "one constantly discovers details of the utmost beauty and skill, as well as discovering new depths of great richness within one's inner being."

Tyranowski was a friend and teacher

Cracow, March 15, 1947
Jan Tyranowski (born Feb. 9, 1901) has died of lung infection in the hospital, where he has been for the past year. He was the founder of The Living Rosary, and a veritable seedbed for priests, among them Karol. He also had an extraordinary gift: if a sick person came to see him, by the power of the spirit alone, he could take their sickness unto himself, leaving the other healed. His confessor saw him as "a spiritual alpinist ..., an evangelical pearl, not to be covered with the dust of forgetfulness." Karol will see to that.

Firm hand with Polish Church

Poland, November 28, 1947
Jozef Cyrankiewicz, the Polish prime minister, who has been in power since February 8, does not intend to tread lightly with the Church. He firmly warns against any "attempt [aiming to] delay or upset the process of political consolidation." After Bierut's election to the presidency of the Republic by the Diet, on February 5 – by 443 votes out of 444, despite 28 deputies voting against him – Cyrankiewicz put a ban on all opposition to "the people's State."

More rigged elections in Poland

A well-guarded voting station...

Poland, January 19, 1947
Elections in Poland are all the same. Last year the semblance of a general referendum on constitutional and economic issues returned a yes vote of 91 %. Tonight, the turnout for the parliamentary elections has been given as 90 %, most improbable, as is the supposed result of 80.1 % for the Democratic Front, that is to say in favor of the Communists. The only real opposition to Boleslaw Bierut's regime is the Polish Peasant party led by Stanislaw Mikolajczyk, which has been virtually wiped out: it obtained, or was only allowed to obtain, 10.3 % of the vote. At the same time, over one hundred of its members are currently in prison for offences connected to their political opinions.

Wojtyla impressed by French worker-priests

Paris, August 5, 1947
Father Wojtyla is leaving the Polish seminary at Rue des Irlandais today, where he has been staying, along with Father Stanislaw Starowiecki. They are going to Belgium, to continue their journey which has so far taken them to Lourdes and Marseilles. On July 8, he signed the visitors' book in the Basilica of Notre-Dame-de-la-Garde "Charles Wojtyla, student in Cracow and Rome." While in Marseilles, he also met some worker-priests – priests who, since 1943 and the publication of *France, a Missionary Land?*, had taken jobs in factories in order to be more effective in re-Christianizing the workers. He met Father Jacques Loew, a Protestant who became a Dominican, who now works as a docker. Karol was full of admiration for all of them. In Paris itself, he made a discovery which would no doubt surprise even the most hardened of Parisians. It is, he said, "marvellous how good the Metro is for meditating!"

On July 2, 1947, Karol receives his theology degree, with flying colors, from the International University, Angelicum, in Rome.

Student days in Rome are over

Poland, June 15, 1948
Father Wojtyla has mixed feelings about returning to Poland: he is glad to be back home, but sad to leave Rome, a city he enjoyed, where he learned a great deal and was particularly impressed by the erudition of his professors at the Angelicum. While at this popular Dominican Catholic university, Karol was lucky enough to have Father Reginald Garrigou-Lagrange as a professor. He has devoted his life to the thoughts of St. Thomas Aquinas, and has just published *A Synthesis of Thomist Thought*, the definitive book on the subject. Karol's French improved a lot in Rome, living at the Belgian College.

Father Wojtyla becomes assistant pastor in rural parish

The presbytery at Niegowic, which Karol shares with the parish priest.

Niegowic, July 28, 1948
Father Kazimierz Buzala, the parish priest of Niegowic, was notified, in a letter from the archbishop dated July 8, that his assistant pastor, Stanislaw Wincenciak, was to be replaced from today by Karol Wojtyla. To get to Niegowic, some eighteen miles east of Cracow, Karol had first taken a bus, then hitched a lift in a cart, and then walked the last part across the fields. This had not prevented him from arriving on time. "When I arrived, I knelt down and kissed the earth." Karol had acquired this unusual gesture from the parish priest of Ars, St. Jean-Marie Vianney. The incumbent priest showed him round the wooden church, and his simple lodgings in the house opposite.

Tough task ahead for Mgr. Wyszynski

Warsaw, November 12, 1948
Monsignor Stefan Wyszynski, aged 47, is the youngest of the Polish bishops. He has, nonetheless, been chosen by Pope Pius XII to become primate of the Polish Church. He succeeds Monsignor August Hlond, who died in Warsaw on October 22 (b. July 5, 1881). Mgr. Wyszynski, former archbishop of Lublin, will need all the strength of character for which he is renowned, as his main task will be to resist the assaults continually made upon the Polish Church by the Communist regime. Since summer, there has been a ban on the distribution of all Catholic publications, and numerous priests accused of carrying on "subversive activities" have been arrested.

Theology doctorate brings end to studies

Poland, December 16, 1948
At last Karol Wojtyla's doctorate of theology has been confirmed. His marks (dated November 24) are excellent in every subject. It was in Rome, on June 14, that he defended his thesis, entitled *The Problems of Faith in the Works of St. John of the Cross*. It earned him the extremely rare mark of 50 out of 50, with the comment *Magna cum laude*. St. John of the Cross (1542-1591) was the founder, in 1563, of the Order of Discalced Carmelites. On several occasions Karol has been tempted to join this Order, to be able to lead a life of pure contemplation, according to the precepts of its founder: "One must renounce everything which is not God."

95% of Poles are now Catholic

Poland, 1948
Never before has Poland been so unified from a religious point of view. This is due to the ravages of war, which have led to the death of three million Jews. In 1938, there were 3,114,000 Jews in Poland, or 9.8% of the population. In certain *voïvodies* (administrative regions), the proportion of Jews recorded in urban areas, such as Lublin, reached 40%, or even 50%, as in certain cities in Polesia and Wolyn. The National-Socialist regime reduced them to near on zero. The Polish episcopate had, unlike those in other Eastern European countries, flatly refused to compromise with the Germans. This, together with the sheer weight of the Catholic Church, makes direct confrontation with it almost impossible for the present government.

Father Wojtyla has no time to get bored: he cares for 5,500 souls in his parish, spread over thirteen villages.

Wojtyla's arrival leads to increase in congregation

Niegowic, 1949

All it needed was one man to transform the rural parish of Niegowic from its recent torpor and poor church attendance, to its newfound religious fervor. This man is, of course, Father Wojtyla. Naturally, he is thrilled that the church is no longer big enough to hold the Sunday crowds. He has already got plans to build another church, if the incumbent agrees. It is the young who are particularly motivated, so Karol has founded two associations which combine both spiritual and other activities, including cross-country walking and drama. Nor does Father Wojtyla mind getting a bit of mud on his boots in order to visit the peasants of his parish.

Like the majority of rural churches, the one at Niegowic is made of wood.

His secretary is roughed up

Niegowic, 1949

Stanislaw Wyporek, Father Karol Wojtyla's helper, who relieves him of much of his administrative work, had a close shave the other day. He arrived one morning, his face and body all battered and swollen. The previous evening some men in a car had forced him to get in with them and had taken him to a deserted spot, where they had beaten him up. The young man had already refused to collaborate with the political police, so some thugs had been sent to teach him a lesson. It would appear that Father Wojtyla's activities are starting to be noticed and frowned upon by the Socialist regime.

The 'Reds' are applying pressure

Poland, February 1949

Cardinal Adam Sapieha estimates that the time has come to attempt to hold discussions with the Communist regime. Since the party Congress last December, and the ensuing fusion of the Communist and Socialist parties, the regime has been on the offensive against the Church. The Cardinal has written to Boleslaw Bierut, the president of the Republic, to ask if negotiations can begin, to try to settle the differences – to put it mildly – between Church and State. There is little hope of success, as the Party has let it be known that it will no longer tolerate "attempts to exploit the religious convictions of the faithful for the sowing of discord, [nor] reactionary tendencies ... under the guise of the defence of the faith." The State has taken over the youth organizations set up by the Church; prayers in school have been suppressed; and Feast Days and Sundays (especially at the usual mass times), have been usurped for all manner of demonstrations which naturally require the obligatory presence of the entire population. Keen for action, the Communist youth organizations have found a new outlet for their enthusiasm: enforcing the removal of all crucifixes from classrooms. The primate of Poland, Monsignor Wyszynski, has a long way to go before his troubles are over.

First article published by 'a young priest with large wings'

Father Wojtyla uses the press to share his experiences of France with others.

Cracow, March 6, 1949

The editorial director of *Tygodnik Powszechny*, Jerzy Turowicz, likened Father Wojtyla's appearance in the editorial offices the other day to that of "a young priest with large wings." The bird was a good omen. He brought him an article on the worker-priests in France. It was overlong and rather out of date, as it had been written in 1947, but nonetheless sufficiently intriguing for Turowicz to publish it on the front page of his newspaper. The title, written in French (*Mission de France*), refers both to *France, a Missionary Land*, written by Fathers Godin and Daniel in 1943, and to France Mission and Paris Mission, two seminaries set up by Cardinal Emmanuel Suhard, archbishop of Paris, in an attempt to check the move away from Christianity in France. Father Wojtyla agrees with the basis of the worker-priests' work: that the intensity of faith is inversely proportional to the level of industrialization of the areas concerned. He defines three levels of religious adherence in France: firstly, where faith is still deeply felt and solid, as in Brittany; secondly, where religious practice is no more that a habit; and thirdly, where faith has all but disappeared, as in the large urban centers, like Marseilles and Paris. He admires the worker-priests for trying to convince through example. The "first fruits" of their work are looking hopeful.

Excommunication for Communists

Rome, July 13, 1949
Any Catholic who succumbs to the "materialist and atheist doctrine" of Communism will be automatically excommunicated. The same goes for collaborators of this "intrinsically perverse" ideology, as Pius XII has defined it. The decree from the Congregation of the Holy Office is aimed both at Catholics in Western Europe, particularly in Italy, where Christian charity is often confused with class struggle (equally true in France among the supporters of the worker-priests), and at the faithful of Eastern Europe where, except in Poland, compromise is no longer possible. For example, last December, the primate of Hungary was arrested for threatening the safety of the State, for treason and for currency irregularities!

Pope Pius XII stands firm in the face of Communism and ethical issues.

Conception must remain natural

Rome, September 29, 1949
Catholic doctors are regularly confronted with problems of conscience in the face of ethical issues. At the IVth International Congress of Catholic Doctors, Pope Pius XII was quite categoric: "The desire to have a child which, in itself, is perfectly legitimate, is not sufficient to make the use of artificial means of procreation legitimate." Although the possibility of artificial conception first arose in the late 19th century, the Church refuses to consider it. Only God can give life. The "right to have children" does not exist.

Father Wojtyla to hit ski slopes

Poland, December 1949
When Father Wojtyla arrived at the Church of St. Florian of Cracow last September as the new assistant pastor, his reputation as someone who understood the young had already preceded him. The parish priest, Father Tadeusz Kurowski, asked him to hold seminars for the town's students. He was invited to do the same thing by the Daughters of Nazareth, in Warszawska Street. The sisters in charge there have also asked him if he would accompany the pupils skiing this winter. He has accepted. The young girls will laugh, as he can barely ski!

Vatican State does not recognize Israel

Vatican, December 9, 1949
The Vatican is certainly not in favor of Israel's admittance today to the United Nations. The Holy See made no pronouncement at all when the Jewish State was created, but during the ensuing Israeli-Arab conflict, it allowed its sympathy for the Palestinians to be understood. Despite recently putting pressure on Catholic countries to oppose Israel's candidature for the United Nations, the Vatican has nonetheless negotiated a separate status for Jerusalem and the Holy Places. It remains to be seen how relations between Israel and the Vatican will develop.

The parishioners of Niegowic are sad to lose their young pastor

Niegowic, August 17, 1949
The decision taken on August 4 by the dean of the diocese of Niegowic, His Eminence Kazimierz Buzala, comes into effect today. It concerns Father Wojtyla who has been transferred to the parish of St. Florian of Cracow. Father Tadeusz Rybka will replace him. "Please be kind enough to send us a letter of good conduct for Karol Wojtyla," the prelate asked of Niegowic's parish priest. Father Wojtyla has nothing to fear. It is thanks to him that a new stone church is currently under construction to replace the 12th century wooden one. The painted image of Mary is the only thing to be retained and transferred to the new building. Karol's diary recounts his own deep respect for the Holy Father. On April 3, 1949, he wrote: "We Catholics should see the Pope as the descendant of Jesus."

Wojtyla knew how to enliven his parishioners' existence with theater performances and various sporting activities.

Age 29   Age 32

Rome, November 1, 1950.
Pius XII proclaims the dogma of the Assumption in his Papal Bull *Munificentissimus Deus*. This decision was taken after consultation with all of the episcopates.

Hungary, November 7, 1950.
The religious orders are dismantled by the Communists.

Poland, January 27, 1951.
The brutal intervention of the authorities in ecclesiastical affairs almost succeeds in causing a schism within the Polish Church, but Cardinal Stefan Wyszynski manages to avoid one.

Peking, February 21, 1951.
The People's Republic of China, proclaimed on October 1, 1949, promulgates harsh decrees to repress "counter-revolutionary" movements. Catholics are forced to practice their religion clandestinely, while priests and bishops are harried.

Cracow, July 23, 1951.
Death of Cardinal Adam Sapieha (born May 14, 1867).

Vatican, December 15, 1952.
Publication of Pius XII's encyclical *Orientales Ecclesia*, on the churches of Eastern Europe which are suffering increasingly severe repression. Cardinal Jozsef Mindszenty, primate of Hungary, condemned in February 1949 to forced labor for life, is the symbol of this repression.

Father Wojtyla finishes writing *Our God's Brother* after 5 years

Cracow, early 1950
For five years Karol Wojtyla has been tied to this work, *Our God's Brother*. It aims to reach the depths of man's nature, through the life of Adam Chmielowski (1846-1916), or Father Adam as he was called. While the character's life is recounted in a historical fashion, Karol states that "mere history is insufficient to say everything there is to be said about him," since every attempt at piercing the depths of man's being goes far beyond the simple perspective of relating facts. The author knows that his task is not easy, that it draws on probability. But the latter, he writes, is "forever the expression of a sought-after truth," and it is that which counts.

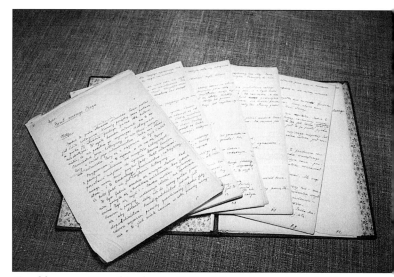

Karol began writing this play in 1945, while at the seminary in Cracow.

When priests go walking in civilian clothes

Poland, 1950
When Father Wojtyla suggested the idea of a trip to the mountains, his friend Father Mieczyslaw Malinski accepted at once, little knowing what was in store! Dressed in hiking clothes, they set off into the Beskidy Mountains, in southern Poland. They climbed and climbed, for what seemed like an eternity ... and then they were lost. It was nightfall and they did not even have a torch. At last they came to a village, found the presbytery and awoke the priest to ask for shelter. He was not best pleased at these two young men with no identification, so he sent them off to sleep in the storeroom.

Church and State conclude armistice

Warsaw, April 19, 1950
The truce lasted four days. On the fifth, after the agreements made with the Polish Church, the authorities announced by decree the setting up of an Office for Denominational Matters. Firmly under the control of the political police, it is empowered to ensure that sermons stick strictly to religious affairs. It has also unofficially been given the task of finding any excuse possible to keep the clergy divided. On April 14, however, the Church and the State came to a *modus vivendi*, granting Polish Catholics a far greater degree of liberty than in any other country in the Eastern bloc. If the Church agrees to show "loyalty" to the State – in other words, not to openly oppose such things as the current move to collectivization, for example – then she will be allowed to exercise her pastoral duties in many fields, including the press and publishing. By the same token, catechism has been re-established in State schools, and the university of Lublin, a Catholic faculty, has been permitted to continue operating. Furthermore, the Church has been allowed to set up chaplaincies in both barracks and prisons, a totally unprecedented event in the rest of the Eastern bloc. Ever doubtful, the Vatican has referred to this as a "master stroke for Soviet-Polish power."

Poems by "Andrzej Jawien" hit front page of *Powszechny*

Cracow, September 10, 1950

Apart from Jerzy Turowicz, editor in chief of *Tygodnik Powszechny*, nobody knows the real identity of this Andrzej Jawien who, for the second time, has had a poem published on the front page of the newspaper. The first poem, the *Song of the Brightness of Water*, appeared on May 7. Despite its apparently pagan title, Karol Wojtyla, the real author behind this pseudonym, was directly inspired by Jesus's words in St. John's Gospel: "Whosoever drinketh of this water shall thirst again; but whosoever drinketh of the water that I shall give him shall never thirst." This time his three-part ode is entitled *Mother*, Christ's mother, but, between the lines, his own is ever present: "There are such moments when the first flash/ reveals deep in a mother's eyes the mystery of man/ like a touch of the heart behind a thin wave of sight./ I remember such flashes, they passed without trace,/ leaving just enough space in me for simple thought." Karol's poems all seem to have something in common: they all seem to combine the worldly with the metaphysical.

"Matka" ("Mother") is one of Karol's most moving poems.

Worn shoes and threadbare cassock

Cracow, January 23, 1951

The young girl climbed the steep and narrow staircase leading to the organs of the Church of St. Florian. All she knew about Father Wojtyla was from the description given to her by her friends at the Daughters of Nazareth boarding school. As she reached the last steps, she saw a pair of "worn out shoes and an old, threadbare cassock": "Immediately, I knew it must be him." She was right. Karol Wojtyla is not the kind of priest to worry about appearance, least of all his clothes. His personal aura is what people notice, the inner strength which he radiates is what attracts young people to him. Father Wojtyla was in search of voices, preferrably in tune, to sing some canticles in a week's time, on February 2. The young girl had come to assure him that she and all her friends would be there if, before then, somebody would teach them to sing the parts. That was no problem. The young man playing the organ, a certain Joachim, would be only too pleased to teach them the rudiments of singing.

April 8, 1951: Karol reckons he has more studying to do. He writes a curriculum vitae, which serves as the basis for his future ecclesiastical career.

Permission granted: Father Wojtyla can take up studying again

His flock follow him faithfully

Cracow, September 1, 1951
Following Cardinal Sapieha's death on July 23, his post has been temporarily filled by Mgr. Eugeniusz Baziak, who himself has been made deputy administrator of the diocese of Cracow. It was he who accorded Father Wojtyla two years' leave. This should afford him the time to dedicate himself completely to his thesis, *Evaluation of the Possibility of Constructing a Christian Ethic based on the System of Max Scheler.* Scheler (1874-1928) was a German philosopher who examined the relationship between God and individuals, and the morality that ensued. If Karol's thesis does well, it will give him the automatic right to teach at university.

Karol is sad to leave the Church of St. Florian, after two years there.

Cracow, Spring 1952
Despite having been relieved of all pastoral duties, Father Wojtyla still continues to say mass. He does so at the Church of Our Lady in Rynek Square where the market is held, in the heart of Cracow. "His" students join him every Wednesday, at 6 in the morning, and sometimes more often, as in Holy Week. Sometimes they also walk around the outside of the church, deep in thought, reflecting perhaps on the sermon he has just delivered to them, much in the same way as the peripatetics who used to walk around listening to Aristotle as he delivered his revered teachings.

'Patriotic priests' and reactionaries

Poland, April 1952
Founded at the beginning of 1947, the Pax Association has just been officially recognized by the regime. To the initiated, this measure is seen as pure form, since they know that from the outset Pax has always been under the control of the political police. For the regime, this recognition allows for the pretence of open-mindedness and greater tolerance towards religion. One of Pax's other aims has always been to sow discord among the ecclesiastical hierarchy, by introducing what are known as "patriotic priests," as opposed to those others who refuse to toe the line, who are immediately qualified as reactionaries. The latter are in the majority, following to the letter the Church's orders forbidding them to join Pax. Several hundred "patriotic priests" have nevertheless been recruited. They provide the authorities with precious information on the dealings of members of the Church and their flock, on one occasion even getting themselves into trouble with the Church by publishing some petitions without clearly stating that the signatories were members of Pax. Since May 1950, these priests have even had their own review, *The Voice of the Priesthood.* The Church continues to seek to neutralize them, without a schism forming within its ranks. Such is the delicate task of the primate of Poland.

The Daughters of Nazareth followed the call of their favorite priest all the way to the Rynek, to pray at 6 am.

The Communists bolt the door on Poland

Stalinization is all but complete

Poland, May 1952

If it were not for the resistance of the Church and the majority of her clerics, the process of Stalinization in Poland could be said to be all but complete. The "masses" are being indoctrinated to distrust existentialism, as well as "a West which is corrupt [and] degenerated by cosmopolitanism." The young are taken in hand from a tender age: the teachers, most of whom have been replaced, and the textbooks, which have been rewritten from a Socialist point of view, raise the children in absolute respect for the "great sister nation, Russia." Everything to do with the Russian occupation of Poland has been suppressed, and the learning of Russian in school has been made obligatory from the age of ten onwards. Collectivization is at its height, except within agriculture, where the peasants are still resisting strongly. The Six Year Plan aims to create an "army of workers" for industrial production.

Recalcitrants end up in prison

Poland, June 1952

The choice is simple, even if it is not stated quite as strongly as in other Eastern bloc countries: the system does not permit the expression of unfavorable opinions, in whatever field, including cultural and artistic. Those who do not share the State's views are forced to keep silent. The rare fearless ones, those who cannot resign themselves to silence, find plenty of time to meditate on their future while getting to know the regime's jails. Woe betide all those who are caught listening to *Radio Wolna Europa (Radio Free Europe)*, a station created by Poles in the United States, which receives considerable American financial assistance. This radio station, which has been transmitting since May 3 in Polish, is the only glimmer of freedom that the Poles can enjoy, the only source of non-controlled information.

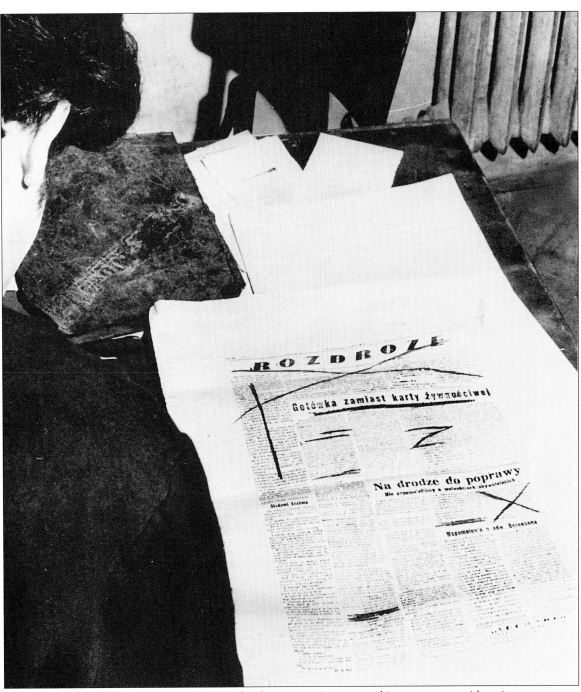

Censorship, cautiously introduced in July 1946, has become omnipresent: nothing can appear without its stamp.

Poland becomes a people's democracy: Stalin wins the day

Warsaw, July 22, 1952

Like the other Eastern European countries who came under the power of the USSR at the end of the Second World War, Poland too has now become a people's democracy. She has adopted a Constitution based on, if not directly copied from, that which has underpinned the Soviet Union since 1936, albeit without reference to the dictatorship of the proletariat. The Constitution appears to offer all the guarantees of democracy, including protection of freedoms, be they of religion, of the press or of associations. However, closer inspection reveals a clause which can overrule all others, if necessary. All rights and freedom may be suspended if abused, in other words, if they are considered "to undermine the interests of the workers." "The supreme organ of power of the State" is Parliament, which chooses the head of State, and which cannot be dissolved. Stalin has had long meetings with Boleslaw Bierut on this, and should be totally satisfied with the outcome. Stalin's wishes are Bierut's commands.

A nonconformist curate nicknamed 'uncle'

Poland, summer 1952

Strange as it might seem, Karol Wojtyla had reached the age of 32 without ever having seen a crocus! His students, by now a tight-knit group centered around him, were so amazed by this, that they decided to take him to Zakopane, in the Tatras, where they were sure to find crocuses in abundance. When at the last minute the boys were unable to come, Karol decided that rather than put off the expedition to another Sunday, he and the girls should just go. But once in the train, alone with five young girls, dressed as he was in golfing trousers, Wojtyla realized that he did not really look like a priest. He thought the public would be shocked if they realized that behind the Tintin-on-holiday façade there hid a priest. So he asked the young girls to refrain from calling him "father" in public. Just then, as other people started getting into the train compartment, one of the girls had the idea of calling him "Wujek," "uncle." He smiled and replied naturally. That was that. The subterfuge had been established, in all innocence, without threatening either the Faith or the Church.

When distances are too great, a bicycle is just the job.

How does one ski when one has no money? Nature provides the answer.

Wojtyla never passes up an opportunity to spend time with the young.

Karol in characteristic pose during one of his expeditions. While the great outdoors is important to him, it can never be as important as his Bible.

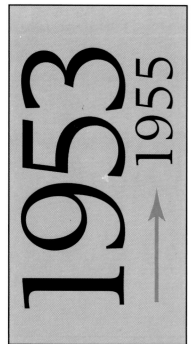

| Age 32 | | Age 35 |

Moscow, March 5, 1953.
Death of Joseph Stalin (b. December 21, 1879).

Poland, March 7, 1953.
The town of Katowice, in Silesia, is renamed Stalinogrod.

Cracow, March 8, 1953.
Publication of *Tygodnik Powszechny* is suspended after its refusal to praise Joseph Stalin.

Czestochowa, April 6, 1953.
After the wedding of two of the members of Karol Wojtyla's youth group, they all leave for Czestochowa and promise to meet there every year.

Vatican, September 15, 1953.
Pius XII puts an end to the worker-priest experiment.

Poland, September 28, 1953.
Polish bishops, under duress, issue a statement disowning Mgr. Wyszynski.

Vatican, May 29, 1954.
Pius X is the 70th pope to be canonized.

Lublin, July 19, 1954.
The Catholic University asks Father Wojtyla to teach ethics, from September. He accepts.

Washington, September 28, 1954.
Lieutenant-Colonel Jozef Swiatlo, deputy director of the 10th department of the ministry of public security, defects to the West, and reveals the extent of the repression in Poland.

Vatican, June 8, 1955.
The weekly review of the Catholic Pax Movement is inscribed in the Index, judged as being beholden to the Communists.

The State brings priests to heel

Poland, February 9, 1953
The decree promulgated by the Council of State today covers "the creation, assignment and suppression of ecclesiastical posts." All nominations, irrespective of rank, must be previously approved by the authorities. If the Church chooses to ignore this, she runs the risk of her priests and bishops being deposed. By the same decree, the Polish Church is obliged to give its allegiance to the People's Republic of Poland. Worse still, the Polish Church is called upon to disown any clerics who have "committed, upheld or concealed an illegal action, prejudicial to public order." This amounts to the State claiming the right to deny the secrecy of the confessional. Contrary to the tradition of the Church, her buildings can no longer be considered as places of sanctuary.

Episcopate replies 'Non possumus'

Poland, May 8, 1953
The episcopate has addressed a plea, clearly and simply, to the State in reply to its decree of February 9. The statement, given to Boleslaw Bierut and signed by every bishop in Poland, calls upon the Communist leadership to revoke its measures. It asks the State: 1. to permit God to be present again in schools; 2. to cease using Pax and other State-controlled movements to divide the ranks of the clergy; 3. to grant the press its freedom again, especially those Catholic organs which, since March, have almost all been banned or censored to the point of making publication impossible; 4. to stop its "meddling in the affairs of the Church" which, for example, goes as far as attempting to modify even the liturgy. On this day, deliberately chosen in celebration of the Feast of Saint Stanislas, the episcopate ends its statement with the following words: "One must obey God rather than men. ... If suffering is to be our lot, it will only be for Christ and for His Church. We have no right to put upon the altars of Caesar that which belongs to God. *Non possumus.*"

Wyszynski is arrested

His Corpus Christi sermon was the final straw for the Communists.

Warsaw, September 27, 1953
Monsignor Wyszynski went too far. At 10.30 pm yesterday, armed men marched into the episcopal palace, told him he was under arrest and took him away with them at gunpoint. The reason for this extreme action, which the State knows will make it unpopular, was the primate's sermon given on the Feast of Corpus Christi, in which he stated his opposition to "the intolerable attempts by the Communists to oust religion from individual and social life." Mgr. Wyszynski had also refused to disown the archbishop of Kielce, Mgr. Czeslaw Kaczmarek, who was found guilty six days ago of spying on behalf of the Vatican and the United States.

In September 1954, Father Wojtyla spent several days kayaking on the River Brda and discovered that it was an immensely enjoyable sport. Rising early, his day always began with a solitary swim. Then he said mass for his young followers, on an improvised altar: upturned kayaks. As for the crucifix, it was made from a couple of crossed paddles.

Wojtyla at last a professor

Cracow, October 1954

Karol Wojtyla has at last been granted a proper teaching post. He has been entitled to call himself professor since the *viva voce* of his philosophy thesis last year. At that time he was given several hours' teaching and allowed to hold seminars for the 4th year students in the theology faculty. This faculty has however just been closed down by the Communists. The reputation of his communicative abilities has nonetheless won him the Chair of Ethics at Lublin University. This establishment is the only Christian university still allowed to operate within the Communist-controlled countries. Despite his apparently casual manner and unselfconscious behavior, Wojtyla is extremely aware of the climate of oppression: the rector and nine of the professors have all recently been arrested.

Prisons packed with dissidents

Poland, 1955

Emblematic as it is of the repression suffered by the Church, Monsignor Wyszynski's sudden house arrest must not be allowed to overshadow the 2,000 other Catholics, priests and lay members alike, who are in prison. Out of the country's 33 bishops, 9 are in detention, as are nearly 900 priests. The regime is taking advantage of the situation to close over a third of all churches. Land, schools, publishing houses and printers are being confiscated or closed down. On top of this are the tactics to infiltrate the Church. Pax and the "patriotic priests" are busy everywhere. They have acquired a monopoly on Catholic publications. The majority of the faithful are unaware of these power struggles, except in so far as they see churches being closed. However those prisoners arrested for their religious beliefs are but a fraction of the overall number imprisoned for their opinions. There are currently 70,000 people stagnating in jails or Communist camps. However, a few voices have started to be heard, denouncing these appalling excesses.

The Eastern bloc countries unite to sign the Warsaw Pact

Molotov's signature gives the USSR military control over Eastern Europe.

As a result of long hours of solitary meditation, Karol has exceptional powers of concentration. He is often to be found in this attitude.

Warsaw, May 14, 1955

Albania, Bulgaria, Czechoslovakia, Hungary, Poland, Romania, East Germany and the Soviet Union have all signed a treaty of cooperation, mutual assistance, defence and friendship. Its terms are virtually identical to those of the Atlantic Pact. The treaty anticipates a unified command led by a field marshal to be named by the Kremlin. East Germany will not participate in the military section of the Warsaw Pact: its people's militia is not deemed to be a proper army. Though heavily weighted in favor of the Kremlin, the Pact nonetheless stipulates that it will cease to have a *raison d'être* the moment a proper treaty for the security of Europe is signed.

The post-Stalin era: freedom at last?

Poland, August 1955

More than two years after the death of the dictator, the Stalinist ice age seems to be starting to thaw, slowly but surely. On August 14, Warsaw hosted the World Youth Festival. After ten years of painful cultural confinement, the young at last had the opportunity to discover new forms of cultural expression, some of which came from the West. It is the young and the intellectuals who are the prime movers in this very cautious thawing process. Meanwhile, in Silesia, Mgr. Wyszynski has also found better conditions. He can now receive newspapers, and is even agreeably surprised by their contents. Led by Communist reformers and left wing Catholic intellectuals, an offensive has been launched against some of the more obvious excesses of recent years. It is only in its very earliest stages, but already some criticism is starting to appear in the official press, for example on the misdeeds of over-rapid industrialization, on the purges, and on the privileges of the ruling class. The works of foreign writers are starting to appear in translation, including those by Kafka, Hemingway, and Sartre. This spring a club opened in Warsaw, which was immediately taken up by *Po prostu*, the official student body. Its success is such that it has been forced to find larger premises for its meetings.

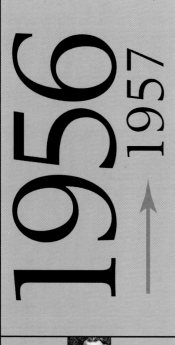

Age 35 Age 37

Poland, June 29, 1956.
Jozef Cyrankiewicz, the prime minister, announces: "Anyone who dares to raise their hand in objection to the people's regime can be certain that that same power will cut off that hand in the interests of the working class [and] in the interests of the nation."

Warsaw, October 28, 1956.
Released from house arrest, Mgr. Wyszynski, primate of Poland, returns to the episcopal palace, to be greeted by a large crowd.

Lublin, December 10, 1956.
Karol Wojtyla takes up the Chair of Ethics at the city's Catholic university.

Poland, December 12, 1956.
Mgr. Czeslaw Kaczmarek, bishop of Kielce, is freed, having been condemned in 1953 to twelve years of forced labor. His trial is annulled.

Cracow, December 1956.
Tygodnik Powszechny is published again.

Warsaw, May 31, 1957.
Death of the Polish poet Leopold Staff (b. November 14, 1878).

Poland, October 26, 1957.
End of the Tenth Plenum of the Central Committee of the Communist party. Wladyslaw Gomulka, its secretary general, announces the return to order: "Influenza cannot be cured by tuberculosis. Dogmatism cannot be cured by revisionism. The revisionist wing should be expelled from the Party."

Suspicious death of Boleslaw Bierut

Moscow, March 12, 1956
Boleslaw Bierut died yesterday of a heart attack. He had remained in Moscow after the XXth Congress of the Communist party in February, hospitalized with bad influenza. In spite of official communiqués about pneumonia, Warsaw abounds with rumors. The Poles, unaware that Bierut was ill, were completely taken by surprise over his death. His closest relations had rushed to his bedside to be with him at the end, but the Soviets had refused them access to his room. Even his personal doctor had been prevented from participating in the autopsy. The public need no more evidence to speculate on a possible suicide or even an assassination.

Mass attracts one million pilgrims

Czestochowa, August 26, 1956
Despite all threats, nearly a million pilgrims made the journey to be present at this mass. Held in honor of the three hundredth anniversary of the Virgin's Coronation, it was said jointly by those Polish bishops miraculously not in prison – there are only 34 of them. The crowd was impressive, calm and dignified. A message was read out from Mgr. Wyszynski, and then the primate's empty throne was symbolically paraded in the procession, as a protest against his continued internment.

Khrushchev calls tanks off

Poland, October 20, 1956
At 2 am the columns of Soviet tanks rolling toward Warsaw received the order to turn back, to re-cross the border and to return to their bases. Khrushchev had relented. For the past month, the Kremlin had been most anxious about the direction the de-Stalinization process had taken in Poland. Led by Gomulka, the Communist party "liberals" had gained the upper hand over the hard-liners. Free rein had been given to critics. Gomulka calmed Moscow's anger, proclaiming his own loyalty.

Poznan flares up

The army wants to contain the nascent insurrection. A curfew is proclaimed.

Poznan, June 30, 1956
The insurrection is over. According to official sources, confrontations and riots caused 55 deaths and 300 wounded in two days. Witnesses give a figure three times bigger. It all began on June 28, very early in the morning, when the workers at the railroad factory – one of the largest in Poland, with 15,000 workers – decided to go on strike. For several months now the atmosphere at the factory has been appalling: increased production, reduced overtime and wages. The demonstration started from the factory and grew as it crossed the city. In no time at all, the demonstrators were singing hymns and forbidden patriotic songs. The regime was at a loss. The Soviet-backed hard-liners eventually won the day: their troops brutally crushed the uprising, sparing no one in their path.

On October 21, 1956, Wladyslaw Gomulka becomes first secretary of the party's central committee. Three days later, he gives a speech in Warsaw, before 400,000 people. He tries to reconcile the aspirations of the people with his own policy, justifying the presence of Soviet troops on Polish soil by the threat posed by West Germany's rearmament program. The crowd chants the names of Wyszynski and Katyn.

Soviet tanks bring Hungarians to heel

Budapest, November 4, 1956

This morning, at dawn, a thousand Soviet tanks rolled into Budapest. The insurgents, supported by the majority of the population, were quickly forced to admit they were outnumbered. It was Janos Kadar, the new Party secretary, who had called the Soviets to the rescue. The uprising, begun on October 23, called for free elections, an end to censorship, freedom for the press and the denunciation of the Warsaw Pact. Pushed aside in 1955, Imre Nagy, a reformist, had been brought back to power, but already his days are numbered. Preoccupied with the Suez Crisis, the West ignored the calls for help. The uprising was crushed bloodily.

Students vote him 'the most intelligent and most saintly of all'

The nonconformism of the teacher-priest is enormously successful.

Lublin, early 1957

Named to the Chair of Ethics at the city's Catholic university nearly three years ago, Karol Wojtyla goes there once a week to give his courses. The students have recently started giving marks to their numerous professors. Whether lay or religious, they are all of an extremely high level, which helps to explain the university's ever-growing success. However, at the end of the informal vote, it is the young Professor Wojtyla who comes out top: the majority of students consider him to be "the most saintly and most intelligent" of all the professors. This verdict is confirmed by Father Malinski, who assists him with his lessons. He confirms the effect of Wojtyla's warm and generous teaching.

Catechism taught in schools again

Warsaw, December 7, 1956

Cardinal Wyszynski, primate of Poland, has signed an accord with the Communist regime. This new compromise annuls the extremely restrictive and anti-religious edict of 1953. From now on, the political authorities are only required to be consulted over the appointment of bishops and more senior prelates. The Catholics also received satisfaction on the crucial issue of religious education. Catechism classes are once again permitted in schools, if the parents so request. The teachers will be selected by the episcopate. Chaplaincies are to be reinstated in hospitals, prisons and army bases. For its part, the Church has undertaken to give its support to the government in creating what it calls a "people's Poland."

Catholic elite form own clubs

Poland, February 1957

The Church is cooperating fully with the government's detente policy, if only for the Church's own survival. Increased freedom has allowed organizations such as the Catholic Intelligentsia Clubs (KIK) to develop and open over twenty-five branches, the most active being those in Warsaw and Cracow. It is a question of linking up with other "patriotic Catholic" organizations, controlled by the government. In Warsaw it is the review *Wiez* (*The Link*), run by young intellectuals grouped around Tadeusz Mazowiecki, which unites independent Catholics. In Cracow, the core of the KIK is made up of the staff of *Znak* and *Tygodnik Powszechny*. Christians, some of whom have come via Socialism, they sometimes upset the clergy.

'The Drama of Word and Gesture'

Cracow, April 7, 1957

This Sunday *Tygodnik Powszechny* has a long article by Andrzej Jawien, Karol Wojtyla's pseudonym, on dramatic art and the theatrical work of Mieczyslaw Kotlarczyk. Entitled *The Drama of Word and Gesture*, the article pays homage to a man who, even under clandestine conditions during the war, gave his all to dramatic art. Deprived of the means to enact things, Kotlarczyk remained convinced that "the living word of man is the essential element." Elsewhere in the article, Jawien continues: "It is important to state that these new relations between word and gesture go far beyond the theater, to pierce as deep as the heart ... of man and of the world."

On August 26, 1957, Pius XII blessed a copy of the picture of the Black Virgin of Czestochowa before it commenced its nine-year peregrination around Poland, to celebrate a thousand years of Christianity in Poland.

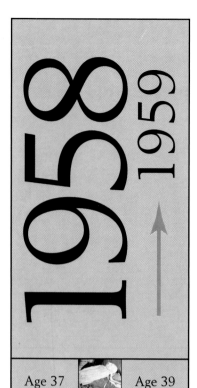

1958 1959

Age 37		Age 39

Malatya, Turkey, January 9, 1958.
Birth of Mehmet Ali Agça.

Poland, February 19, 1958.
New attack on Church by the Communist regime, via the government newspaper, *Trybuna Ludu*, which violently denounces the "fanaticism and intolerance" of the Polish clergy.

France, September 28, 1958.
The Constitution of the 5th Republic confirms its strictly lay status.

Castel Gandolfo, October 9, 1958.
Death of Pope Pius XII (b. March 2, 1876).

Vatican, March 1959.
During Lent, John XXIII removes the mention of "perfidious Jews" from the Good Friday liturgy.

Krasnik, July 1959.
Confrontations occur between the army and the inhabitants of the working class suburb of Lublin, who are building their own church.

Warsaw, August 1959.
Richard Nixon, vice president of America, calls his visit to Poland "the most moving experience of all my travels overseas," referring to his overwhelming welcome from the Poles, unlike that accorded to Khrushchev the previous month.

Cracow, November 27, 1959.
Death of Maria Anna Wiadrowska (b. 1880), Karol Wojtyla's godmother and maternal aunt.

Cracow, December 29, 1959.
Death of Jan Piwowarczyk (b. January 29, 1889).

Prostrate on floor, talking to God

Poland, July 1958
Back from a long walk just as night was falling, Karol Wojtyla knocked at the door of a convent. He asked to pray in their chapel and was admitted. Several hours later, when he had not returned, one of the sisters opened the chapel door and saw him lying on the floor, his arms spread out in the shape of a cross. She assumed he was a penitent, and left him alone. Still later, finding him in the same position, the mother superior asked him if he would like to share their supper. Karol replied that the train for Cracow left at midnight, and that he had "a lot to say to God" before then.

The army storms a monastery

Czestochowa, July 21, 1958
Two hundred soldiers stormed the monastery of Jasna Gora, seizing all the publications and religious propaganda they could find. The truce between the Church and the State, and the more relaxed atmosphere, were short lived. Since the beginning of the year, the Communist regime has been making moves to enforce the strict limits it places on freedom of expression. There has been a marked increase in the number of trials and acts of intimidation against those priests whose sermons clearly do not please them.

Twenty years on from high school

Wadowice, September 14, 1958
Twenty years on, the 1938 class of graduates are back at the Marcin Wadowita High School to celebrate this important anniversary. Karol Wojtyla and his old classmates found their old classroom. There were some empty seats, due to the inevitable ravages of the war, the deportations, the emigrations and the general political upheaval that Poland has undergone in these two decades. Karol was pleased to find Halina Krolikiewicz, the director's daughter, with whom he had shared his early theatrical experiences.

Surprise telegram announces nomination

The telegram's good news fires a burst of spontaneous enthusiasm.

Swieta Lipka, July 4, 1958
Karol Wojtyla was on a trip to the lake region of Mazurie with a group of young people. It was a combination of canoeing holiday and spiritual retreat. A telegram arrived for him. Surprised to have been tracked down, he was even more surprised by its contents: Pope Pius XII had named him assistant bishop to Mgr. Baziak and titular in charge of the episcopate of Ombi (an ancient diocese which no longer exists). He departed for Warsaw immediately, in order to have his nomination ratified by Mgr. Wyszynski and to give him his acceptance. He promised to rejoin the trip in a few days, as soon as all the ecclesiastical formalities had been sorted out.

On October 28, 1958, exactly one month to the day after Father Wojtyla's consecration, Cardinal Angelo Giuseppe Roncalli is elected pope, under the name of John XXIII.

Consecration of Poland's youngest ever bishop

The ceremony took place in Wawel Cathedral. The application of the chrism, a holy oil composed of olive oil and balm, was a powerful moment for all.

Cracow, September 28, 1958

Today's consecration ceremony for Poland's youngest ever bishop – he is only 38 – was marked by great simplicity and solemnity. When Mgr. Eugeniusz Baziak, current apostolic administrator for Cracow, raised the immaculately white miter above Karol Wojtyla's head and touched him with it, a ray of sunshine shone through the stained glass windows of Wawel Cathedral. Some saw this as a sign. His nomination came as a great surprise to many people. Karol was not among those favored for the post, partly because of his age, and partly because he was considered to be too involved in his research and the theological aspects of the priesthood to be able to find the time for this essentially pastoral role. When Wojtyla came to Wyszynski's office on July 4, to hear the primate personally pronounce his nomination, it was the latter who was surprised by the clear determination of this young and athletic-looking priest. He had been expecting the usual signs of hesitation: he thought Karol Wojtyla would at least ask for time to consider his appointment, or would make endless protestations of modesty. Wyszynski even had ready his replies to such protestations, renowned as he was for his dislike of time wasting. Instead, he was amazed to hear Wojtyla reply: "I accept. Where do I sign?"

His motto: Totus tuus

Cracow, October 1958

Like every other new bishop, Karol Wojtyla had to choose a motto. He took his, *Totus tuus* (All for you), from a 17th century French Saint, Louis-Marie Grignion de Montfort, whose work had greatly impressed him. It had taught him that popular piety, devotion to the Virgin and mystical spirituality all go together.

John XXIII announces forthcoming synod

Rome, January 25, 1959

It was from the vast basilica of San Paolo Fuori le Mura, that Pope John XXIII announced his intention to convoke a synod. Since the new pope has been considered to represent continuity, this announcement came as a surprise. Inspired by the enthusiasm currently running through the Churches of several countries, the Pope believes that the Church should renew its pastoral vision. For many theologians, it is vital to close the glaring gap that exists between the Church's infrastructure, her doctrine and her way of putting across her message, and the social and evangelical realities of the 20th century. What is more, this synod will be ecumenical.

Bishop Karol Wojtyla still goes kayaking

Poland, September 1959

Since his promotion, Karol Wojtyla has in no way abandoned his friends and the young. He still goes off with them in the summer, in the utmost simplicity, walking, kayaking, praying and celebrating mass every morning in the open air. The altar is improvised from upturned kayaks and the crucifix from crossed paddles. At night, he is always the first to start singing folk or religious songs, when sitting round the camp fire. The only real changes that have occurred since he became a bishop are symbolic bonuses: he has swapped his two-seater kayak for a smaller one-seater, and he now has the far from negligible privilege of a tent all to himself.

Vatican, June 5, 1960.
Pope John XXIII creates a Secretariat for the Promotion of Christian Unity.

Langres, March 18, 1961.
Jacques Gaillot is ordained priest in Haute-Marne.

USSR, April 12, 1961.
The astronaut Yuri Gagarin states: "I did not see God. The sky was empty!"

Rome, January 3, 1962.
Fidel Castro is excommunicated.

Cracow, May 24, 1962.
Death of Stefania Adelayda Wojtyla (b. Dec. 16, 1891), Karol Wojtyla's half-aunt, daughter of Maciej Wojtyla and his second wife Maria.

Cracow, June 15, 1962.
Death of Mgr. Eugeniusz Baziak (b. March 8, 1890).

Poland, December 7, 1962.
Death of Anna Sanak, née Kaczorowska (b. April 1, 1891), Karol Wojtyla's maternal aunt.

Cracow, December 27, 1962.
Death of Robert Kaczorowski (b. April 26, 1887), Karol Wojtyla's maternal uncle.

Rome, June 3, 1963.
Death of Pope John XXIII (b. November 25, 1881).

Poland, June 23, 1963.
Stanislaw Dziwisz is ordained priest.

Poland, August 15, 1963.
Mgr. Wojtyla catches the scepter which falls from the hand of the Virgin of Ludzmierz as it is carried past him. Mgr. Wyszynski, who is beside him, says: "Karol, the Virgin has just handed you the care of the Universal Church."

Wojtyla's *Love and Responsibility* grants a place to pleasure

Poland, 1960
In his recently published book *Love and Responsibility*, Mgr. Wojtyla, assistant bishop of Cracow, reveals an extraordinary degree of acumen and understanding of marital issues. This essay is an extremely convincing attempt to find a new Christian sexual ethic. The book's keystone is the responsibility of the individual. Naturally, sexuality is considered only within the context of marriage. Wojtyla is one of the first prelates to approach this subject without any sense of taboo or the use of convoluted terminology. In this domain, he will no doubt have drawn upon his long discussions with the young, with his walking companions and with his students in Lublin. What

differentiates man from an animal, are the moral demands engendered by the sexual act. To exclude the purpose of procreation from this act is to go against the very person and wishes of God. These demands do not, however, forbid pleasure between husband and wife. But this pleasure, that is to say the necessary sexual satisfaction of both partners, must be shared. It is in this light that Karol Wojtyla writes, with regard to frigidity, that it is "usually the result of egoism in the man, who failing to recognize the subjective desires of the woman in intercourse, and the objective laws of the sexual process taking place in her, seeks merely his own satisfaction, ... sometimes brutally."

Antidote for Wojtyla's anemia: exercise

Cracow, 1960
With several projects on the go, and numerous peripheral activities, it is perhaps not surprising that Mgr. Wojtyla recently suffered a sudden attack of weakness. According to his doctor, Dr. Stanislaw Kownacki, it is due to anemia, which he puts down to trying to do too much. He prescribed him some tonics and a health-inducing diet. But in order to avoid a repeat in the years to come, he advised him to ensure he takes two weeks' holiday in winter and the same in summer. He specifically added, however, that these holidays must be a time for "lots of intense activity, plenty of movement." Cross-country walking and skiing would seem to fit the bill perfectly.

Dr. Kownacki prescribes lots of exercise for Mgr. Wojtyla.

Nowa Huta fights for its own church

Nowa Huta, April 28, 1960
Official interference with religious freedom has intensified. Nowa Huta, a new town on the outskirts of Cracow, dedicated to steel and the construction of Socialism, has no place of worship. Petitions have failed to change this, so the workers have bought some land on which to build their own church. They then erected a cross there while awaiting the building permit. When the army came to remove it, on the pretext that the land was needed for a school, they were met by a furious crowd. After violent exchanges, the ensuing riot was brutally crushed.

Public education to be secular again

Poland, July 1961
A recent law voted by Parliament reverses the compromise of 1956. It stipulates that public schools must once again be entirely secular, explicitly stating that catechism can no longer be taught within schools. From now on, any religious education must take place in a church or some other parish building. Mgr. Stefan Wyszynski was obliged to accept this clampdown, but he has nonetheless refused to let catechism teachers be submitted to State inspections.

Archbishop Baziak's death propels Mgr. Wojtyla to forefront

Cracow, June 17, 1962
The death of Eugeniusz Baziak, archbishop of Cracow, has led to the diocese's assistant bishop, Karol Wojtyla, being nominated to the post of vicar capitular. This is equivalent to a diocesan administrator, when an episcopal seat remains empty. Current differences between Church and State mean that the post will not be filled in a hurry, as the authorities have to be consulted over all high-ranking nominations. This prerogative, at first a mere formality, has become a powerful tool for the Communist regime. Given the decline in relations between the primate and the government, Karol Wojtyla's interim post looks set to last some while.

As an interim measure, Mgr. Wojtyla is made vicar capitular of the diocese.

Wojtyla at inauguration of Vatican II

Rome, October 11, 1962
2,400 bishops from throughout the world, wearing their miters and ceremonial albs, filed into St. Peter's Basilica in a long procession. Pope John XXIII will celebrate mass there in a short while, and give the opening speech of the Council. Both the Catholic Church and her faithful have great expectations for this Council. John XXIII said as much himself when he convoked it, stating that Catholicism was going to be brought up to date. Representatives from the "Church of silence" who are fighting for survival in the Communist countries, were present and welcomed with great respect. Among them was the primate of Poland, Cardinal Wyszynski, and a little-known bishop, Karol Wojtyla.

2,400 of the world's bishops have answered Pope John XXIII's summons to the Second Vatican Council.

Inheritor sought for Tyniecka Street

Cracow, December 27, 1962
Karol Wojtyla's maternal uncle, Robert Kaczorowski, has died. Ten days ago, his maternal aunt Anna Sanak, née Kaczorowska, died. Their deaths leave the house at 10 Tyniecka Street empty, with no obvious inheritor around. Karol knows the house well, for it was here that he and his father lodged when he moved to Cracow to attend university. It was also here that in 1941 the Kotlarczyks took refuge when they were being hounded by the Nazis. The archive service at the Town Hall is searching its records to see if it can come up with the name of a legal inheritor.

Worrying report for the police

Poland, 1963
A report has just been completed by a colonel with the secret political police force, concerning the far-reaching effects of the Church on the lay community. Its conclusions are rather alarming for the regime, much less so for the Church. The Catholic network is expanding fast throughout the whole country. Relations between intellectuals and clergy have never been as fruitful as now, thanks to bishops like Karol Wojtyla. Marriages and baptisms are on the increase, as is the Cult of the Virgin. The police must act soon.

Eulogy from fellow academic

Cracow, February 1, 1963
Karol Wojtyla had invited thirty friends to his house. Most of them were from *Znak*, or *Tygodnik Powszechny*, or from the Catholic intelligentsia club (KIK). They were justifiably pleased with the success of these clubs and so-called intellectual circles. In a fit of enthusiasm, Professor Jozef Mitkowski went as far as to say: "In our own bishop, we can discern the lawful successor to one of the apostles." With a barely perceptible smile, but amused and flattered, Karol replied: "Yes, but which one?"

▷

Publication of Pope John XXIII's encyclical *Pacem in terris*

Vatican, April 11, 1963

Pope John XXIII is the first pope to have addressed an encyclical to "All Men of Good Will," rather than just to all Catholics. While *Pacem in Terris* has the defense of peace as its central priority, the pope has gone far beyond his predecessors in extolling the creation of a "public authority with worldwide powers, [that is to say] a juridical-political organization of all peoples in the world." Referring to the "universal, inviolable and inalienable rights" of the 1948 Universal Declaration of Human Rights, the pope felt it was a question of pushing the United Nations to "adapt its structures." He went on, in the same text, to call "urgently ... that the arms race should cease," whatever the cost of so doing.

John XXIII with Mgr. Wyszynski. The pope's health is deteriorating rapidly.

Church's fury over Communist rumor

Warsaw, August 28, 1963

The Polish episcopate is furious. It has circulated a letter to every priest throughout the country rebutting the suggestion that the Polish Church is "one of the most reactionary in the world." The accusation had been made by the Communists in a well-informed, anonymous statement, written in Italian, sent to all the members of the Vatican Council, pointing out the disparity between the Council's innovatory projects, and the archaic attitude of the Polish Church, with its "excessive and morbid cult of the Virgin, bordering on heresy." Luckily, the success of this clever plan, which managed to worry many souls, was short-lived.

Mgr. Wojtyla derives great strength from his moments of contemplation.

Paul VI is elected pope

Vatican, June 21, 1963

It was not until the sixth ballot that Giovanni Battista Montini was elected pope. Born in Brescia in 1897, he was ordained priest in 1920. In 1954 he became archbishop of Milan, and he acquired his cardinal's purple robes in 1958. He was in charge of Catholic students during the Fascist period, and was one of the mainsprings of the renewal of Vatican diplomacy at the end of the war, under Pius XII and then his successor, John XXIII. Known to be discreet and effective, he has made numerous trips to South America and Asia, and to the United Nations headquarters in New York. He also helped organize the Second Vatican Council.

It took six rounds of voting to elect Giovanni Battista Montini as pope.

Father Rubin looks after his compatriots

Rome, October 21, 1963

Karol Wojtyla and his old friend, Father Malinski, are both staying in the college on the Aventino for the second session of Vatican II. It is the most perfect setting, with cypresses and a shady garden, a sports ground, a terrace overlooking the rooftops of Rome, and excellent Polish-Italian food. To make their stay even more pleasant, they have been graced with the presence of the college rector, Father Wladyslaw Rubin. A native of Lvov, he settled in Rome after many tribulations. He is a great connoisseur of the Eternal City, and is thrilled to be able to fulfill the role of invaluable and charming mentor to his two compatriots.

Wojtyla goes on trip to the Holy Land

West Bank, December 15, 1963

Taking advantage of a break between sessions of Vatican II, Karol Wojtyla and several other Polish bishops hurried off to the Holy Land. Their ten-day trip started in Cairo. From there, in a plane, they followed the Israelites' route on their exodus from Egypt, flying over the Red Sea, before touching down in the Promised Land. They visited Jerusalem and then Bethlehem for a late night mass at the sanctuary of the Church of the Nativity. They went on to the Lake of Tiberias, Jacob's Well and Capernaum. There, where St. Peter had had his vision, Karol saw, in flesh and blood, a Franciscan preaching in Polish, in front of the icon of Czestochowa!

Between two sessions of Vatican II, Mgr. Wojtyla returns to Poland. Here he is on a pastoral visit to the Chocholowska valley, in the south of the country.

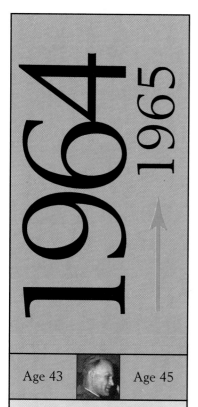

Age 43   Age 45

Vatican, January 13, 1964.
Paul VI nominates Karol Wojtyla as archbishop of Cracow, after an 18-month vacancy.

Vatican, May 19, 1964.
Paul VI creates a Secretariat for Non-Christians.

Vatican, June 23, 1964.
Paul VI reminds the cardinals that despite widespread use of the pill, the Church still remains hostile to all means of artificial contraception.

Vatican, September 14, 1964.
Start of third session of Vatican II. Of the 61 Polish bishops and archbishops only 17, including Karol Wojtyla, are able to leave Poland to attend.

Moscow, October 14, 1964.
Leonid Brezhnev succeeds Nikita Khrushchev as leader of the Soviet Union.

Vatican, November 30, 1964.
Karol Wojtyla has his first private audience with Paul VI.

Arricia, near Rome, January 31, 1965.
Mgr. Wojtyla helps prepare *Gaudium et Spes*, one of the major documents of Vatican II, which searches for an understanding of the Church in today's world.

Vatican, November 18, 1965.
A committee is to examine the possible beatification of Pius XII and John XXIII.

Holy See, December 7, 1965.
In a *Motu proprio*, Paul VI transforms the Congregation of the Holy Office into the Congregation for the Doctrine of the Faith.

First papal visit to the Holy Land: following in Christ's steps

Jerusalem, January 5, 1964
No pope has previously traveled beyond the confines of Europe. Paul VI has chosen to break with this tradition by visiting the cradle of Christianity. His trip started in Amman, where he was greeted by King Hussein. He was then driven to Jerusalem by car, crossing from Jordan to Israel at an entry point opened specially for the occasion. At Megiddo, the pope was greeted by top Israeli officials. Paul VI was at pains to insist that he was there as a pilgrim rather than as a head of state; he did not even mention Israel's name once. On the Mount of Olives he formally embraced Athenagoras I, Patriarch of Constantinople, and together they solemnly recited the Lord's Prayer.

Enthusiastic crowds fill the narrow streets of Jerusalem to greet Paul VI.

Wojtyla is archbishop

Poland, March 8, 1964
To accompany his enthronement and his solemn entry into Wawel Cathedral, Karol Wojtyla decided to add a display of magnificence rarely seen in the drab circumstances of Communist Poland. Millions of people gathered in and around the building, considered to be the symbol of Polish Catholicism. Adorned with the damask chasuble given by Queen Anna Jagellon, the 17th century miter of Archbishop Andrzej Lipski, Jan Malachowski's cross, and the ring of Maurus, who died in 1118 and was the fourth successor of Saint Stanislas, the archbishop's sumptuous apparel represented a thousand years of Polish Catholicism. The head of state, who still has a right of veto over such high-ranking appointments, almost certainly accepted Wojtyla because the regime considered him to be the most susceptible to following their dictates. Only time will tell ...

After the induction ceremony, outside Wawel Cathedral, Cracow.

Vatican II speech gets him noticed

Vatican, October 28, 1964
The archbishop of Cracow opened his second speech at this session of the Council amidst a hubbub of inattention. He began with several previously expressed comments on the Church and the world and the president of the session was on the point of stopping him, when he quickly and skilfully captivated his audience and silenced all the noise in the auditorium. In a loud and distinct voice, he clearly explained that the Church should no longer pose as the sole dispenser of Truth and Goodness, for in so doing, she risked losing in the void the very lessons that this Council was trying to elaborate. She should, he went on, be in the world and not above it. If the Church wants to be heard, and most of all understood, she must abandon the "ecclesiastical" and doctrinal tone which she uses and abuses in relation to her faithful. She should be by their sides, in the midst of them, to help them discover the Truth by themselves. It is only in this way that the world, whose lamentable state everyone bemoans, will be capable of discovering the potential of Christian action. The Church must alter her teaching: she should encourage Revelation and no longer dictate it. Wojtyla's powerful words will have won over even those who formerly knew nothing of him.

Visit to a source of true ecumenism

France, September 1965

Mgr. Wojtyla is not one to waste time. In between two sessions of Vatican II, he visited the church of Paray-le-Monial. Saint Marguerite-Marie Alacoque (1647-1690) had a visitation from Christ in the chapel of the convent there. Mgr. Wojtyla went on to meet Brother Roger in his ecumenical community at Taizé. For nearly a decade, the young from all over the world have flocked to Taizé, seeking a more meaningful existence in the community's renunciation of material goods and in its totally ecumenical way of life, far removed from the riches of the official Church. Vatican II would later reintegrate Taizé into the Church.

Interviewed by Radio Vatican

Holy See, October 20, 1965

As a result of a much-appreciated intervention on collectivism and atheism during a working session of the Council, Mgr. Wojtyla has just given his first interview with Radio Vatican. He discussed a subject which, as a Pole, he knows only too well: religious freedom and the many dangers that threaten it. Coming from a country which is burdened, against its will, by the yoke of Communism, he knows the importance of this principle, and the sacrifices which are made in order to achieve it. For this reason, he hammered home the point that no human being should be persecuted, morally or physically, for their faith. However, he reminded his radio audience that the Church should set a good example, as had the rector of Jagiellonian University, Pawel Wlodkowic, at the Council of Constance (1414-1417). Referring to the colonizing and "evangelizing" of the Teuton Knights, done in the name of the Cross, Pawal Wlodkowic warned the Council participants against recognizing those conversions made by the sword or by force. It was at this same Council of Constance that Jan Hus (1372-1415), the Czech reformer, had his death sentence confirmed. The Church must learn from its own history.

Hectic schedule for an archbishop who takes his job seriously

Wojtyla's Cracow office is a reflection of his personality: austere and simple.

Cracow, 1965

The new archbishop's day begins at 5.30am and ends around 11pm. He rises and says mass before having breakfast. His day is then one long series of work sessions, either on his own or with his team of helpers, and long periods of saying offices and meditation in his chapel or in the cathedral. He sometimes allows himself a ten-minute siesta, but if he sleeps for fifteen minutes he wakes up with a start saying "Oh no, I've slept five minutes too long!" However, his pastoral visits and the long meetings with his numerous diocesan committees take up most of his time. As metropolitan archbishop, Mgr. Wojtyla is in charge of five dioceses: Cracow, Katowice, Kielce, Tarnow, and Czestochowa. He spends so much time traveling from diocese to diocese that his driver, Jozef Mucha, has installed a sort of desk in the car, so that he can continue working en route. He has four briefcases which never leave his side, two of them full of books.

Paul VI addresses the United Nations

New York, October 5, 1965

It is an historic event. Paul VI is the first pope ever to have spoken at the United Nations General Assembly. President Johnson traveled to New York specially to greet him. Paul VI's speech was about the universal nature of brotherhood. "The real threat to peace does not come from progress, nor from science, but from man himself," he said. His speech received great acclaim. He went on to meet the Soviet foreign minister, Andrei Gromyko.

The media treats Paul VI's presence in New York as an event.

Catholic olive branch to Jews

Vatican, October 28, 1965

After two years of long and bitter discussion, the Declaration *Nostra Aetate* has finally been adopted by the Council. This document lays out the Church's new policy toward non-Christian religions. It decrees, in particular, that "the Spirit blows where it will," and that "the rays of that Truth" which enlightens all men are found in other religions. It brings to an end the principle which, for centuries, has determined the attitude of the Church in the face of all other beliefs: "Outside the Church, there is no salvation!" The Declaration has already left some people questioning the validity of the Catholic Church's missionary and evangelical work. The passage about the relationship with Judaism received the most comment. The basis of Christian anti-Semitism, that ancient accusation launched against the "God-killing people", has been abandoned. The Church does not approve of anti-Semitism, declaring that there is no hostility between Christianity and Judaism. ▷

69

Polish request for forgiveness

Warsaw, November 18, 1965

Karol Wojtyla was one of the main authors of the letter sent to the German episcopate by the Polish bishops. The document was also signed by the twenty-five Polish Council Fathers. The letter was inviting the Germans to participate, "in a brotherly but solemn way," in the forthcoming major festivities in celebration of the thousandth anniversary of Poland's existence, with the aim of bringing an end to the ill feeling between the two nations. One sentence greatly astonished many Poles and made the government furious: "We forgive and ask your forgiveness." To which the Communists replied: "We have not forgotten and we shall not forgive!"

Jurek and Lolek meet up in Rome

Rome, November 20, 1965

Karol Wojtyla met up with his childhood friend, Jerzy Kluger, who at the time had been called Jurek, while he, Karol, had been called Lolek. The two men had not seen each other since the autumn of 1938. It was Jerzy who had spotted Karol's name in a newspaper, while passing through Rome. He was not sure if it was Lolek and had left a message. When they met, Jurek addressed Karol formally, but seeing him laugh, they soon embraced each other like old times.

Excommunication of 1054 is lifted

Vatican, December 7, 1965

A new step towards true ecumenism has been taken. Pope Paul VI has effectively annulled the decree of 1054 which excommunicated the Orthodox Church. Meanwhile, in Istanbul, Athenagoras I, Patriarch of Constantinople, read out the joint declaration lifting all the mutual anathemas exchanged by the two Churches that same year, in order to "erase them from the memory." This double gesture theoretically puts an end to one of Christianity's major upsets, the Great Schism.

Vatican II is over after three years

Vatican, December 8, 1965

"It is impossible to address those who are outside the Church, those who attack her, those who do not believe in God, in the same language as those she considers as her faithful." These are words of experience, for Mgr. Wojtyla has spent the past twenty years in the midst of a hostile environment. Having started the Council in a rather hesitant way, as one of the youngest bishops present, he has meanwhile been nominated as archbishop and has himself made a considerable contribution to the decisions of Vatican II. The Council drew to a close this evening, with the final session in the presence of 81 government delegations. Sixteen texts (constitutions, decrees and declarations) have been adopted, but their influence on the evolution of the Church is difficult to measure, because some of them appear to predict a veritable revolution. Such a one is Schema XIII, *Gaudium et Spes* (a *Pastoral Constitution for the Church in the Modern World*), which caused much lively debate but which ended up being adopted by 2,309 votes to 75. This was in part due to Karol Wojtyla's ardor and great powers of persuasion in his brilliant defense of the text written by Mgr. Montini, before he became Pope Paul VI. The archbishop of Cracow made an equally passionate speech about *Dignitatis Humanae* (*Declaration on Human Freedom*), which states that "the human person has a right to religious freedom." Viewed in an international context, this text appears to be a straightforward call to the Eastern bloc to allow Catholics free exercise of their faith. Looked at more carefully it could be seen as a double-edged weapon. Despite its adoption by a large majority the fact remains that many Catholics, represented by Mgr. Lefebvre at the Council, interpret it as a brutal, unapostolic break with the Church's desire to convert. This was not the view of the Church Fathers for whom an ecumenical approach now takes precedence, much to the satisfaction of Mgr. Wojtyla. Far from putting himself alongside the "retrogrades" or "conservatives," Mgr. Wojtyla came across strongly as a forward-looking intellectual, open to the problems of the contemporary world, to the point where he sometimes finds himself out of step with the Polish primate, Mgr. Wyszynski. One such example was when the latter asked the Council to condemn Communism outright, and Karol Wojtyla did not back him up. It remains to convert Vatican II's decisions into deeds, notably the reform of the liturgy, which will certainly confuse the faithful for some time to come.

Mgr. Wojtyla has taken part in every session of the three-year Council.

Polish episcopate still misunderstood

Poland, December 10, 1965
The Polish episcopate's letter to the German bishops continues to be misunderstood. Worse still, it has provoked a deluge of outraged reactions in the press and the media. This campaign, orchestrated and blown up by the State, ignores the fact that the letter enumerates in great detail all the offences done to the Poles by the Germans, from the Teutons through to the Third Reich. The bishops are accused of putting victims and torturers on the same plane. "We shall never forgive" has become the slogan of the Church's enemies. Mgr. Wyszynski has had to denounce the misrepresentations and explain that in the Church's eyes pardon can only be reciprocal.

Letter questions archbishop's allegiance

Cracow, December 24, 1965
Like all the Polish bishops, Karol Wojtyla has been attacked over the letter to their German counterparts, but he has also been personally slandered. In a letter published in the *Gazeta Krakowska*, the local newspaper, he has been basely accused by the workers of the former Solvay factories, where he himself worked during the war, of having been a "collaborator" throughout this period and of working for the National Socialists. Outraged, the archbishop replied to these accusations very bluntly, revealing just how hurt he was by them. Sadly the press has not given the same coverage to the bishop's defence as to these calumnious charges.

In December 1965, Mgr. Wojtyla becomes the pope's trusted man in Poland. They share the same views on the Church's need for a new dynamism.

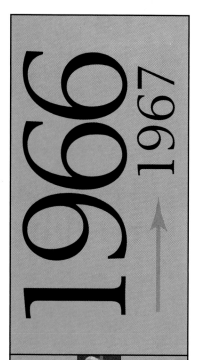

1966 1967

| Age 45 | Age 47 |

Poland, February 10, 1966.
The episcopate publishes a second letter explaining the meaning of the one sent to the German bishops. It denies accusation of treason and talks about "reciprocal understanding."

Cracow, May 7, 1966.
High mass at Wawel Cathedral to celebrate 1,000 years of Christianity in Poland.

Wadowice, July 2, 1966.
Karol Wojtyla celebrates a mass for the 100th anniversary of the Marcin Wadowita High School.

Vatican, 1967.
Paul VI creates an Office of Economic Affairs for the Holy See.

Cracow, April 11, 1967.
Karol Wojtyla signs a petition asking for the reopening of the Rhapsodic Theater, which had yet again been closed down.

Louvain, July 24, 1967.
Death of founder of the Young Christian Workers, Mgr. Cardijn (b. November 12, 1882).

Albania, November 22, 1967.
Enver Hoxha, the Communist leader, issues a decree stating that a "scientific battle" must be fought against the "religious aftermath" found in Albania.

Warsaw, November 25, 1967.
First of several performances of Adam Mickiewicz's play *The Forefathers' Eve* at the Narodowy Theater.

France, December 19, 1967.
Adoption of the Neuwirth Law legalizing contraception.

Vatican recognition of Anglican Church

Rome, March 24, 1966
Dr. Michael Ramsey, the archbishop of Canterbury and the spiritual leader of the Anglican Church, is on a visit to the Holy See. At the end of their meeting, Paul VI, in a far-reaching gesture, invited the archbishop to bless the crowd with him. This gesture was seen as the Holy Father's implicit recognition of the validity of the ordination of Dr. Ramsey. The two men have agreed to set up a joint Anglican-Catholic international commission to speed up the process of bringing together the *Ecclesia Anglicana* and the Vatican.

Index of banned books is abolished

Vatican, April 9, 1966
The *Index Librorum Prohibitorum* (*Catalog of Prohibited Publications*) has been abolished. A symbol, since its creation in 1571, of the Church's desire to control the minds of its faithful, it was last published in 1949, but was regularly updated. This century 16 authors have been inscribed in it, including André Gide, Jean-Paul Sartre, Simone de Beauvoir and Nikos Kazantzakis. Though special dispensation can be granted to those who can demonstrate their need to read a banned book, the avoidance of anti-religious books remains a moral requirement.

Need for younger clerics recognized

Vatican, August 12, 1966
Conscious of the need to rejuvenate the clergy, especially in the light of Vatican II and the spiritual demands issuing from it, Pope Paul VI has just published a long-awaited *Motu Proprio*. Its recommendation that bishops and priests retire at 75 is a deliberate act aimed at accelerating this process of rejuvenation and preventing the stagnation of their minds and bodies. However, in order for this to be effective, the number of recruits to the priesthood must increase. At present there is little sign of this happening.

One thousand years of Polish Christianity

Mgr. Wojtyla replaced Paul VI for the celebratory mass in Czestochowa.

Poland, May 3, 1966
Nearly half a million people flooded into Czestochowa to celebrate the thousandth anniversary of Poland's conversion. This was despite the many obstacles put in their way by the Communist authorities, such as roads and railroads blocked or under repair, and intimidating threats at work. The Polish episcopate had invited Paul VI to attend the celebrations, but he had not been granted a visa by the Polish State, upon orders from the Kremlin. No matter. Archbishop Wojtyla stepped into his shoes to celebrate a pontifical mass during which he renewed the 1555 vow dedicating Poland to the Virgin. The fervor within the sanctuary was palpable. "All of us" he said, "Polish bishops and God's people, we grant forgiveness."

On September 4, 1966, the Black Virgin of Czestochowa, which was being carried through the entire country, was stopped at Katowice by Communist demonstrators. In this anniversary year, they are particularly concerned to put a halt to the people's piety. Mgr. Wojtyla was forced to turn back.

The new church at Niegowic is consecrated by its archbishop

The new church is much bigger.

Mgr. Wojtyla's former congregation flocked to welcome and thank him.

Poland, September 25, 1966
Karol Wojtyla is back in the small parish where he had been assistant priest at the end of the 1940s. It was largely thanks to him that the attendance had increased so markedly, soon outgrowing the old church.

Sixteen years later, the new church that he had fought hard to get permission for, is complete. And he is back to consecrate it. As for the old church, it is still there, but not for long. Being made of wood, it can be dismantled, and it has another cus-

tomer waiting for it. The parish of Metkow, about thirty miles away, east of Cracow, is in need of a church but has been refused building permission. But no such permission is needed to put up a church which is already built!

Holy Places under Jewish control

Jerusalem, June 27, 1967
The Israeli parliament, the Knesset, has adopted a law guaranteeing free access to the Holy Places, alongside severe sanctions to be applied to those hindering such access. It is only 5 days since the Knesset unanimously approved the annexation of the eastern part of Jerusalem, while declaring it "irreversible and non-negotiable." On June 8, following a lightning war, Israeli troops led by Moshe Dayan seized all the Old Town, both the Arab and Christian sectors, previously controlled by Jordan. The Israeli vote concerning access to the Holy Places is still a long way from satisfying the wishes of the Vatican. Since the creation of the Jewish State and the partition of the city, the Papacy has been petitioning for international status for the Holy City. It is the main obstacle to closer links between the Vatican and Israel. Paul VI is determined to guarantee a Christian presence in Palestine.

Nothing can prevent him from spending time alone in the midst of nature.

Police report on Mgr. Wojtyla

Warsaw, 1967
The description of Karol Wojtyla given by a secret police agent, a specialist in religious matters is, if not flattering, nonetheless surprisingly full of insight into the prelate's character. He says Wojtyla is "one of the few intellectuals among the Polish episcopate." He continues: "Unlike Wyszynski, he easily reconciles popular piety with Catholic intellectualism ... So far, he has not got involved in activities opposed to the State. He has shown little interest in politics." The report recommends a course of action aimed at ultimately dividing the two clerics. Wojtyla is, according to the agent, flexible, and should not therefore be attacked; neither should he be openly supported.

An encyclical for developing nations

Rome, March 26, 1967
"The new name for peace is the development of peoples ..." reckons Pope Paul VI. His latest encyclical, *Popularum Progressio* (*Development of Peoples*), published today, acts as a reminder to people of their rights to self-determination. It also stresses the need for the former colonial powers to participate in such a "development that demands bold transformations." "It is for each one to take his share in them with generosity," he firmly suggests.

Gomulka revives anti-Semitism

Poland, June 19, 1967
Having already condemned "Israeli aggression" and all the expressions of sympathy that the Israeli victory had aroused within Poland itself, the first secretary, Gomulka, launched a violent counterattack with strong overtones of anti-Semitism. Before the Congress of Trade Unions, he derided the "Zionist milieu of Poland's Jewish citizens," and reiterated that a Pole can never have more than "one motherland." This diatribe is the starting point for a State campaign of anti-Semitism.

Raised to cardinal in Sistine Chapel

Vatican, June 28, 1967
The archbishop of Cracow is one of 27 cardinals named by Paul VI. For Karol Wojtyla, it is undoubtedly recompense for his intense pastoral activity in Poland, which has proved him to be one of the most effective executors of the Council's decisions. This afternoon, all the new cardinals were given their red birettas by the pope. They donned their cardinals' vestments in the sacristy (Sala dei Paramenti) and, led by the doyen of the Sacred College, they processed into the Sistine Chapel. There, seated in front of them, the pope pronounced the sacred words: "For the glory of the all-powerful God and for the glory of the Church, accept this sign of the dignity of cardinal through which you will become the defender of the Faith and pledge your blood." In accordance with ancient tradition, each cardinal was assigned a church in Rome by Pope Paul VI. Karol Wojtyla was given San Cesareo, a beautiful building near the Baths of Caracalla. Mgr. Wojtyla owes his rapid rise to the position of cardinal to the vigor of his evangelical message, which is crystal clear, straightforward and extremely precise.

Meeting with de Gaulle passed up in support of Wyszynski

Cracow, September 8, 1967
Charles de Gaulle is the first French head of State to visit Poland. He already knows the country a little, having served here as a military adviser from April 1919 to January 1921. He even managed to speak a few words of Polish to the Council president, Edward Ochab, who met him at the airport. Accompanied by the minister of education, Alain Peyrefitte, he gave an address to the students at Jagiellonian University today. As the authorities have refused permission for the primate of Poland, Mgr. Wyszynski, to have a meeting with General de Gaulle, they suggested he might like to see the archbishop of Cracow instead. However, Karol Wojtyla himself has declined the honor, purely out of solidarity for Mgr. Wyszynski, replying that he is "committed to other engagements." De Gaulle did not take offence, considering it an elegant and honorable action.

A warm welcome was accorded the French president upon his arrival.

Archbishop defends Polish culture

Cracow, July 31, 1967
The Rhapsodic Theater has been banned by the authorities, having twice previously been forced to close. Established by Mieczyslaw Kotlarczyk, this drama company is renowned for supporting Christian playwrights and using the theater as a means for discussing metaphysical issues. Karol Wojtyla acted with them as a young man, as well as writing and directing plays for them. Having signed a petition for them in April, he said the following about this new decision: " A great wrong has been done to Polish culture. It is proof that there is no freedom of thought in our country."

Paul VI determined to modernize Curia

Vatican, August 15, 1967
Paul VI has just published a new Apostolic Constitution, *Regimini Ecclesiae Universae*, which chiefly aims to modernize the Curia. This desire came across clearly in many of the speeches at the Council. For his part, the pope has succeeded in overcoming the resistance of the Roman prelates. Certain archaic organizations have been suppressed, like the Datary and the Secretariat of Briefs to Princes. Others have been promoted, like the Secretariats for Christian Unity and for Non-Christians.

Together or not at all ...

Vatican, September 29, 1967
"Only together can we come to the synod; we constitute a united delegation of the Polish episcopate." This was how Cardinal Wojtyla was obliged to justify his absence from the first Assembly of the Synod of Bishops, due to open in Rome. His statement is a protest against the Communist State's refusal to grant an exit visa to Mgr. Wyszynski, the primate. This decision illustrates the extent to which relations between the Church and the State have come to a head, against a background of social and economic problems.

As is to be expected from someone of his dynamic character, the newly created cardinal Wojtyla is pursuing a vigorous program of pastoral visits.

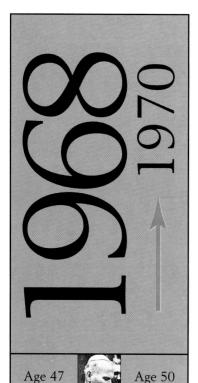

Wadowice, January 9, 1968.
Mgr. Wojtyla attends Father Jan Pawela's funeral.

Rome, February 18, 1968.
Mgr. Wojtyla takes possession of the Church of San Cesareo as part of his cardinalship.

Warsaw, April 11, 1968.
General Wojciech Jaruzelski becomes minister of defense.

Vatican, June 26, 1968.
Paul VI announces the discovery of the remains of St. Peter.

Poland, July 1968.
15,000 Jews have fled the country since April.

Vatican, November 2, 1968.
In reply to Paul VI's statement that "Poland needs a saint," Karol Wojtyla suggests Father Maximilian Kolbe.

Vatican, May 2, 1969.
Mgr. Jean-Marie Villot becomes secretary of State for the Vatican.

Switzerland, June 6, 1969.
Mgr. Lefebvre founds the Society of St. Pius X, in Fribourg.

Uganda, August 2, 1969.
Paul VI is the first pope to travel to Africa. He says: "Africans, you have [become] your own missionaries."

Cracow, December 1969.
The Polish Theological Society publishes *The Acting Person*, an essay by Mgr. Wojtyla.

Vatican, October 19, 1970.
The Holy See recognizes the legitimacy of the Warsaw government by asking the representative of the Polish government in exile to leave.

Renowned for trusting everybody and never losing his temper

Cracow, 1968
Cardinal Wojtyla is determined not to use the Archbishop's Palace in the center of the old part of Cracow as his residence, but he nonetheless uses it for his work and has already made his mark there. The opinion of those around him and those who work for him is unanimous: he is exceptionally pleasant to be with and to work for. Every morning he still says mass before breakfast, at 7am. He prays, meditates and writes until 11am. Then his appointments begin. After lunch, the afternoon is mostly taken up with administrative matters for the diocese. Fathers Mikolaj Kuczkowski and Stefan Marszowski, his two chancellors as well as his closest collaborators, never cease praising his calm and hard work. His secretary, Sister Jadwiga, confirms this, although she feels that sometimes he places his trust a little too readily in those he does not know.

The cardinal knows how to be as close to his people as to his collaborators.

'Muscovite scoundrels' given notice

Warsaw, January 30, 1968
The police violently dispersed the students demonstrating around the statue of the Polish playwright Adam Mickiewicz. They had been there since the end of the last performance of *The Forefathers' Eve* given at Narodowy Theater. The play is a 19th century classic from the repertoire of Polish theater. Its current success has irritated the authorities since the play opened in November. The piece does in fact contain quite a few anti-czarist tirades and retorts such as: "Moscow has always sent us scoundrels!" The applause this incited and the obvious parallels to be drawn with the present situation, led the minister of culture to limit the number of performances, in the first instance, and then to ban them altogether. The students, who are largely responsible for the play's success over the past two months, and who demonstrated their anger in opposition to this ban, are certain that tonight's arrests will not break their determination.

Student demonstrators are forcibly put down by the police.

Metaphysical cause of Church's crisis

Cracow, February 1968
When Karol Wojtyla was helping write Vatican II's final document, *Gaudium et Spes*, he had met France's two most influential theologians of the time, Fathers Yves Congar and Henri de Lubac. They were equally struck by the powerful impression the young archbishop from Cracow made on them. Like them, he was a specialist in ethics and moral theology. At the time of the Commissions' work for Vatican II, they had particularly noticed Wojtyla's charisma and the clarity of his speeches. Wojtyla has kept up a correspondence with Father de Lubac. He has just told him that, whenever possible, he is working on his book which deals with "the metaphysical sense and the mystery of the Person." According to him, the crisis currently striking the Catholic Church is due more to metaphysics than morals: "The evil of our time consists ... in a sort of degradation, or a disintegration of the fundamental uniqueness of each human being ... We should oppose it [not] with sterile arguments [but] with a recapitulation of the sacred mystery of the person."

Church comes to aid of students

Poland, March 28, 1968
After two months of restlessness, the student movement has calmed down. The State is taking advantage of the lull to purge the universities. But the fever which has caught hold of the students has in no sense gone away. The movement's aspirations are voiced in their Declaration, a veritable manifesto explaining the nature of true, democratic socialism. The university managed to face up to the Communists for a short while, thanks partly to the unfailing support of the Church. Six days ago, an episcopal communiqué, clearly bearing the hand of Mgr. Wojtyla, was published denouncing police repression, accusing the official media of distorting the facts, and demanding the liberation of those students still in prison, among whom is Jacek Kuron, detained for "Zionist schemings."

Paul VI condemns contraception

Vatican, July 29, 1968
In October, 1964, the question of birth control had been removed from the agenda of the Council, which left the final decision in the hands of the pope. Four years later, after many delays, the encyclical *Humanae Vitae* offers a long-awaited reply for millions of Catholics. Paul VI's position is made quite clear: in the name of the principle of natural law established by God, he is opposed to all forms of chemical or artificial contraception. Only the temperature method (Ogino), approved in 1951 by Pope Pius XII, remains legal. The pill is not actually mentioned anywhere in the encyclical, but it is foremost in people's minds. Catholics in Western Europe and America are deeply upset by this decision. Back in 1966, the Church's commission of experts had recommended that these precepts be reformed. The encyclical ban is perhaps more of a personal decision. Paul VI is known to have consulted Cardinal Wojtyla, author of a book on marital morals, *Love and Responsibility*. There is no doubt Wojtyla's theses influenced the pope's convictions.

Celebrating mass does not need an actual church ... and he proves it.

Skis and paddles complete the move

Cracow, January 10, 1969
Cardinal Wojtyla has been tricked. It was well known that he did not wish to make the Archbishop's Palace his residence. He preferred

His new residence, the Archbishop's Palace, at 3 Franciszkanska Street.

to remain in Kanonicza Street, near Wawel Castle. So while he was away, his secretary, Stanislaw Dziwisz, moved his belongings. Cardinal Wojtyla gave in gracefully and moved the last of his belongings himself, including his skis and the paddles which he always takes with him on his canoeing trips. His clothes had been simple to move: his wardrobe consisted of no more than three black cassocks, four red ones, and three pairs of heavy shoes. The episcopal palace is just beside the Franciscan Church where he often goes by himself to pray, and near the Planty, the tree-lined avenues where, as a student, he often used to go for walks. Mgr. Wojtyla's diocese is roughly 5,000 sq. miles, with 327 parishes, nearly a thousand priests and over 600 monks and nuns. He has already broken one tradition: that of an archbishop taking his meals alone. His close co-workers enjoy having their meals with him. In fact everyone has nothing but praise for him.

The Red Army invades Prague

Czechoslovakia, August 21, 1968
"Socialism with a human face" and the "Prague Spring" are living their last hours. Polish, East German, Soviet, and Hungarian tanks rolled into Czechoslovakia during the night, seizing strategic points within the major cities. The Polish first secretary, Wladyslaw Gomulka, has been one of the most outspoken supporters of the Soviet leaders, continually pushing for military intervention to put an end to this "counterrevolution." The only one to seriously favor moderation was Janos Kadar, the Hungarian, but he was forced to bend to orders from the Kremlin. Poland is directly involved by dint of her proximity to Czechoslovakia. Also, after all the student agitation last March, the Polish Communists are obsessed with the fear of unrest spreading, of the Czechs somehow escaping from the lap of Socialism. Although, in Warsaw, news of the Soviet invasion has provoked remarkably little protest, the Czech affair has nevertheless served to confirm general anti-Soviet sentiment.

Cassock and kippa for the synagogue

Cracow, February 28, 1969
Karol Wojtyla was met in Szeroka Street, at the synagogue entrance, by Maciej Jakubowicz, president of the small Jewish community in the city's Kazimierz district. Cardinal Wojtyla had expressed a wish to make contact with Cracow's Jews, while on a visit to the parish of Corpus Domini. Jakubowicz and Wojtyla had a long conversation before entering the synagogue where, on the eve of the Sabbath, a small crowd had gathered to pray. Wearing just his black cassock, with the traditional kippa on his head, Wojtyla joined the faithful in prayer. Afterwards, the cardinal and Maciej Jakubowicz visited Cracow's other synagogue, , which contained no crowd, just one man praying alone. At a time when the Communist regime is stirring up the still smouldering embers of anti-Semitism, Cardinal Wojtyla is speaking out in favor of reconciliation.

'You cannot pigeonhole him, he's even a bit mischievous'

His speeches are noted at synod

North America, September 1969
This is what a Canadian journalist had to say about Cardinal Wojtyla at the end of his trip to Canada and the United States: "He's the most likeable man I've ever met. ... You cannot tag a label on him. He's even a bit mischievous. Just like a close member of the family!" Cardinal Wojtyla was concerned to show the Polish émigrés that their country had not forgotten them. Thus, he set out to meet the *Polonia*, the Polish diaspora, in all its vastness across the United States and Canada. At first he was somewhat surprised by their way of life, but after a while he warmed to the lack of formality in their relations with one another, as it seemed to suit his own character remarkably well.

His unwavering supporters treat him almost like a Hollywood star.

Vatican, October 28, 1969
This time both Cardinal Wojtyla and Cardinal Wyszynski were granted visas to attend the synod in Rome. The head of each country's episcopate was present to discuss the issue of collegial structure within the government of the Church. Drawing upon his Polish experiences and his recent American tour for inspiration, Cardinal Wojtyla's speeches did not pass unnoticed. He talked about Christian communities and groups, about their dynamics, and the need for a "collegial structure." At the end of which he was asked to be part of the committee in charge of writing the final declaration summarising the deliberations.

Paul VI alters the rules for electing a pope

Holy See, November 21, 1970
Paul VI's *Motu proprio* recently modified the conditions for electing a pope. Entitled "Ingravescentem Aetatem," it limits the number of cardinal members of the Sacred College to 120. It is they who elect the new pontiff at the time of a conclave. Paul VI has also imposed an age limit. From now on only cardinals under the age of eighty can elect a pope. Those in their eighties will of course remain cardinals but will be excluded from conclaves. Since Pius XII, the period allowed for the Holy See to remain vacant has been limited to 18 days, after which a conclave must be called. In the interval, the Church is ruled by a cardinal called the camerlengo.

On May 18, 1969, the cardinal lays the foundation stone for the Church of Nowa Huta. Donated by the pope, the stone comes from St. Peter's.

On May 18, 1970, Mgr. Wojtyla celebrated his 50th birthday. He returned to his birthplace for the occasion. He consecrated the new church bells, bought by Father Edward Zacher, his catechism teacher in the 1930s.

Price rises spark insurrection in the Baltic

Poland, December 17, 1970

For the past four days, several towns along the Baltic coast have been in a state of insurrection, which the Polish authorities persist in calling "anarchic plots, counterrevolution and outbursts of hooliganism." It all began on the morning of Saturday 12th, when an increase in prices of between 10% and 30% was announced on the radio, affecting all basic necessities and foodstuffs. This news was particularly badly received in view of the approaching holidays. The following Monday, tools were immediately downed at the naval dockyards in Gdansk. Delegates from the Party came to explain the reasons for the price rises, but were shouted down and beat a hasty retreat. Processions started forming, making their way through the town to rally other workers, calling for the abolition of the price rises and for Gomulka to resign. To the north of Gdansk, in Gdynia, Elblag and Szczecin, the same scenarios were occurring. The army and the police reacted with brutality, firing on the demonstrators. In spite of keeping the region in almost total isolation, the government is still paranoid about the possibility of the contagion spreading.

After 48 hours of rioting in Gdansk, there are already five dead and 33 seriously wounded. It is an uprising.

Homage to an old sporting friend

Cracow, December 20, 1970

Today's *Tygodnik Powszechny* has an obituary of Jerzy Ciesielski, who died in an accident on the Nile on October 9, with two of his young children. The tribute is written by Karol Wojtyla, an old friend of his. It was Ciesielski who had originally encouraged Karol to go canoeing, patiently teaching him and helping him overcome his initial fear. The cardinal recalls, in the article, their numerous expeditions together, and their lengthy conversations on marriage, on the vocation, and on their love of nature. He also remembers those open air masses, said "in a forest, beside a lake, experiencing together that strange osmosis of the Mystery of the Redemption and the Mystery of the Creation." Karol Wojtyla has lost one whose "life and words were in perfect harmony."

Gierek replaces Gomulka after riots and brutal repression

Gierek is in favor of resolving the crisis, as are the Soviets.

Warsaw, December 20, 1970

Wladyslaw Gomulka has signed his own letter of resignation from his hospital bed. Abandoned by the Soviets, he could see no other solution to popular unrest than the continued use of the most brutal repression. Two days ago, some members of the governing body, centered around Edward Gierek, had come to realize that while repression brings calm, it does not get rid of the causes of worker discontent. For them, only the removal of Gomulka, ill and suffering from fits of increasingly idiosyncratic behavior, would resolve the problem. The Soviets had no desire to intervene, but clearly saw the explosiveness of the situation, and wrote a letter dissociating themselves from all Gomulka's repressive action. Even according to official sources the riots have caused 45 deaths and 1,200 wounded. The truth will be even grimmer.

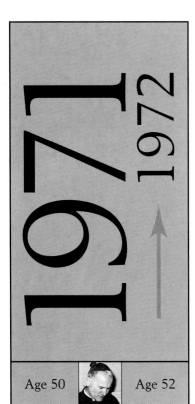

1971 1972

Age 50 — Age 52

Warsaw, January 20, 1971.
The government announces the reconstruction of the Castle, destroyed by the Germans. A bishop will be assigned to the works committee.

Poland, January 27, 1971.
In response to the government's goodwill, the Church calls the faithful to "pray for the nation."

Switzerland, June 6, 1971.
The foundation stone for the seminary of the Society of Saint Pius X in Ecône is laid by Mgr. Lefebvre.

France, September 2, 1971.
The front page of *Le Monde* announces the marriage of Father Jean-Claude Barreau.

Warsaw, November 10, 1971.
Visit of Mgr. Casaroli, head of the Vatican's diplomatic service.

Warsaw, December 11, 1971.
General Jaruzelski joins the Party's political office.

Nowa Huta, December 25, 1971.
Despite the ban, Karol Wojtyla celebrates midnight mass outside by candlelight.

Poland, January 1, 1972.
The New Year message given by Mgrs. Wyszynski and Wojtyla ends: "The life of the nation cannot develop within an atmosphere of terror."

Vatican, March 25, 1972.
New rules are issued for appointing bishops, which include consulting diocesans.

Poland, June 1, 1972.
Richard Nixon is the first American president to visit Poland.

Church and State near reconciliation

Warsaw, March 3, 1971
Mgr. Wyszynski, Poland's Primate, and Piotr Jaroszewicz, the prime minister, met earlier today for the first high level discussions to be held between Church and State for ten years. They will hopefully bring to an end the rupture between the two parties. The *modus vivendi* which has prevailed up till now – really more of a "cold coexistence" – should be replaced, thanks to the renewed contact, by a partnership which is at least constructive for both parties, if not overtly friendly. Since his nomination in December, Prime Minister Jaroszewicz has made increasingly positive overtures toward the Catholic hierarchy and has announced the forthcoming complete normalization of relations with the Church. On January 25, the Church's legal ownership of nearly 7,000 buildings and places of worship was recognized. Several previously refused building permits for churches have subsequently been granted, and censorship of religious publications has been considerably reduced.

Role in Secretariat of bishop's synod

Vatican, October 5, 1971
Mgr. Wojtyla has been elected to the Council for the General Secretariat. He was chosen on the second ballot, by 115 votes out of 184, and he thus becomes the third-ranking member of the permanent synod secretariat. The latest synod started five days ago, and is primarily dedicated to world justice and the priesthood. While the debates on justice raised no real surprises, those on the future of vocations were considerably more heated. Faced by the present crisis in vocations, and by the ever-growing demands of modernists for modification of the rules of the priesthood, Cardinal Wojtyla clearly pointed out that it is not the Church which is in crisis, but man himself. He reminded his audience that personal vocation remained first and foremost a response to the call of Christ, and that the ardent demands of this call must not be allowed to be sacrificed to the ephemeral.

Father Kolbe beatified thanks to Wojtyla

The Cardinal put forward Maximilian Kolbe as the most saintly of Poles.

Vatican, October 17, 1971
Thousands of Poles have managed to obtain visas to be here on this cold but sunny morning, for the mass in celebration of the beatification of Father Maximilian Kolbe. The ceremony is being conducted by Pope Paul VI in person, assisted by Mgr. Wyszynski and Mgr. Wojtyla. It was upon Wojtyla's suggestion that the Holy Father commenced the beatification process for Kolbe, a Franciscan who, in Auschwitz, was condemned to starvation in a cell with a dozen other prisoners. Cardinal Wojtyla also gave some urns containing a little bit of earth to several of the bishops. The earth is from the extermination camps at Birkenau and Auschwitz.

Mgr. Wojtyla likes to meditate in the simplest of places, like in this former Franciscan church almost directly opposite the Archbishop's Palace.

Wojtyla supports celibacy for priests

Vatican, November 6, 1971
Cardinal Wojtyla is back in Rome to take part in the second synod dedicated to the priesthood, which began on September 30. Confronted with the modernist suggestions of the Dutch bishops, Karol Wojtyla restated his view that celibacy and the priesthood are and must remain one. He explained that: "It is by this giving of himself that the priest discovers his identity and his place within society ... This call, insisting that the priest follows Christ in a perfect state, explains the link between the priesthood and celibacy. ... This sign must be visible and understood through his priests."

Jews and Catholics at the same table

Paris, December 16, 1971
"For twenty centuries, Jews and ... representatives of the Church have not been seen to sit together at the same table." This was said by one of the participants at the first assembly of the International Committee for Liaison between Catholics and Jews, which took place amidst great emotion in the Central Consistory in Rue Saint Georges. The delegations were made up of five members from each side, and were led by the Chief Rabbi, Arthur Hertzberg, on the one hand, and the archbishop of Marseilles, Monsignor Roger Etchegaray, on the other hand.

St. Stanislaus patron saint of the Poles

Cracow, April 9, 1972
Every church within the diocese heard Mgr. Wojtyla's letter on the occasion of the 900th anniversary of the nomination of Stanislaus of Szczepanow (the future St. Stanislaus) as bishop of Cracow. In the letter, the life of "he who will remain the patron saint of faith and has been accepted as such ... by the Polish soul," serves as an example for the whole nation. The cardinal also asked the country to participate in the renewal of the Church, as enjoined by Vatican II.

Christmas 1972: Cardinal Wojtyla shares the unleavened bread with Chamberlain Tadeusz Novak. He is the first archbishop to practice this 17th century tradition, borrowed from the Jews. The Poles have adopted the habit of breaking the bread as a sign of sharing and fraternity.

Believers should link faith to morality

Cracow, May 8, 1972
Alongside the opening of the synod of Polish bishops, Mgr. Wojtyla has published a study based on his own experience at the head of the diocese of Cracow. Simply entitled *The Foundations of Renewal*, it looks at how to put into practice the teachings of Vatican II. It questions both the Polish Church and the faithful on the means of accomplishing one's duties as a believer, on fully realizing oneself "within the Church." One must "link faith to morality," making pastoral effort equally the business of the laity, so that they themselves open up to others and become involved in the spirit of communion both through their words and their deeds."

Surrounded by scientists, Cardinal Wojtyla listens to the latest findings concerning the tomb of King Kaziemierz Jagellon in Wawel Cathedral.

Inauguration of Cracow synod

Cracow, May 8, 1972
To coincide with the anniversary celebrations for Saint Stanislaus, a synod of the archdiocese of Cracow was inaugurated today. In the year since it was announced, study groups have been set up in every parish within the diocese, to discuss themes such as the priesthood, youth and marital life. This group work perfectly illustrates Cardinal Wojtyla's desire to involve the faithful in discussions on the Church. At the ceremony, Wojtyla declared: "During the course of these study groups, ... we wish to be deeply receptive to the council's contributions, to do our best."

Special mass said in Auschwitz

Auschwitz, October 15, 1972
Karol Wojtyla celebrated the first anniversary of the beatification of Maximilian Kolbe before a crowd of 200,000. It was the first time the government had authorized mass to be held on the site of the camp. Addressing his somber congregation, Mgr. Wojtyla said: "We are ... here to participate in the sacrifice of Christ, in the millions of sacrifices of those men who gave their lives. ... Their ashes are under our feet."

Possibility of non Italian pope raised

Venice, November 1972
Mgr. Albino Luciani, patriarch of Venice, was receiving a group of French pilgrims. One of them asked him if, after four centuries of Italian popes, he could imagine having a non-Italian pontiff. He replied: "I can see at least two. ... The first is the best among us, but he cannot be pope. In a century which has given rise to Auschwitz, the pope cannot possibly be an Austrian. His name? Cardinal Koenig: [he is] archbishop of Vienna. As for the second, he is the bishop of Auschwitz. [I am referring to] a young Polish cardinal." His name? "He's called Wojtyla." None of the French there had ever heard of him.

Poland, January 1973.
The Church protests against the adoption of a law "on the education of the young and their participation in the building of Socialism."

Holy See, January 16, 1973.
Golda Meir is the first Israeli head of State to be received by the Vatican. She meets Paul VI to discuss the status of Jerusalem.

Vatican, March 27, 1973.
Cardinal Wojtyla participates in the Sacred Congregation of the Clergy.

Warsaw, April 19, 1973.
The commemoration of the 30th anniversary of the insurrection of the Warsaw ghetto takes place in the Yiddish Theater, a sign that the policy towards the Jews is evolving.

Vatican, May 10, 1973.
Paul VI receives Chenouda III, head of the Coptic Church.

Warsaw, January 1974.
The new minister of religions, Kazimir Kakol, states that the role of the Church must limit itself to "the sacristy" and that he does not want any "evangelizing outside the Church."

Italy, May 13, 1974.
The Church speaks of its consternation after the referendum passing the law on divorce.

Vatican, June 21, 1974.
Karol Wojtyla participates in the anniversary ceremonies of Paul VI's consecration, as well as for the consecration of his friend Andrzej Deskur.

Cardinal Wojtyla enjoys traveling to far corners of the world

Poland, March 9, 1973

Cardinal Wojtyla is back home again after a busy month traveling to the other side of the world. He departed from Fiumicino, Rome's airport, on February 6, arriving on the 7th at Manila, with stops in Karachi and Bangkok. His stay in the Philippines was a great revelation to him, since it is an enclave of Catholicism in the midst of Muslim and Buddhist countries. The Cardinal celebrated mass on the evening of his arrival, and was struck by the piety of some of the faithful who advanced up the middle of the nave on their knees. Then the Polish delegation flew off to Port Moresby, New Guinea's capital. There, the cardinal encountered several Polish missionaries, all from the Society of the Divine Word. The local missionaries sang some very beautiful songs in dialect. After Papua New Guinea came Australia, where the Eucharistic Congress was being held – the main reason for this Antipodean journey. Wojtyla was feted in Melbourne, Sydney and Brisbane, by the famous *Polonia*, the Polish community found in every country with immigrants, which even has its own priests. Everywhere he went Wojtyla was received at the *Dom Polski*, the Polish House. The archbishop of Cracow made a loop down to New Zealand and back to Melbourne, where he celebrated a mass in honor of all the ethnic groups of Australia. Psalms and prayers were read out in fifteen different languages!

An absolute must on an Australian tour: a visit to a kangaroo reserve.

His reception in Papua New Guinea was overwhelmingly friendly. Mass was said in Latin, Polish and dialect.

The Acting Person to be translated

Cracow, July 29, 1973
Anna-Teresa Tymieniecka had been wanting to meet the archbishop of Cracow, ever since she had first read his work *Osoba i Czyn* (*The Acting Person*), published in 1969. As a specialist in phenomenology and a philosophy lecturer in the United States, she was forever recommending the book to her students. She has even undertaken a translation of it. While in Poland, she wanted to meet the author to encourage him to expand his ideas in a fuller version of the work. The daughter of Polish aristocrats, Anna-Teresa had left Poland in 1946 to study in Paris. She settled in America in 1954, and is married to one of the advisors to Richard Nixon.

Wyszynski steps up his resistance to the Communist regime

Poles see the Wyszynski-Wojtyla tandem as their best hope for freedom.

Warsaw, January 1974
Cardinal Wyszynski, the primate of Poland, recently delivered several brilliant homilies clearly illustrating his changed attitude with regard to the regime. Through his voice, the Church has indicated that it is no longer content to just provide moral resistance, but wishes to be involved in the political debate. His sermons discuss relations between men, on the one hand, and economics and power on the other. He also says about productivity: "Materialistic values cannot hide man's mission from him, the significance of his humanity, the dignity of the human person." The primate also attacks the omnipotence of the State, the influence of its organizations over the young, and the uniformity of thought which it produces.

700 years since death of Aquinas

Italy, April 24, 1974
Cardinal Wojtyla took part in a number of events celebrating the seventh centenary of the death of St. Thomas Aquinas. Some were held in Rome, others in Rocca Secca, his birthplace, in Fossanova Abbey where he died, in Naples and in Aquino. They commemorated the life of a man who was responsible for the most important synthesis of Medieval Christian thought, and who sought to reconcile faith and reason, a project dear to Wojtyla.

Some say sexuality is overdiscussed

Poland, June 1974
Many people, both lay and Church members within Poland and abroad, are concerned by Mgr. Wojtyla's seeming preoccupation with the matter of sexuality. In these post-Council times and after publication of *Humanae Vitae*, it has certainly become a burning issue. In the Western world, the clergy are more in touch with the ever-increasing tide of marital problems and breakdown. For Karol Wojtyla, these issues are crucial, but his answers are not really what was hoped for. In 1960, *Love and Responsibility* stated his opinion on the importance of love and the sexual act within the life of a couple. But this act of love takes place within the divine order of things. Sexuality must therefore be matched by a moral requirement. It is within marriage, and only there, that sexuality can fully flourish. But sexuality needs self-control and the ability to listen to one's partner. Another struggle equally preoccupying the mind of Cardinal Karol Wojtyla is the "culture of death," which has led to his vigorous rejection of abortion, as well as contraception.

Firm rejection of liberation theology

Vatican, October 26, 1974
Begun on September 27, the third session of the synod has just ended. Dedicated solely to evangelism, the synod was the forum for some extremely lively debates, both for and against liberation theology. This movement is very active in South America, where Marxist principles are used to justify the involvement of priests in the defense of the poor. Cardinal Wojtyla has responded that Marxism does not leave the Church any chance of existing.

Lefebvre opposed to Vatican II

France, November 21, 1974
Mgr. Lefebvre, head of the Church's traditionalist fringe, has published a manifesto in which he takes up all the reproaches that their movement has already made to the Council. He refers to Vatican II as an act of "robbery," the "liberals' sleight of hand" which neither John XXIII nor Paul VI opposed even when they did not agree. The Council should have been dogmatic, not "pastoral." The pope should refuse to advance ecumenism and should argue his own infallibility in matters of dogma, as stated in Vatican I.

In 1974, Mgr. Wojtyla takes part in a top-level meeting of the Catholic newspaper *Tygodnik Powszechny*.

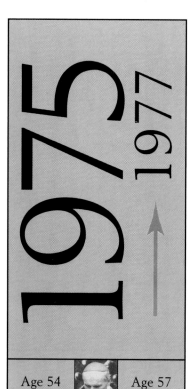

Age 54   Age 57

France, January 17, 1975.
Legalization of abortion.

Warsaw, May 12, 1975.
Large gathering in Wawel
Cathedral for the 40th
anniversary of the death of
Jozef Pilsudski.

Rome, June 26, 1975.
Death of Mgr. Escriva de
Balaguer (b. January 9, 1902),
founder of Opus Dei.

Vatican, July 22, 1976.
Mgr. Lefebvre is suspended *a
divinis.*

Poland, September 9, 1976.
The Church agrees to Edward
Gierek's call for co-operation,
on condition that the repression
of the workers ceases.

Lourdes, February 1, 1977.
Death of Mgr. Jean Rodhain
(b. January 27, 1900), founder
of the *Secours Catholique.*

Paris, February 27, 1977.
Mgr. Lefebvre's followers
occupy the Church of
St. Nicholas du Chardonnet.

Rome, March 15, 1977.
End of the synod at which Mgr.
Wojtyla presided in the absence
of the titular president.

Mainz, June 23, 1977.
Mgr. Wojtyla is made doctor
honoris causa at the university.

France, July 1, 1977.
Mgr. Wojtyla presides over a
meeting of Polish Catholics.

Poland, November 1977.
The KOR creates a mobile
university designed to oppose
official teaching.

Paris, December 6, 1977.
Death of Raoul Follereau
(b. August 17, 1903), a key
figure in the fight against
leprosy.

Institute of the Family is founded

Cracow, February 9, 1975
The highly critical comments arising
from the publication of *Humanae
Vitae* in 1968, led Cardinal Wojtyla
to submit the issue of Catholic con-
jugal ethics to moral theologians.
For years they held informal debates
and meetings, but they lacked an in-
terface with the outside world. This
is why the Cardinal decided to create the Institute of the Family. From
the outset, it engaged with the views
of moralists and doctors in debates
such as "A look at all aspects of in-
terrupting a pregnancy." The unequivocal opinion on this issue was
that this form of "destruction is a
serious wrong."

Yalta's frontiers not to be altered

Helsinki, July 31, 1975
Thirty-five heads of government and
state today signed the final act of the
Conference for Security and Cooperation in Europe (CSCE). It is a
diplomatic victory for the Socialists.
In exchange for a few minor concessions on human rights, made to the
West, Leonid Brezhnev has gained
recognition for his doctrine of the
inviolability of Europe's frontiers,
inherited from the Yalta carve-up,
and for the notion of limited
sovereignty. East and West seem to
have their spheres of influence
frozen forever.

Conclave rules are altered again

Vatican, October 1, 1975
Romano Pontifici eligendo is the
name of Paul VI's constitution,
which takes up and refines all previous clauses and decisions to do with
a vacancy in the Holy See and the
election of a pope. The plenum of
120 cardinals is maintained, as is the
age limit of 80 years. The pontiff can
be elected by vote (with a majority
of two-thirds plus one), or by accla-
mation. In order to assure secrecy
of the ballot and freedom of the
electors, any indiscretion about the
deliberations of the conclave will be
punished with excommunication.

Polish Church on the offensive

Poland, November 25, 1975
The government has relaunched its project to reform the Constitution of 1952. Uppermost among the amendments are the Catholics' duty of loyalty toward the State, the inclusion in common law of the fact that Poland is a "Socialist State," and the subordination of citizens' rights to duty toward the State. Battle cries were immediately raised among Polish intellectuals. The Church has put up an equally rebellious front. The episcopal council has publicly declared that this is yet further proof of the "totalitarianism of the Marxist-Leninist ideology of the Party and the State."

Encyclical on how to preach the Gospels

Vatican, December 8, 1975
Evangelii Nuntiandi, Paul VI's latest encyclical, reminds Catholics that the Church's principal mission is the transmission and propagation of the Christian message throughout the world. But the methods of spreading the Gospels must take account of the changes within society, which "oblige all of us to revise methods, to seek ... how we can bring the Christian message to modern man. For it is only in [this that he] can find the answer to his questions ..." Disorientated and hungry for the truth, humanity awaits.

Premarital chastity next for discussion

Cracow, February 1976
The Institute of the Family, created by Cardinal Wojtyla as a center for exchange and reflection for Catholic theologians and doctors, is already organizing its third working session. The first session discussed and condemned the use of contraception. Now the committee is discussing the issue of premarital chastity. It is a precept which modern societies, including Christian ones, seem to have forgotten, but which is Cardinal Wojtyla's warhorse. He says it must be seen as a development rather than as an outdated restriction.

Mgr. Wojtyla is chosen by the pope to preach before the Curia

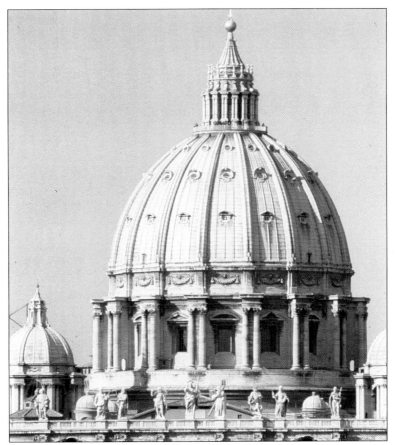
The Basilica of St. Peter's is at the heart of the Vatican State.

Vatican, March 13, 1976
Mgr. Wojtyla has just finished the last of twenty-seven sermons which he has given in the past week in the Chapel of St. Matilda. Paul VI did him the signal honor of entrusting him with the homilies for the Lent offices. Thus, for the past seven days the members of the Curia have been preached to by Karol Wojtyla, while the pope, who has not been well, stayed in the antechamber. The pontiff had no cause for regret. Even though the Polish cardinal had only had two weeks to prepare his talks, this did not show. He spoke in Italian, as advised by the pope. For those high-ranking prelates who did not already know him, he clearly displayed his exceptional qualities as a theologian as well as his skills as an orator. The title of his sermons was *Christ, Sign of Contradiction*, a subject of great importance to him. In them he was able to develop his view of the Church's place within modern societies, particularly within so-called liberal and tolerant systems which, in fact, undermine the very teachings of Christ. Mgr. Deskur, Wojtyla's Roman mentor, had good reason to be proud of him.

The conflict between Church and State is never-ending. On May 19, 1976, the minister of religions, Kakol, said: "The Poles' piety is superficial, emotional. [They] know nothing about dogma. It does not interest them at all."

Celebrity trip around the US to meet the *Polonia*

Harvard gives red carpet treatment

Boston, July 27, 1976
Cardinal Wojtyla has just delivered a lecture to the Harvard Divinity School thanks to an invitation from its director, Dr. George Hunston Williams, and many a good word from the philosopher Anna-Teresa Tymieniecka. Nothing had been spared in the organization: a car with chauffeur to greet him and 250 guests at the dinner given in his honor – no small achievement considering that it is only specialists who normally show any interest in Polish matters, and that Wojtyla himself is completely unknown. Cardinal Wojtyla spoke about his philosophical works, about phenomenology, about Husserl and St. Thomas Aquinas, and about the English translation of his work *The Acting Person*, which Anna-Teresa Tymieniecka is responsible for. His lecture aroused much interest, even in the media: the *New York Times* wrote a eulogistic article about it. Since his arrival in the US with his secretary Stanislaw Dziwisz, he has been constantly feted, with no sign of the enthusiasm waning.

An American souvenir: Father Malinski is on the cardinal's right and his secretary, Stanislaw Dziwisz, on the far left.

Human hunger in all its aspects

Philadelphia, August 8, 1976
Having had two weeks of rewarding philosophical discussions and contact making, Cardinal Wojtyla then took part in the 41st Eucharistic Congress in Philadelphia. Mother Teresa and Dom Helder Camara, the founder of the church of the poor, were also present. The sessions were dedicated to "humanity's different forms of hunger: hunger for God, for bread, for freedom, for justice, for truth and for peace ..." Karol Wojtyla talked about religious freedom. Interviewed by German television, he voiced his admiration for the joyful expression of faith in the US: "It's simpler, and more sincere ... We Europeans have made Christianity too intellectual."

Ever-growing popularity in the United States

United States, September 1, 1976
Mgr. Wojtyla's American tour is transpiring to be even more fruitful than hoped for. He has had long discussions with the most eminent members of the *Polonia*, the famous Polish community in exile, such as Mgr. John Krol, the archbishop of Philadelphia, and the great expert on Eastern Europe, Zbigniew Brzezinski. In each of the dozen cities he has visited, he has been warmly welcomed, as in Chicago, where there are 1.5 million Polish Americans, out of a grand total of 25 million throughout the US. During a cocktail party, Father Hendrik Houthakker, carried away by the general euphoria, introduced Karol Wojtyla as "the next pope."

Wyszynski's roses: a thorny gift

Warsaw, August 3, 1976
Cardinal Wyszynski, the primate of Poland, received a bouquet of 75 roses for his 75th birthday, sent with a telegram from none other than the Communist regime! This apparent sign of affection should not be misinterpreted. The Communist State has quite simply decided to favor the continued presence of Mgr. Wyszynski at the head of the Polish Church, with his policy of nonconfrontation, rather than Mgr. Wojtyla, whom they see as a rabble-rouser. The regime even went as far as to intervene directly with the Holy See to ask if Wyszynski could stay on despite the age limit. So it would seem that Wyszynski can do no wrong, and Wojtyla is the baddy.

Paul VI concedes meeting to Mgr. Lefebvre

Castel Gandolfo, Sept. 11, 1976
The Christian philosopher, Jean Guitton, a friend and confidant of Paul VI, interceded with the pope for him to receive Mgr. Lefebvre, who was suspended *a divinis* in July. This suspension did not stop the French prelate from celebrating mass in Lille last month in front of eight thousand faithful. Paul VI, keen to avoid an unwanted schism with the traditionalist wing of the French Church, had high hopes for their meeting. But Mgr. Lefebvre was intransigent in his view that liberalism had invaded the Roman Church and perverted its doctrines. In some of his demands, he barely stops short of renouncing the Holy Father. The gulf is as wide as ever.

Intellectual support for the workers

Poland, September 23, 1976

"To defend persecuted workers and victims of denials of justice." This single phrase sums up the objectives of the signatories of the petition of the Committee for the Defense of the Workers (the KOR). They are fourteen for the moment – young intellectuals and prestigious figures, Christian Democrats, Socialists or those with no political attachment – led by Jacek Kuron, Jan Jozef Lipski and Antoni Macierewicz. Their motive is the witch hunt by the law and the police against those workers, in Radom and in other cities, who have demonstrated against the price rises.

St. Martin's Church becomes a sanctuary

Cracow, June 17, 1977

Karol Wojtyla has spoken out yet again against repression. He clearly stated that "the solution is not to increase police manpower... Only one road leads to peace and national unity: that of absolute respect for the rights of all citizens and all Poles." In Warsaw, the men and women who had been on hunger-strike since May 25, have ended their protest against police violence. The police, however, have not yet dared to effect entry into the Church of St. Martin, which has been the protestors' sanctuary since the start of the strike.

The intolerance of atheists denounced

Rome, October 29, 1977

Cardinal Wojtyla is taking part in the bishops' synod on catechism and the role of religious education. He made a speech violently condemning the current show of official atheism in the Communist bloc countries. Speaking of Poland, he said that the authorities' intolerance and aggressive attitude toward religious education had forced parents to take the education on themselves. According to Wojtyla, it should be the State's task to assure complete religious freedom for its citizens.

Cardinal Wojtyla is revolted and sickened by police misconduct

On May 15, 1977, Mgr. Wojtyla consecrated the first church of Nowa Huta, in Mistrzejowice, a suburb of Cracow. The struggle surrounding the construction of this church dates back twenty years. Its success is seen as a symbol of the enduring passion of believers.

Cracow, May 15, 1977

Cardinal Wojtyla cannot hide his sorrow and pain. For, while he is consecrating the first church of Nowa Huta, in Mistrzejowice, he knows that the streets of Cracow are packed with thousands of mourners attending the funeral of Stanislaw Pyjas, a student from Jagiellonian University, who was found dead eight days ago. The militia stated that he had fallen down some steps while drunk. However, not only were there no steps near where his body was found, but also his wounds were those commonly associated with having been beaten up. It just happened that Pyjas was an active member of the KOR, and his friends reported that he had received numerous threats over the past weeks. Yesterday, as a precaution prior to the funeral, several members of the KOR were arrested by the political police. This did not discourage those taking part in today's mass, who filed through the old town in silence. A statement was read out in Wawel Cathedral asking for the creation of a "true and ... independent representative body for students." Subsequently, the first Committee of Student Solidarity has been formed. The rest of the world is watching with interest.

Lack of funds for Polish Church

Warsaw, December 1977

Even if the Church did have funds, the regime would not let it use them as it pleased. As the media is strictly supervised by the government, it is difficult for the Polish Church to convey its message except within the churches themselves. There is no Catholic daily newspaper, and all other publications are firmly controlled. The three weeklies can only publish 200,000 copies in total. (In France, where religious practice is far lower, its publications exceed a million copies.) All the churches under construction are running into numerous administrative problems. And this year the Church was only able to print 300,000 catechisms for nearly eight million schoolchildren; that is one between 26. No matter how oppressive things may be, religious sentiment is still alive.

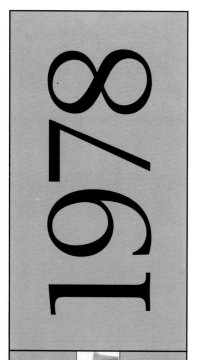

Age 57   Age 58

Warsaw, January 6.
In his Epiphany sermon, Mgr. Stefan Wyszynski asks for the Polish Church to have access to the media.

Cracow, February 21.
Mieczyslaw Kotlarczyk dies (b. May 6, 1908).

Katowice, early March.
Creation of the first founding committee of a free trade union.

Rome, May 9.
Aldo Moro, president of the Christian Democrats, is found assassinated.

Manchester, England, July 25.
Birth of Louise Brown, first test-tube baby.

Vatican, August 27.
Mgr. Wojtyla says that John Paul I is "the ideal man for this role. Thanks to his piety and humility he is open to receiving the Holy Spirit."

Vatican, August 30.
The pope receives Mgr. Wojtyla.

Vatican, September 17.
The pope confides that "if I had known that I would one day be pope, I would have learned more."

Vatican, September 20.
The pope states that it is false to believe that "where Lenin lies, so does Jerusalem."

Holy See, September 27.
John Paul I reveals that he has already been operated on 4 times.

Italy, October 17.
According to *La Stampa*: "The Soviets would rather see Solzhenitsyn made secretary general of the UN, than a Pole become pope."

58th birthday celebrated in Rome

Rome, May 18
Karol Wojtyla celebrated his 58th birthday at Mgr. Andrzej Deskur's residence. The two compatriots have remained good friends ever since their student days. Deskur has lived in Rome for thirty years and lets Wojtyla share his intimate knowledge of the Roman Curia. The Secretary of State for the Vatican, Mgr. Jean-Marie Villot, was the guest of honor at the meal. He surprised all present by saying that he thought Wojtyla was the only person capable of getting a majority vote.

The people's right to their 'opium'

Poland, June
100,000 miners gathered in Piekary Slaskie for their national pilgrimage. The presence of Cardinal Wojtyla made them even more fervent. His sermon was wildly applauded. In clear and direct language, he showed the extent of his fighting spirit, which naturally delighted them. Wojtyla reproached the State for doing away with Sunday as a day of rest, for doing its best to prevent the construction of churches, and for restraining the growth of the Catholic press: "It is said that faith is the opium of the people; I say that it is the right of workers! What is man, if not the son of God?"

Many see Wojtyla as *papabile*

Rome, August 24
In Rome's heavy summer heat, the entire Vatican is preparing for the imminent conclave. This morning, while celebrating mass, Cardinal Wojtyla heard a nun's voice say during the bidding prayers: "Lord, we pray that you will elect Cardinal Wojtyla as pope." The Cardinal did not react, but the phrase nonetheless proves that he is considered eligible, or *papabile*, as the Italians say. He is not one of the favorites, but his name is circulating both within the Polish colony and among certain cardinals, including Franz Koenig, primate of Austria.

Continuity in Vatican

Paul VI dies from heart attack

Castel Gandolfo, August 6
Paul VI (b. September 26, 1897) died today in the papal summer residence. He suffered a lingering death, having been weakened by months of poor health. He was pope for 15 years and 46 days. Less popular and charismatic than his predecessor, John XXIII, with whom he had helped prepare Vatican II, he nonetheless displayed the same simplicity. And he knew exactly how to impose and put into action the Council's teachings. Paul VI was the first pope to speak before the United Nations in New York, and it was he who inaugurated papal visits to foreign countries. But the success of the aggiornamento must not disguise the crisis opened up between the Church and society by his encyclical *Humanae Vitae*.

Albino Luciani becomes Pope John Paul I

Vatican, August 26
The cardinal archbishop of Venice, Albino Luciani, has been elected pope after just four rounds of voting – the shortest conclave in the history of the Roman Church. He chose the name John Paul I, in memory of his two predecessors: "I have neither the wisdom and kindness of Pope John, nor the education and aptitude of Pope Paul, and yet ... I find myself in their place." His mother cleaned dishes in a poorhouse, his father was a mason and a militant Socialist. Known for his gentleness and humility, he answers the needs of the Curia and the Church: a pastor and an apostle of spiritual unity.

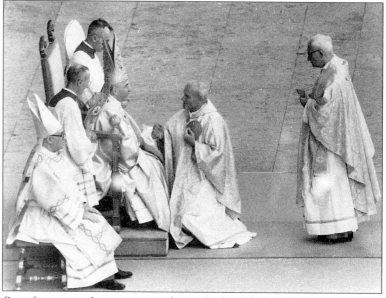

Son of a mason, the new pope is the cardinal archbishop of Venice.

Swimming and canoeing far from Rome

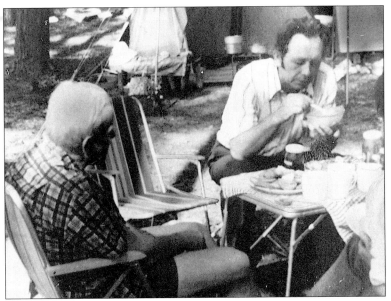

Wojtyla with Professor Gabriel Turowski, in between canoeing trips.

Poland, September

Karol Wojtyla has returned to his homeland, not least to recover from the pressure and pace of Rome. He and his old friend Father Malinski set off for an eight-day trip in the mountains, swimming and canoeing. Malinski, who has adopted the habit of calling Karol "Wujek," is amazed at the latter's stamina: at 58 years old, he can still quite happily swim both ways across a lake that is half a mile wide, without even pausing for a rest!

Nikodim dies in the pope's arms

Vatican, September 5

Since his investiture two days ago, John Paul I has not ceased receiving foreign delegations invited to the ceremony. The new pope made a highly significant stand at the investiture mass: he refused to wear the tiara, symbol of the political and monarchic powers of the papacy. This was however overshadowed by the event which took place in the Holy Father's private library. In a closed session with the pope, the metropolitan of Leningrad suffered a heart attack and died in the pope's arms. Still shaking with emotion, John Paul I later confided that the Orthodox archbishop had previously "just spoken to him about the Church, full of love."

Reconciliatory visit to West Germany

The two inseparable cardinals arrive for their mission in West Germany.

West Germany, September 25

This is the first time since the end of World War II, that such a high-level meeting has taken place between the Polish and German episcopates. Championed and organized by the archbishop of Cracow, it was really a voyage of rediscovery and reconciliation. Naturally Mgr. Wojtyla was part of the Polish delegation led by Mgr. Wyszynski. The mood was one of compromise without surrender. Karol Wojtyla made a strong impression upon his German hosts, through his sheer knowledge and his desire for forgiveness. He had asked for these "two Christian peoples" to cast off the burden of history and to forgive each other. This last point was received with ambiguity within Poland: what had the Germans to forgive them for?

20th anniversary of investiture as bishop

Cracow, September 28

Twenty years ago today, Cardinal Wojtyla was appointed a bishop, becoming the youngest bishop in Poland. He celebrated a high mass for the occasion, which also just happened to be the feast day of St. Wenceslas (duke of Bohemia from 907 to 929, who was assassinated by his brother, a pagan, for having converted the country to Christianity). Yesterday, Karol spent the day as he used to when a child, at Kalwaria Zebrzydowska. He had purposely told no-one of his visit to the Sanctuary of Our Lady, as he did not wish for any formality. There he meditated, by himself, on "the great secret of faith hidden deep within Kalwaria".

▷

John Paul I does not awake on the 34th day

Wojtyla upset by pope's sudden death

Cracow, September 29

Cardinal Wojtyla had adopted the habit of having his breakfast next to the kitchens in the episcopal palace, after saying mass in one of the chapels of Wawel Cathedral. It was there that his chauffeur, Jozef Mucha, informed him of the death of John Paul I. Stanislaw Dziwisz saw him blanch and freeze in mid-gesture. Shortly afterwards, Wojtyla excused himself with the pretext of a headache, and went to his chapel, where he spent the next few hours alone. The news of the sudden death of the Holy Father had been given out by Radio Vatican at 7.42 am. John Paul I (b. October 17, 1912) had died of a heart attack during the night, worn down by the sheer weight of the duty which he considered to be his as pope.

Too conscious of his papal duties

Cracow, October 1

Throughout the sermon in memory of Pope John Paul I, given by Karol Wojtyla in the Church of Our Lady, the tension and emotion steadily rose. "We expected such a lot from him," the Cardinal said. "We had put so much hope in him. His very humanity appeared to answer our hopes. His moment had hardly come, and yet it already showed signs of great promise. Politicians and heads of State agreed that he brought ... a new style to the Apostolic See. A style founded on great simplicity, great humility, ... on a deep respect for man. This he inherited from his two predecessors but, from the outset, he stamped it with his own being." Already, on September 17, in Mogila, the pope had devoted an entire sermon to the responsibility that "the very great honor" of being pope entailed. He said that it was "a very heavy cross, a cross for the whole human family, ... a cross for all those tensions and all those dangers which can only be vanquished through justice and love."

100,000 faithful applaud after procession

Vatican, October 4

Outside St. Peter's, in the pouring rain, 100,000 people took part in the funeral of John Paul I. The long, simple ceremony began at 4 pm and proceeded without a hitch. After the cardinals had donned their miters and the coffin had been raised to be taken back inside the basilica, the Romans began clapping. This ancient tradition means just one thing: it is the Romans' way of telling their bishop that he will live on forever in their hearts. With the coffin back inside St. Peter's basilica, the knell began to be tolled.

It is the second time in two months that he has had to choose a pope.

One of the favorites for succession

Vatican, October 13

Being a favorite or even simply a candidate is not easy for anyone to live with, cardinal or not. Having already been evoked at the previous conclave, Karol Wojtyla's name has resurfaced. The *papabile* cannot put himself forward, nor campaign in any way. He just has to leave things up to the Holy Spirit ... or his earthly helpers. In Wojtyla's case, it was Archbishop Andrzej Deskur, expert in Vatican affairs, who took charge of everything. As in August, he had the support of Cardinal Franz Koenig, primate of Austria, as well as of all those who wished to get away from the traditional election battle between Italians, or between candidates from the Church's conservative and progressive factors. The fact that Karol Wojtyla had never associated himself with either of the Curia's camps played in his favor, neither was he totally unknown to them. Ever since he had made his brilliant speeches before Vatican II, he had been viewed as a great intellectual who was also a man of immense moral strength.

Habemus Papam: Joannes Paulus II

Hitch-hiking to the next conclave

Rome, October 14

His concern for others outweighs all else, even in the run-up to a conclave. Karol Wojtyla had rushed to the bedside of his old friend Andrzej Deskur, in the Gemelli clinic, as soon as he heard the news of his heart attack. Before returning to the bustle of the city, he spent a short time relaxing on a Tyrrhenian beach. As a result, he missed the bus for Rome ... and had to hitch-hike.

Chosen after eight rounds of voting

Vatican, October 16

At 6.43 pm Cardinal Pericle Felici appeared on the balcony of the Basilica of St. Peter's and pronounced the famous Latin words "Habemus Papam." After this, he proclaimed Karol Wojtyla's election to the thousands of faithful gathered in the square below. He who a few hours before was totally unknown outside religious circles, is the first non-Italian pope since 1523 and the first Polish pope. To speak of surprise would be an understatement. But the amazement of the Italians soon gave way to enthusiasm and joy when, at 7.15 pm, the former archbishop of Cracow appeared on the balcony to bless the crowd. He addressed them in Italian, saying: "Even if I cannot express myself in your ... in our ... language, if I make mistakes, please correct me." Two days earlier, after high mass, the 111 voting cardinals went into conclave in the Sistine Chapel. Sworn to total secrecy and cut off from all contact with the outside world, they sleep in small austere cells within the Borgia apartments. The two main Italian *papabile*, the modernist Giovanni Benelli and the conservative Giuseppe Siri, were quickly ruled out. It was then that Cardinal Franz Koenig, archbishop of Vienna, made his move and put forward the name of his candidate, the young Polish cardinal. On the 8th round, Karol Wojtyla obtained 99 votes: he had been elected!

For the past two conclaves, the prelates who burn all the papers and documents used for the election, and who have to stoke the stove from whence the white smoke issues if a pope has been elected (or black if not), have used a smoke-producing device in the chimney, in order to avoid the slightest ambiguity.

The world could not believe its eyes: the man who appeared on the balcony of St. Peter's Basilica was Polish.

Reactions in Poland: Catholic joy and Communist irritation

Warsaw, October 17
Poland awoke this morning still stunned by yesterday's news that Karol Wojtyla, the archbishop of Cracow, had been elected pope, taking the name of John Paul II. In the evening, the churches and squares in the old part of town thronged with rejoicing crowds. Holding candles, the young Catholics danced around the statue of Adam Mickiewicz in the Rynek Glowny in the center of Cracow. Happiness had swept away the disbelief of the first few moments. As for the authorities, their courteous messages of congratulations barely disguised the Communists' irritation. Their statements all tallied: Karol Wojtyla had never submitted.

The news spreads quickly to the furthest corners of the country.

Pope's message: 'Be not afraid'

Vatican, October 22
Over 300,000 spectators filled the square in front of St. Peter's, with its magnificent Bernini colonnade, to be present at the enthronement mass for the new pope. Heads of State, kings, patriarchs of the Orthodox Churches, England's archbishop of Canterbury – they were all present. The high mass began at 10 am. One and a half billion people were able to watch the ceremony which was relayed by 44 television stations. They saw Mgr. Felici place the pallium around the pope's neck. Since John Paul I had abandoned the use of the papal tiara, this white woollen vestment remained the sole sacred emblem worn by the pope as a symbol of his power. One by one the cardinals knelt before the new pope as a sign of obedience. Stefan Wyszynski, primate of Poland, had barely knelt down before John Paul II helped him up and embraced him, thanking him with all his might. He did the same for the archbishop of Prague, Frantisek Tomasek, who had suffered emprisonment at the hands of the Communists. The mass went on till 2 pm, so great was the rejoicing. John Paul II's call to all Christians was perhaps the most moving moment of all. From behind the altar his words rang out vibrantly: "Brothers and sisters, be not afraid! Open wide the doors for Christ." He repeated several more times: "Be not afraid!"

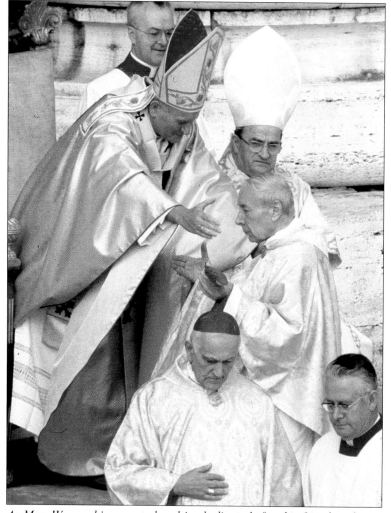

As Mgr. Wyszynski comes to kneel in obedience before his friend at the enthronement ceremony, the new pope leans forward to embrace him and says: "Without you and your faith, there would be no Polish pope."

Pope still dazed over own election

Rome, October 17
One of John Paul II's first visits was to the bedside of his old Polish friend, Mgr. Andrzej Deskur, still suffering from his recent heart attack. The Holy Father was not able to talk to the man who had initiated him into the esoteric ways of the Vatican, because he was still unconscious. Having come to the clinic without any security guards, he had to be reminded, at the end of his visit, that he should bless all those present. At the top of his voice, and smiling, he said to the nurses: "It's not finished, I've got to bless you ... They are teaching me how to behave like a pope!"

Giscard's meeting was with another!

Vatican, October 26
Valéry Giscard d'Estaing was the first overseas Head of State to be received by John Paul II. This was more of an accident than a sign of great ardor. Giscard had arranged a meeting with John Paul I, and his successor, John Paul II, simply decided to honor the engagement.

Eighteen miles of cheering crowds

Castel Gandolfo, October 27
Never before has a pope attracted such crowds along the road from the Vatican to Castel Gandolfo. The entire length of the eighteen-mile route separating the Eternal City from the papacy's summer palace in the Alban Hills, including right up the Via Appia, was lined with thousands of the faithful, cheering and waving. John Paul II quickly decided to stand up in order to return their greetings, which obliged his vehicle to advance at a snail's pace. The enthusiasm that his election has aroused shows no sign of abating. For the past ten days the Holy Father has demonstrated his eagerness to show his faith and to reach out to the faithful. At his summer palace, hundreds of young children offered him yellow and white birds: the Vatican's colors.

His first pilgrimage outside Rome honors the Virgin Mary

Mentorella, October 29

For his first pilgrimage as pope outside Rome, John Paul II has chosen the Marian sanctuary of Mentorella, 25 miles away, deep in the countryside. This magical place, at a height of 4,000 feet, is doubly significant for the pope. Firstly, it is devoted to the Virgin, the center of his personal devotion, and secondly, for the past century it has been inhabited by Polish priests and monks of the Congregation of the Resurrection, founded in Paris in 1836. The Holy Father knows the place well, as he has been there several times, most recently on October 7, when he climbed the last six miles on foot. "Here, far from everything, ... one can speak quietly to God," he said.

The sanctuary of Mentorella houses a monastery of Polish monks.

Five Poles in the Pope's service

Vatican, November

When John Paul II took possession of the private apartments which had been assigned to him, he decided to surround himself with people and things which would, in some small measure, remind him of Poland. He chose five Polish nuns to look after his everyday needs. Sister Germane is his cook: she alternates Italian and Polish cooking. The pope's favorite beer, *Zywiec*, is brought directly from Poland. Sister Fernand does the shopping, Sister Eufrosyna looks after the Holy Father's private correspondence, Sister Mathilda is in charge of his wardrobe. Their mother superior is sister Tobiana.

The Soviets have not lost all hope

Moscow, November 4

Since his election, the Soviet leaders have been watching the new pope closely. The director of the Institute for a World Socialist System has just submitted an unusually perceptive report. John Paul II is certainly described in it as being an adversary of Socialism, but it also predicts that he will avoid head-on attacks. In addition, it says his known hostility to the Communist bloc is likely to be somewhat compensated for by his probable denunciation of the plight of workers and peasants in several Capitalist countries.

His thoughts are with his people

Vatican, November 4

On the occasion of the feast of his patron saint, St. Charles Borromeo (Karol in Polish), John Paul II has sent a letter to his former catechism teacher, Father Zacher, parish priest of Wadowice. In it, he thanks Zacher for having him in his thoughts today. He also assures him that his own thoughts are very much with those people who showed him the deep mysteries of the Faith, and with his parents, his friends, his teachers and everyone for whom he will always remain Karol Wojtyla, a Pole to the depths of his soul.

Nuns should keep wearing their habits

Vatican, November 10

The pope has been in audience with Rome's nuns and clergy since yesterday. He brought them together to tell them his view of their particular mission, and to alert them to the vocational crisis currently hitting the Italian clergy. The thousands of nuns present expressed their enthusiasm in an unusually demonstrative manner, given the surroundings. Then the pope admonished them to keep wearing their habits: "The purpose of our vocation should be clear from our dress. Do not be ashamed of it."

Visit to Rome's Communist mayor

Rome, November 12

John Paul II is starting to strip away some of the old pontifical finery and introduce a breath of fresh air into Roman practices. He barely listens to the advice of the Curia Monsignori. This morning, on his way to San Giovanni di Laterano to officially take possession of the basilica, which forms part of the Vatican State, the Pope stopped at the Capitol to see Carlo Argan, the Mayor of Rome. He is a former art-historian and, more importantly, a Communist, but this did not prevent the Pope from embracing him.

Pope needs a new pair of legs!

Rome, December

John Paul II is a sportsman. All those around him and all those who knew him in Poland as Karol Wojtyla agree on this aspect of his character. Above all, he adores mountain sports. Watching some skiing on television, he said: "It's all very well, but I can no longer do that. ... I am rusty. I need a new pair of legs." Then, with an amused look, he continued: "It's a sport that is especially suited to small people: they have less far to fall than tall people!" His humor is certainly far from rusty.

On November 10, 15,000 nuns gathered in the Vatican and applauded the pope. The joyous scenes which ensued had never been seen before.

Unhealthy rumors started in Italy

Rome, December 9

Having failed to find the pope guilty of the usual Polish vices, such as alcoholism, two journalists have just published a book, *Il Pastore venuto da lontano* (*The Pastor from Afar*), which contains gossip which has inevitably hit the front page of this morning's *Corriere della Sera*. Their "enquiry" concludes that Karol Wojtyla had a love affair in his youth. They even suggest that the pope is a widower! John Paul II and his old friends denied all this in vain, as the rumors swell, seeking to destabilize this dynamic pope.

Santo Domingo, January 25.
En route to Mexico, the pope's plane touches down in the Dominican Republic, where the pope kneels down and kisses the ground.

Poland, March 3.
The pope's trip to Poland is confirmed; Brezhnev failed to force the Polish authorities to cancel it.

Vatican, March 9.
Death of Cardinal Jean-Marie Villot (b. 1905), secretary of State for the Vatican.

Vatican, April 30.
Mgr. Agostino Casaroli succeeds Cardinal Villot.

France, June.
Karol Wojtyla's play *The Jeweller's Shop* is published in French, with a preface by Jean-Louis Barrault.

Vatican, June 30.
For his first consistory, John Paul II names 14 new cardinals, including Mgr. Casaroli, and two Poles, Mgr. Wladyslaw Rubin and Mgr. Franciszek Macharski, his successor as archbishop of Cracow.

New York, October 5.
John Paul II declares: "It is my plan to go to the Holy Land, and my great hope is to do so soon."

Orléans, November 10.
Jean-Marie Lustiger is named bishop of Orléans.

Moscow, November 13.
The central committee of the Communist Party decides "to act against the Vatican's policy in the Socialist States."

Stockholm, December 8.
Mother Teresa is given the Nobel prize for Peace.

Eighteen-hour days for pontiff

Vatican, 1979
In the space of just a few months, the Holy Father has established a gruelling daily routine to cope with his round of pontifical duties. As in Cracow, he gets up at 5.30 am, does a few exercises, has a quick shower, prays and meditates before going to mass at 7 am. There are frequently guests at mass, which is a new departure. He then has breakfast with some of them at 8 am. After that, he works until 11 am in his office. Late morning is taken up with meetings with his colleagues and secretaries, as well as with private audiences. A relaxed lunch, often with guests, begins at 1.45 pm. The pope then returns to his office to continue working, alone, until 6.30 pm. Matters to do with the Holy See keep him busy until 8 pm. After dinner, he returns to his office to prepare his papers with his secretaries for the following day. The pope goes to bed around 11 pm, after saying compline, having a final meditation and a private prayer. And every Friday, he goes to confession.

Popemobile for modern pope

Vatican, 1979
While the pope has already made it quite clear that he will make no concessions on the doctrinal issues of Catholicism, he is aware of the urgent need to adapt papal practices to the modern world. The sedan chair has been replaced with the "popemobile", a high, clear-topped vehicle, for maximum visibility.

Mediator between Argentina and Chile

Vatican, January 24
At the request of the military juntas in both Santiago and Buenos Aires, John Paul II has agreed to arbitrate the border dispute between Chile and Argentina concerning the islands in the Beagle Channel. The quarrel dates from 1820, and confrontations have already occurred in the Andes and Tierra del Fuego.

Mexican trip a success despite warnings

The Mexican people's joy is recompense for the president's icy greeting.

Mexico, January 31
At the end of the day, the Mexican authorities are the only ones not to have benefited from the country's first papal visit. John Paul II has just departed for Rome, and can pride himself on having thwarted his entourage's pessimism. He was there to open the General Assembly of the Bishops of Latin America in Puebla. When he arrived on January 26, the Pope was given an icy reception by President Jose Lopez Portillo, just as his advisors had warned him to expect from a State renowned for its anticlericalism. Addressing him as "Mr Wojtyla" the president told him dismissively: "Go and join the people of your faith." But the fervor of the 91% of the population who are Catholic won out. There were four million faithful cheering him all the way to the sanctuary of Our Lady of Guadaloupe. At every stop, the Mexicans displayed enthusiasm and jubilation. While warning the bishops against any involvement other than purely religious, the pope also pleaded the defense of the rights of the Indians.

Redemption and dignity for mankind

The encyclical is run off the presses of the Vatican's official newspaper.

Vatican, March 15
The pope wrote his first encyclical in Polish, and it was then translated into Latin. *Redemptor Hominis* (*The Redeemer of Man*) introduces John Paul II's Christian Humanism. He describes man's place in the modern world, explaining that he must be at the heart of every set of values. The pope takes issue with all economic systems, and makes no distinction between them. He says they cause suffering, subservience and alienation, and distance individuals from Christian values, both moral and spiritual. The encyclical is explicitly addressed to all human beings, not, as is usual, just to Catholics. In addition, John Paul II has done the unthinkable, and written his encyclical in the first person – yet another sign of his desire to get closer to the faithful.

Message of fraternity and support to ten million Poles

Cracow, June 10

The pope has rekindled the Poles' sense of pride. Despite television censorship and warnings given out by the Polish and Soviet authorities, crowds of faithful flocked to hear the pope speak on his eight-day visit, drawing renewed energy and hope. Years of propaganda had convinced the Polish Catholics that they would go down in history as losers. Their isolation has been shattered by the pope's visit, which has also proved that their aspirations are shared by others and that they have not been forgotten by history. Welcomed by the leader of the Polish United Workers' party, Edward Gierek, the pope visited Cracow, Nowa Huta, Czestochowa, Jasna Gora – the religious heart of Poland – Auschwitz, "the Golgotha of the modern world", and Wadowice, his home town. His message of hope was addressed to all Slav Christians, which will not exactly please Moscow. One in three Poles traveled to see the Holy Father. There can be no better proof than this of what people are hardly daring to start to think and have not yet dared to express: that Communism is built on sand.

His visit unleashed the enthusiasm of the people and the fear of the regime.

Dziwisz remains the pope's confidant

Vatican, June 18

Stanislaw Dziwisz, aged 40, has been retained by John Paul II as his personal secretary, a post which he held in Cracow. However, the post does not exist within the Vatican, so he has officially become "chaplain to His Holiness" and second assistant priest. Father Dziwisz entered Mgr. Wojtyla's service in 1966. As his private secretary and chamberlain, Dziwisz is the pope's advisor, his messenger and his privileged confidant. His task is to steer the notoriously unpunctual pope to the right place at the right time. He also organizes his meetings and the visits of Polish friends and acquaintances.

No liberalization in this Church

Vatican, December 18

It appears that the Holy Father does not wish to hear any discord in matters of theology. Indeed, the Pope has effectively approved the condemnation of Hans Küng, who has been relieved of his teaching functions in Tübingen and stripped of his title as Catholic theologian. Since 1967, this Swiss has been in the sights of the guardians of Church dogma. He has questioned the very structures of the Church. His latest work, entitled *Infallible? An Unresolved Inquiry*, takes issue with a dogma dating from Vatican I (1870): that of the infallibility of the pope. Four days ago, a Flemish Dominican, Edward Schillebeeckx, was questioned for hours by three experts. He had come under fire from the Congregation for the Doctrine of the Faith. In his book, *Jesus: An Experiment in Christology*, he states that the Gospels should not be taken literally, and he questions the resurrection of Christ!

The pope around the world
1. January 25 to February 13: Santo Domingo, Mexico, Bahamas.
2. June 2 to 10: Poland.
3. September 29 to October 8: Ireland, United States.
4. November 28 to December 1: Turkey.

Mixed results from his transatlantic trip

Washington, October 8

The pope's first North American trip ended on a rather discordant note. Yesterday, in the Church of the Immaculate Conception, before 5,000 nuns, over two-thirds of whom were dressed in normal clothes, John Paul II had to face up to the first truly anti-establishment speech of his pontificate. Sister Theresa Kane, president of the Leadership Conference of Women Religious, addressed the pope bluntly on "women's suffering" and the need for "their access to all the sacred ministries." She then greeted him with typical American simplicity, far-removed from the reverence shown towards him by all the other nuns that the Holy Father had so far encountered. This frontal attack on the place of women in the Church deeply irritated the Holy Father. However, the rest of his trip could be said to have been a success. His speech on the "inalienable rights" of man, given to the General Assembly of the United Nations in New York, was very well received. His last stop was at the White House, where he had been invited by President Jimmy Carter. He is the first pope to have set foot there.

Open air mass opposite Capitol Hill.

Turkish trip rated high risk

Izmir, December 1

The pastoral visit of John Paul II passed off without encountering any of the threatened disasters. Eight days before, Mehmet Ali Agça, a man linked to the Turkish underworld, escaped from prison where he had been held for assassinating the editor of the newspaper *Milliyet*. Three days later, Agça had a letter published in the same newspaper, in which he threatened to kill the pope if he came to Turkey. In the end, Agça did not act, and John Paul II was able to relaunch theological discussions with the Orthodox Church. He is the first pope to have taken part in an Orthodox mass in the cathedral, St. George at the Phanar, celebrated by Dimitrios I, Patriarch of Constantinople. The pope said that the third millennium "will see the return of that unity broken in the ... second." He also visited Ephesus, where the Virgin took refuge after the Crucifixion.

Age 59 | Age 60

Vatican, February.
The pope attends a performance of his play *The Jeweller's Shop*, whose cast includes Nino Manfredi.

Vatican, February 24.
The pope sends a letter to all bishops informing them of his intention to bring back the giving of communion directly onto the tongue.

Warsaw, June 1.
The government authorizes the distribution of a monthly Polish edition of the *Osservatore Romano*, edited by Father Adam Boniecki.

Gdansk, August 14.
The shipyard workers go on strike.

Vatican, August 20.
During an audience with 900 Polish pilgrims, the pope sings a Polish resistance song from the time of the German occupation.

Poland, September 22.
Creation of the Founding Committee of the free trade unions, which becomes *Solidarnosc* (*Solidarity*).

Stockholm, October 1.
The Nobel prize for literature is given to the Pole Czeslaw Milosz, exiled since 1951.

Vatican, October 17.
First official visit of Elizabeth II, Queen of England and head of the Anglican Church.

Vatican, December 2.
Publication of the encyclical *Dives in Misericordia* (*On the Mercy of God*).

Cracow, December 13.
Premiere of *Our God's Brother*, a play by Karol Wojtyla, written 30 years ago.

John Paul II meets young delinquents

Rome, January 6
The Holy Father's visit to Rome's prison for juvenile offenders was organized by Mgr. Agostino Casaroli who, for many years, has taken a particular interest in rehabilitating juvenile delinquents. John Paul II said mass in front of several dozen young prisoners and their parents. Aged between 14 and 18, they are all in custody awaiting trial. Before the pope shared their meal with them, he asked them to take their futures in hand, speaking to them of pardon, trust and hope.

Convocation of Dutch bishops

Vatican, January 31
John Paul II has finally brought the turbulent Dutch Catholic Church into line. On January 14, all the bishops from the Netherlands were convoked to an extraordinary synod which came to an end today. For the pope, this process was deemed necessary as the Dutch clergy, following the lead given by Dutch society, renowned for its liberalism, had been making bold claims for the ordination of women and for priests to be able to get married. For the pope, these issues are not even open to discussion.

Tragedy at funeral of Mgr. Romero

San Salvador, March 30
El Salvador's bloody civil war has claimed a new victim: the capital's archbishop, Mgr. Oscar Romero. His denunciation of murders by the death squads, as well as his defense of the indigenous peasants, had continually infuriated the ruling oligarchy. Six days ago, a four-man commando assassinated him while he was officiating in a hospital chapel. His funeral, held earlier today in the cathedral in the presence of thousands of people, ended in yet more tragedy. A burst of rifle fire left thirty-five dead and several hundred wounded. Stunned, the congregation slowly emerged with their hands in the air.

Hints at lack of fervor among the French

Paris, June 2
It is 817 years since a pontiff was last in France of his own accord (Pius VII was held prisoner there by Napoleon from 1809 to 1814).

At St. Denis, the pope shows that he too was once a young worker.

Apart from a visit to the sanctuary of St. Theresa in Lisieux, the pope's trip was confined to Paris and the Ile-de-France. On May 30, he was welcomed in the Champs-Elysées by Valéry Giscard d'Estaing, France's president. From then on it was nonstop. He celebrated high mass at Notre-Dame Cathedral. Later that day he met Jacques Chirac, the mayor of Paris, who welcomed "this historic hour." Beneath the Eiffel Tower, the pope stopped and spoke to members of the Polish community, a habit he had adopted ever since his Mexican trip. In front of the basilica in St. Denis, to the north of Paris, he shook hands with young workers. At Le Bourget, in front of a crowd of 300,000 people (one million had been anticipated), the Holy Father called out to them: "France, eldest daughter of the Church, are you faithful to the promises of your baptism?" He then spent a long while with the young Christians in the Parc des Princes. The pope was allowed a break for sightseeing, aboard a *bateau mouche*, before concluding his tour with a speech at UNESCO.

While in Kenya on his ten-day African tour, the pope remarked that without doubt "Christ, in the members of his Body, is himself African."

Brazil, the land of inequality

Manaus, July 12
Twelve cities in as many days, over a distance of 18,650 miles – that was the pace of John Paul II's visit to Brazil, which ended today. In a country renowned for its social inequalities, and better known for its *favelas* than for its dynamism, the pope declared that "only a socially just society has any right to exist." To the peasants he said: "Legitimate ownership of land is a universal right." Liberation theology is widely practised throughout Brazil, most notably by Dom Helder Camara. The pope's address to the bishops referred to this in no uncertain terms: "Your vocation ... clearly and unambiguously forbids adherence to any political group or submission to any ideology."

American Poles give the Holy Father a heated swimming pool

The Swiss Guards' Gallery at Castel Gandolfo is one of the palace's wonders.

Castel Gandolfo, August
Along with much of the aristocracy, who retreat to their hillside villas in order to flee the stifling heat of Rome, the pope is spending the summer at Castel Gandolfo. This magnificent villa was built by one of his predecessors, Urban VIII, in the 18th century. Having fallen badly into neglect, it was totally restored in the 1930s, after the signature of the Lateran Treaty. The villa has an indoor heated swimming pool, given to John Paul II as a present by the Polish community in America who were anxious about his health. With the Alban Hills right behind it, the villa and its terraced gardens look out over the Lazio countryside. Nearby, Castel Gandolfo's model farm provides plentiful dairy produce, vegetables and fruit for the papal table.

Gdansk strikers gain recognition

Gdansk, August 31
As the world's cameras film this historic moment – the signature of the agreement recognizing the existence of the first free union within a Communist state – there are no lack of symbols. The room where the negotiations took place is hung with a portrait of Lenin, the Polish eagle, and a crucifix! When Lech Walesa came to sign, he pulled out an enormous pen with a photograph of the pope on it. This all goes to show that throughout this fifteen-day strike, there have been three major players, not two: the State, the strikers, and the Church. To the eyes of the outside world, as to the Communist government, the calm determination of the strikers owes just as much to the qualities of their leader, Lech Walesa (who wears the Virgin of Czestochowa inside his jacket), as to the discreet but unfailing support of the Vatican and its influential networks.

Is Soviet military action imminent?

Vatican, December
The White House is as concerned about the seriousness of the Polish situation as John Paul II. On two occasions in the past month, high-ranking American officials have contacted the pope to convey highly important information to him. First Zbigniew Brzezinski, National Security advisor to the Carter administration (recently defeated by Ronald Reagan in the presidential election, but still in office), phoned the pope to warn him that Soviet military action was imminent. The pope accepted the principle of issuing Moscow with an ultimatum in the event of an intervention. This was followed by a secret meeting with William Casey, head of the CIA, who showed Jean Paul II photographs taken by American spy satellites, which showed significant troop movements along the Polish border. The Soviets are twitchy, and could strike at any moment.

Poles send pope tree for Christmas

Vatican, December
Twice running makes a habit. Just as last year, John Paul II has received a Christmas tree all the way from Poland. It is a present from the inhabitants of the Podhale region, in the south of Poland. After the festivities, the magnificent tree will be planted in a monastery garden.

The pope around the world
5. May 2 to 12: Zaire, Congo, Kenya, Ghana, Upper Volta, Ivory Coast.
6. May 30 to June 2: France.
7. June 30 to July 12: Brazil.
8. November 15 to 19: FRG.

Lech Walesa is the symbol of the workers' struggle for freedom in Poland.

Rome, December 9: the pope escapes for a session of bowls.

Age 60 — Age 61

Vatican, January.
Alexandre de Marenches, chief of the French Information Services, sends an emissary to warn the pope that an assassination plot is hatching.

Washington, January 20.
Ronald Reagan takes up his duties as president, and decides to retain Zbigniew Brzezinski as his advisor on eastern Europe.

Poland, February 9.
General Jaruzelski becomes prime minister.

Pakistan, February 16.
One hour before the pope's arrival in Karachi, a bomb explodes in the stadium where the crowd awaits him. It kills the man carrying it.

Washington, March 30.
President Reagan is badly wounded in an assassination attempt.

Rome, May 15.
While in hospital, John Paul II hears that the Italian government has voted to legalize abortion.

Rome, May 20.
The pope has his first meal since the attempt on his life: soup with an egg.

Cannes, May 27.
The Palme d'Or at the film festival is given to a Polish director, Andrzej Wajda, for *Man of Iron.*

Castel Gandolfo, September.
Professor Crucitti considers the pope to be too fat for his age, and advises him to diet.

Vatican, November 12.
John Paul II calls for "a Europe which will once again be aware of its Christian roots and its identity."

'The son has come to see his father'

Vatican, January 15
This was what Lech Walesa said when he came to see the pope in Rome. The delegation was twelve-strong, including Walesa's wife, Danuta, Father Henryk Jankowski, the priest who said mass in the Gdansk shipyards during the strike, and Anna Walentynowicz, the crane driver whose dismissal sparked off the conflict. John Paul II took advantage of this meeting to reiterate the importance of union rights and of Solidarity's struggle. But he also took care to specify that this struggle, made valid by "the law of the people," was directed "towards and not against whomsoever."

Reagan surrounded by Catholics

Washington, January 30
Ronald Reagan, son of an Irish Catholic father and a Protestant mother, does not have the usual strong prejudice of the American establishment towards "Papists." Never has a president, not even John F. Kennedy, had so many avowed Catholics around him. Among them are William Casey, the director of the CIA, Alexander Haig, the Secretary of State, whose brother is a priest, General Vernon Walters, and Richard Allen, his advisor for National Security. All hold key foreign affairs posts.

A yellow star on the crucifix

Paris, February 24
The Chief Rabbi of France was not amused when Mgr. Lustiger, named archbishop of Paris on February 2 by the pope, and a convert from Judaism, stated that: "In embracing Christianity, I have not renounced my Judaism; on the contrary, I have completed it." Rabbi Jacob Kaplan replied that "one cannot be both Jewish and Christian at the same time; one must choose." Jean-Marie Lustiger is well aware of the symbolic importance of his nomination. "It is as if suddenly the crucifix had a yellow star on it."

'Military exercises' on Polish soil

Polish airspace is closed as Warsaw Pact maneuvers take place.

Poland, April 23
Warsaw Pact troops have just completed three weeks of major military maneuvers. Neither the Vatican nor the Americans, both of whom have been observing matters very closely, are in any doubt about the prime purpose of all this military movement taking place either side of the Polish frontier. It is a firm warning to the Warsaw government. Stanislas Kania, first secretary of the Workers' party, and the prime minister, General Jaruzelski, know that the Soviets' patience is not boundless. They have been summoned to Moscow on several occasions, to have Leonid Brezhnev tell them that they must put an end to the "counterrevolution." They were given a respite in order to find a Polish solution to the problem. But Jaruzelski's patriotism is certainly being put to the test. With the Hungarian example looming large, he is determined to avoid a bloodbath.

On February 22, in Manila, during his trip to Asia, the pope initiated the beatification process for Lorenzo Ruiz. It was the first time in the history of the Church that this has occurred outside Rome.

John Paul II shot down outside St. Peter's

Warning given of attempt on his life

Vatican, May 13

As usual on a Wednesday, the pope was standing up in his Popemobile as it drove around the vast square in front of St. Peter's for him to give his blessing to the faithful. At 5.17 pm, several shots were heard. John Paul II wavered and collapsed into the arms of Father Dziwisz, his face twisted in pain. Somebody had just attempted to kill the pope. That somebody was quickly found. His name – Mehmet Ali Agça. Back in November 1979, just out of prison, the Turk had publicly promised to kill the Holy Father. Two women were also wounded: Ann Odre, a 60-year-old American from Buffalo, and Rose Hall, 22 years old, from Jamaica. "Mary, my Mother!" were the words which John Paul II kept uttering like a litany.

Wounded in the hand, elbow and abdomen, the pope is supported by his secretary, Stanislaw Dziwisz (right).

Pope's operation lasts over five hours

Professor Crucitti is cautious about his patient's chances of survival.

Rome, May 14

None of the doctors at his bedside yet dares to make an announcement about John Paul II's state. However his operation, which took place late yesterday evening, went well. With serious abdominal wounds, the pope was rushed to hospital by one of the two Vatican ambulances kept at the ready. They reached the Gemelli Clinic in eight minutes flat, where an operating theater and a private room are always available for the Holy Father. His pulse was almost nonexistent, his breathing and blood pressure extremely weak. The pope only lost consciousness upon arrival at the hospital, suffering from very serious internal bleeding. He was rapidly prepared for his operation. A nurse who happened to be listening to the radio at the time of the shooting, immediately contacted Professor Crucitti who was working at another hospital several miles away. He came rushing over to the clinic. The 9 mm bullet had passed within an inch or so of the central aorta before passing out the other side of his body. Before the operation, the pope's secretary gave him extreme unction.

Out of danger in time for his birthday

Rome, May 18

At precisely 1.30 pm John Paul II was brought out of intensive care and taken to a private room. While postoperative complications may yet occur, the pope is definitely on the mend. The morning after his operation he regained consciousness. His personal secretary, the five Polish nuns, and his doctors, had all taken turns, watching at his bedside, awaiting some sign of improvement. Yesterday, at the time for Angelus, the pope said: "I pray for the brother who shot me, and I pardon him sincerely." More than 15,000 telegrams have been sent to the hospital. The pope gave a reproduction of the Black Virgin of Czestochowa to his anesthetist in gratitude.

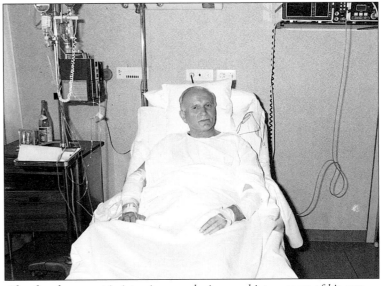
After five days spent in intensive care, he is moved into a room of his own.

The Holy Father is deeply saddened by Wyszynski's death

Rome, May 31
John Paul II is still in hospital, and so is forced to follow the funeral of his mentor, Mgr. Stefan Wyszynski (b. August 3, 1901), on the radio. He died on May 28, but the pope was not told until mass that evening. The news upset him deeply. Without Wyszynski, his own destiny would have been quite different. As for the Poles, they feel like orphans: after the shock of the attempt on the pope's life on May 13, they have now just lost the man who, for decades, kept the Polish Church alive. John Paul II had had a final conversation on the telephone with Wyszynski on May 25. Dying, he had received the pope's blessing. The pope was represented at the funeral by Mgr. Agostino Casaroli.

Mgr. Wyszynski's funeral in Warsaw attracted a vast crowd.

A troublesome convalescence

Rome, June 20
At last the pope's doctors seem to have identified the reason for his lengthy and troubled convalescence. He has a cytomegalovirus. The Holy Father had been allowed back to the Vatican on June 3, to preside over the ceremonies celebrating the anniversary of the Council of Ephesus. But far from improving, his health remained unsteady, with sudden high fevers, and general weakness that no one could satisfactorily explain, despite numerous tests. He had to be brought back to the Gemelli Clinic. Upon arrival, he collapsed into a wheelchair which, when offered, he had at first refused. He must now overcome the virus.

Life sentence for the Turkish terrorist

Rome, July 22
After a seven-hour deliberation, the special Assize Court charged with judging Mehmet Ali Agça, decided to condemn the terrorist to prison for life. After he had shot the pope on May 13, Agça was nearly lynched by the crowd – the police had the greatest difficulty extricating him from the mob. His personality and his motivation have subsequently remained a mystery. He has made numerous contradictory statements: that he had acted independently, in the name of Islam, then that he was working for a secret organization. Despite plentiful rumors concerning a plot by the Soviet secret services, no proof has been found to support this thesis.

The pope's 77 days in hospital are over

Rome, August 14
The lengthy treatment of the pope's cytomegalovirus is finally at an end. John Paul II left the Gemelli Clinic earlier today and will go to Castel Gandolfo tomorrow. From mid-July, his health started to improve visibly. At that point, it was decided to go ahead with the operation to remove the bypass system which had been inserted on May 13, thus hopefully avoiding a third relapse and period of hospitalization. The Pope, nonetheless, still had to press for the operation to take place. He wanted to return to the Vatican free of all health worries, to take up his work, which he reproached himself for delaying, and to celebrate the Assumption with his faithful.

Already pardoned by the pope, Agça awaits the justice of normal mortals.

The faithful often wait outside his hospital hoping to catch a glimpse of him.

An encyclical on man and work

Vatican, September 14
John Paul II's encyclical *Laborem exercens* (*On Human Work*), has at last been published, after the delay caused by the attempt on his life. It recalls the relevance of an earlier encyclical, *Rerum novarum*, which appeared 90 years ago. The pope denounces everything that can lead to alienation. Capitalism and Communism are both equally criticized. The pope argues for "the dignity and rights of those who work ... to ensure authentic progress by man and society." Work done within a community, in his view, constitutes "the very nature of man." "By means of work man participates in the activity of his creator."

Ratzinger is in charge of doctrine

Vatican, November 25
Cardinal Joseph Ratzinger is the new prefect of the Congregation for the Doctrine of the Faith. Replacing the Holy Office after Vatican II, this is the organization whose responsibilities cover everything to do with doctrine, morals, and theological questions. Born in 1927, this Bavarian prelate was an expert at the Council and made a name for himself with his progressive ideas and his broad-mindedness. But as the head of the Congregation, he has to avoid such distractions and work toward gaining respect for dogmas.

The oldest education system in the world

Vatican, November 30
General Vernon Walters has come to the Vatican to show the pope a new series of photographs taken along the Soviet-Polish border by satellite. The Americans are especially interested to see what the Church itself can teach them about the situation inside Poland. Walters, who is acting as President Ronald Reagan's ambassador extraordinary, says that the Church has "the oldest education service in the world [which], for the past thousand years, has never ceased to function."

Short-lived victory for Lech Walesa at Solidarity's first congress

The congress celebrated Walesa's birthday (b. Sept. 29, 1943) "with dignity!"

On December 13, Jaruzelski declared a state of war in Poland. The pope reacted: "Polish blood must not flow." He called for prayers to be said for the Polish nation, while Lech Walesa was put under detention.

Gdansk, October 30
The trade union Solidarity has asked that all strikes end, "because of their uncontrolled nature." The union's first Congress, from September 5 to October 7, saw several opposed factions rear their heads, basically pitching radicals against moderates. The leader of the moderate camp, Lech Walesa, was re-elected head of Solidarity, but only with 50 % of the vote. He must take into account the fact that the rank and file are prepared to go a long way with the strike and their revenge, while the Church and the regime are stepping up their warnings. On December 18, the pope was dining with the primate of Poland, Mgr. Glemp, when they heard that General Jaruselski had taken over as Party leader.

The Vatican reports on nuclear war

Vatican, December 12
Representatives have been sent by John Paul II to Washington, Paris, London, Moscow and the United Nations. They are delegates from the famous Pontifical Academy of Sciences. Their mission is to convey the results of their research into the consequences of a nuclear holocaust for Europe and the whole world. Last February, during a talk on peace given by the pope in Hiroshima, he called upon scientists to work within a moral context.

A candle is lit in the name of solidarity

Vatican, December 24
The idea originally came from a North American pastor. The pope placed a lighted candle in one of the windows of his private apartments. On Christmas eve it was meant quite simply as a "sign of solidarity towards those nations in suffering." Thousands of people throughout the world copied him. The Poles are in the forefront of their thoughts.

> **The pope around the world**
> **9.** February 16 to 27:
> Pakistan, Philippines, Guam, Japan, Anchorage (Alaska).

England, May 28.
John Paul II is the first pope to visit England for 450 years. He meets Queen Elizabeth II and he seals the theological reconciliation with the primate of the Anglican Church, Archbishop Runcie.

Vatican, August 2.
The Holy See sets up diplomatic relations with the Lutheran kingdoms of Sweden, Denmark and Norway.

Warsaw, September 1.
Death of Wladyslaw Gomulka (b. June 2, 1905).

United States, September 15.
After Yasser Arafat's visit to the Vatican, the Chief Rabbi of New York denounces the collusion between "the prince of peace and the prince of terror."

Spain, November 9.
In Santiago de Compostela, John Paul II calls upon Europeans to rediscover their origins, and he refers to himself as "the son of a Polish nation which has always considered itself European in origin, traditions and culture – a Slav among Latins, and a Latin among Slavs."

Italy, November 25.
The Bulgarian Sergei Ivanov Antonov is arrested, suspected of complicity in the assassination attempt upon the pope.

Vatican, November 28.
Opus Dei becomes the personal prelacy of the pope.

Poland, December 31.
Martial law and the state of war are lifted.

John Paul II pays homage to the wisdom of Black Africa

Libreville, February 19
The pope rounded off his African tour with a speech in Gabon, in which he spoke of his conviction that "when Africa was allowed to look after its own affairs, the rest of the world would be stunned by its progress and would learn a thing or two from Africa's wisdom, its joie de vivre and its respect for God." Out of a total population of 450 million in the African continent, there are only 50 million Catholics, but that number is on the increase. The pope visited Benin, Nigeria, and Equatorial Guinea. In Lagos, some Muslim religious chiefs refused to meet the Holy Father. In spite of the heat, John Paul II coped with the journey well – his first since the attempt on his life last May.

The pope is convinced that Africa's future lies in her autonomy.

No politics for prelates says pope

Vatican, March 8
Taking up the issue discussed in his speech to the Mexican clergy, the pope made official his firm opposition to the clergy's involvement in political matters. His position on this has never changed: he refuses any form of political involvement because it too often smacks of Marxism. Priests are therefore banned from all political activity.

Supportive of the workers at Solvay

Italy, March 19
John Paul II's latest encyclical has finally convinced skeptics that he really does take a great interest in the world of work and in social issues. While in Africa, the Holy Father had said that he regarded his own experience of working in a factory as "a blessing on his life." As he visited one of Solvay's chemical factories today, the pope was able to say to the workers, referring to his own experience: "I stand by you, for I once shared your lot. ... My time as a worker I consider as a gift from God. ... When I left the factory to pursue my vocation as a priest, I took with me the irreplaceable knowledge of what the world of work was really like."

Fatima brings him luck

Portugal, May 15
The town of Porto, in the north of the country, was the last stop on the pope's visit. In front of workers he delivered an animated eulogy to "the nobility of the hand that works, to the hand that transforms the world, to the hand that builds a new, more humane society." However the overriding memory from this Lusitanian voyage is that of the Holy Father being attacked, on the day of his arrival, in Fatima. A young fundamentalist priest, Father Krohn, armed with a bayonet, threw himself at the pope, intending to kill him. He was instantly overwhelmed by security guards. Luckily this did not stop the pope meeting Lucia do Santos, the last surviving child to whom the Virgin had appeared in 1917. Now a Carmelite nun, she could at last confide Fatima's third secret to the pope.

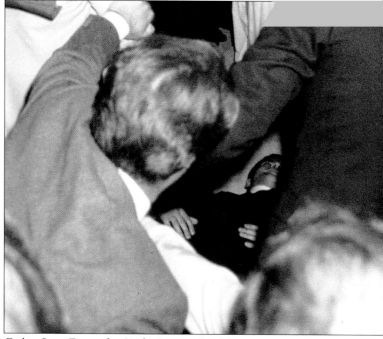

Father Juan Fernandez Krohn is neutralized by security guards.

Pope visits two nations at war: Great Britain and Argentina

Buenos Aires, June 13
Having visited Great Britain from May 28 to June 2, the Holy Father is now in Argentina, after a stopover in Rio de Janeiro. He was greeted by the usual enthusiastic crowds that have now become a feature of his world travels. John Paul II made a special pilgrimage to Lujan, to venerate the Virgin of the Pure and Immaculate Conception. The Holy Father's role as apostle of peace and reconciliation is of particular relevance here as Argentina is currently at war with Great Britain over the sovereignty of the Falkland Islands. The pope says he has come to pray for "all those who have lost their lives, for the victims of both sides and for an honorable and just solution to the conflict."

The capital's welcome for the pope and his "honorable and just solution."

Canonization of Maximilian Kolbe

Vatican, October 10
"By virtue of my apostolic authority I decree that Maximilian Maria Kolbe ... shall henceforth be venerated as a saint." With these words the pope canonized this Polish Franciscan who, in Auschwitz in 1941, had given his life by taking the place of a deportee, Franciszek Gajownizek, who had been condemned to death. Gajownizek was present at the ceremony. Kolbe still arouses controversy, for some say his writings are anti-Semitic. The Church denies this, saying he simply wanted to convert the Jews.

In memory of his brother Edmund

Vatican, December 5
Fifty years ago to the day, Karol Wojtyla learned of the brutal death of his brother, Edmund, victim of scarlet fever. Mundek, as his brother Karol had always called him, worked as a doctor in a hospital in Silesia. The Holy Father has never forgotten that he was not there to hear his brother's dying words. Those close to the pope know that somewhere in a drawer in his office in the Vatican he still carefully keeps his brother's stethoscope, as a sort of relic.

On October 31, the pope ritually kissed the ground as he arrived in Madrid. He was in Spain for the 400th anniversary of Saint Theresa of Avila. His visit came to an end on November 9 in Santiago de Compostela where, in a passionate speech, he urged the peoples of Europe to unite.

Arafat leaves gun in the antechamber

Vatican, September 15
With a smile on his face, Yasser Arafat, leader of the PLO, came out of his twenty-minute meeting with John Paul II. They had conducted it in English, without an interpreter. Wearing his army uniform and his keffieh, Yasser Arafat had left in the antechamber the gun that he always wears at his belt. The meeting raised the Palestine leader's international profile. It was followed by an even-handed press release, recognizing the Palestinians' right to a homeland, as well as Israel's right to security. Jewish authorities and the Israeli government reacted to this immediately: to their mind this visit was an absolute scandal.

80 million dollars for winning souls

Vatican, December 31
The missionary budget is one of four budgets for the Holy See. The others are for the Fabric of St. Peter, the Vatican City, and the Curia, now purely symbolic. Controlled by the Congregation for the Evangelization of Peoples (formerly the Congregation for the Propagation of the Faith), the missionary budget this year is worth $80 million (in 1975 it was $63 million). Half of this goes to the African Catholic mission, and about a third goes to Asia. The Congregation deals with over a third of the world's Catholics, and more than 800 missionary dioceses. There are nearly 250,000 Catholic missionaries throughout the world. This budget is financed by donations, collections and devout foundations and only covers ongoing projects of a strictly missionary nature.

> **The pope around the world:**
> **10.** February 12 to 19: Nigeria, Benin, Gabon, Equatorial Guinea.
> **11.** May 12 to 15: Portugal.
> **12.** May 28 to June 2: Great Britain.
> **13.** June 10 to 13: Argentina.
> **14.** June 15: Switzerland.
> **15.** August 29: San Marino.
> **16.** October 31 to November 9: Spain.

1983

Age 62 | Age 63

Guatemala, March 7.
Addressing the Maya Indians who came to tell the pope of the harshness of their living conditions, he said: "Your indigenous cultures demand the utmost respect ... from all mankind."

Vatican, March 25.
Inauguration of the Holy Year, on the occasion of the 1,950th anniversary of the Redemption of Christ.

Turin, March 25.
The Shroud of Turin is given to the pope by the Italian Royal Family, who have owned it since the Middle Ages.

Cracow, June 22.
John Paul II beatifies Father Adam Chmielowski (1845-1916), artist and art theoretician before becoming a priest. Karol Wojtyla had used him as his central character in his play *Our God's Brother.*

Cracow, June 22.
The pope is made a doctor *honoris causa* of Jagiellonian University.

Vatican, July 8.
Beatification of the 15th century Italian painter Fra Angelico.

Vatican, September 2.
The General Congregation of the Jesuits elect the Dutchman Hans Peter Kolvenbach to the post of General of their order.

Cracow, September 23.
Death of Father Kazimierz Figlewicz, teacher and then confessor to Karol Wojtyla at the time of his vocation.

Oslo, October 5.
Union leader Lech Walesa receives the Nobel prize for Peace.

A new Code of Canon Law

Vatican, January 25
The Holy Father has authorized the publication of *Sacrae Disciplinae Leges.* This new Apostolic Constitution promulgates a new Code of Canon Law. In 1963, John XXIII decided to revise all the Church's laws. Pope Paul VI confirmed his willingness to carry on with this process in 1965. This lengthy undertaking aims to bring the Church's legislation into line with the principles adopted at the time of Vatican II. One of the main aims of modernizing all these principles and processes is to grant a more important role within the Church to women and the laity.

Pope seeks to extend role of cardinals

Vatican, February 2
John Paul II's decision to create 18 new cardinals was pronounced at the second Consistory of his pontificate. Among those selected are Mgr. Jean-Marie Lustiger, Mgr. Jozef Glemp, primate of Poland, and Mgr. Juiljans Vaivods, who is the first Soviet citizen to be made a cardinal (he is actually the apostolic administrator for Riga and Leipaja in Latvia). When addressing the Consistory, the pope expressed his desire to see the role of cardinals extended. For centuries they have been little more than the electors of the pope.

Go-ahead for pope comic book

New York, March 23
Marvel Comics, the super heroes' publisher, renowned for their sci-fi comic books, have just launched their latest title, which is on the life of Pope John Paul II. This project has been done with the pope's full permission, after he had seen and approved another of their books, on the life of St. Francis of Assisi. The text was written by Steve Grant, who was helped, where necessary, by Father Mieczyslaw Malinski, an old friend of John Paul II. The illustrator is John Tartaglione.

Razor-sharp atmosphere in Nicaragua

The portraits of Augusto Sandino and another revolutionary dwarf the pope.

Haiti, March 10
"Something must change here." These were the pope's words at a meeting in Port-au-Prince, in the presence of President Jean-Claude Duvalier. They come at the end of a week-long Central American trip. His stop in Nicaragua on March 4 was the most troubled of the tour. Welcomed by Daniel Ortega, leader of the revolutionary Sandinista junta which came to power after overthrowing the dictator Anastasio Somoza, the pope celebrated mass in the center of Managua. At the airport, he severely berated the government minister Father Ernesto Cardenal, demanding that he clarify his position with regard to the church. The mass, disrupted by Sandinista protestors, was totally chaotic. There remains a total lack of understanding between the pope and the revolutionaries.

John Paul II meets Jaruzelski and Walesa

Poland, June 23
The nature of John Paul II's second trip to Poland, from June 16 to 23, was particularly special. Since the declaration of a state of war, and with all of Solidarity's leaders either

under arrest or in hiding, the Church has become the regime's only interlocutor. The crowds waiting to greet him in Warsaw, Poznan, Katowice, Cracow, Nowa Huta and Wroclaw, were even bigger than on his first visit. In Czestochowa, the Holy Father left a very moving *ex-voto* in the Sanctuary of Jasna Gora: the bullet-riddled white belt he had worn at the time of his attempted assassination in 1981. The pope met General Jaruzelski twice: at the Belvedere Palace in Warsaw, and in Cracow. Everywhere he went his faithful made the victory sign and shouted out "Solidarnosc!" Faced with this pressure from the people, and the insistent demands of the Church, the government has agreed to release Lech Walesa from house arrest. He was thus able to meet the pope in Zakopane for talks which remain strictly private. This high-risk tour has given new hope to the entire nation and renewed the strands of dialog.

Pope's outrage at newspaper report

Vatican, June 24
Renowned for his calm disposition, few have ever seen the Holy Father really lose his temper. However, those who were with him this afternoon when he read the editorial in the *Osservatore Romano*, witnessed just such a thing. The article claimed that Lech Walesa had lost the battle and that he had been abandoned by the pope. Nothing could have been further from the message that the pope himself had tried to put across during his trip to Poland. The Holy Father certainly had something to get angry about – a real stab in the back. The journalist concerned has handed in his resignation.

Charter on family rights published

Vatican, November 24
By publishing a Charter of the Rights of the Family, John Paul II wished to underline the central place of the child within the family unit. The Charter states that: "The activities of public authorities and private organizations which attempt in any way to limit the freedom of couples in deciding about their children constitute a grave offence against human dignity and justice." This stands as yet further proof of the Holy Father's personal interest in and concern for children, whom he sees as the true symbol of hope and innocence.

Freemasons not to be excommunicated

Vatican, November 26
Tomorrow, the new Code of Canon Law comes into force, replacing the one which Benedict XV instituted in 1917. One of the many changes it brings is to allow Catholics the choice of becoming Freemasons without automatically risking excommunication. Cardinal Ratzinger nonetheless wanted to emphasize that the Church was not reconciled with all facets of Freemasonry: certain aspects of the higher ranks of the Masonic Order still arouse some suspicion among the clergy.

John Paul II drinks the water of Lourdes' miraculous fountain

Paying homage to Bernadette Soubirous in the Grotte Massabielle, Lourdes.

Vatican workers on strike over low pay!

Vatican, December 1
The Holy See is experiencing the first strike in its long history. Over 1,500 of the 1,800 Vatican employees have stopped work, at the call of their union, the Vatican Association of Lay Workers (ADLV). There are no real militants among them, but most agree that the wages are too low. This is particularly true now that the numerous privileges that used to make the low salaries more acceptable have been removed (tax-free goods, exemption from personal tax, free medical care). Within the framework of the Labor Office of the Apostolic See, the pope has met a delegation, led by Mariano Cerullo, president of ADLV. The pope hopes to reconcile "the wishes of the personnel with the financial constraints of the Vatican."

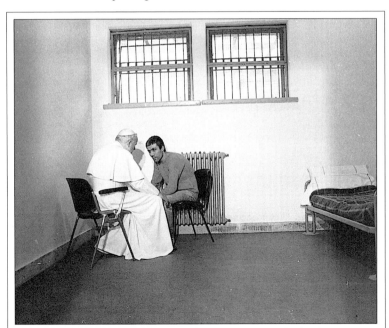

On December 27, the pope visited Rome's prison, Rebibbia, for a twenty-minute meeting with Ali Agça. The Holy Father had already forgiven Agça on a previous occasion. This time he embraced him and offered him a medal of Fatima. Agça repented his action and confided his motive. On departing, the pope replied to journalists: "It is a secret between him and me."

Lourdes, August 14
François Mitterrand welcomed the Holy Father to Tarbes, former archbishopric for the department of Hautes-Pyrénées and currently the seat of its prefecture. The French president had a short discussion with the pope, before his Holiness set off for Lourdes. His pilgrimage to the sanctuary of the Immaculate Conception was also a journey of homage to Bernadette Soubirous, the young shepherdess to whom the Virgin appeared eighteen times in 1858. Together with the 300,000 pilgrims who had come from all over the world, the pope prayed for those who are persecuted for their faith, condemned "to death, to deportation, to exile."

Criticism of rapport with Protestants

Rome, December 11
John Paul II went to the evangelical Lutheran Church of Rome today to take part in a prayer meeting. He is the first pontiff to preach in a Protestant church. His action is a concrete example of the ecumenical approach he repeatedly advocates, and clearly illustrates his continued desire to reconcile and bring together all the Christian Churches. To Mgr. Lefebvre's partisans, this unusual visit must have looked like confirmation of the reproaches that the French traditionalist is forever making towards the papacy. In an open letter to John Paul II, Mgr. Lefebvre, at odds with the Vatican since 1976, denounces the pope's "flirtation" with Protestantism. He accuses him of being "infected by Humanism", and he blames him for collectivizing the decision-making process on issues for which the pope should have sole responsibility, as well as stating that since Vatican II, Rome has spread a false idea of the natural rights of man.

The pope around the world
17. March 2 to 10: Portugal, Costa Rica, Nicaragua, Panama, El Salvador, Guatemala, Belize, Honduras, Haiti.
18. June 16 to 23: Poland.
19. August 14: Lourdes.
20. September 10 to 13: Austria.

1984

Age 63   Age 64

Warsaw, February 11.
The pope manages to pass on, through the Bishop of Warsaw, a breviary and a rosary to Father Jerzy Popieluszko.

Rome, February 18.
Signature of a new concordat with Italy revising the Lateran Agreement.

Vatican, April 6.
Aid to the Church in Need is recognized by the Catholic Church as a universal public association of faithful.

Vatican, April 20.
Publication of the pope's Apostolic Letter, *Redemptionis Anno*, the first official text to mention the State of Israel.

Thailand, May 12.
The pope says: "I defend ethics in order to save politics while others get involved in politics and forget ethics."

Geneva, June 12.
The pope is received by the World Council of Churches, the organization that promotes eucharistic unity between Churches.

Vatican, August 6.
Denouncing the foundations of liberation theology, the pope condemns "the Marxist infiltration in the Church."

Vatican, October 18.
Thanks to the arbitration of the Holy See, Chile and Argentina sign an accord resolving the conflict over the Beagle Channel.

Warsaw, November 3.
Nearly 500,000 people attend Father Popieluszko's funeral in St. Stanislaw-Kostka.

Vatican treasures given more space

Vatican, 1984
Early this year, the pope discreetly inaugurated the new underground rooms in the Vatican. They run underneath the Borgia and Sentinella courtyards, and will house the most precious treasures from the Vatican Library. Since 1954, the Vatican has come under the wing of The Hague Convention which protects goods in times of war. Even so, the rarest and most ancient of the Library's manuscripts have been put onto microfilm and lodged in a secret location in America.

Diplomatic relations reopened with USA

Vatican, January 10
The excellent relations between the Holy See and President Reagan's administration have at last rectified a long-standing anomaly. There have been no official diplomatic relations between the Vatican and the United States since 1867. Despite recent exchanges of information concerning Poland, despite all the synergy and shared interests of the Church and Washington in many Latin American countries, and despite the 1960 election of a Catholic president (Kennedy), it is only now that this oversight has officially been set right.

Fatima looks after him in his chapel

Vatican, March 25
On this Feast of the Annunciation, in St. Peter's Square, John Paul II announced that he had entrusted Russia and Eastern Europe to the Virgin of Fatima. The Holy Father has had the original, three-foot-high statue of Fatima brought all the way from Portugal, and yesterday it was installed in his private chapel, next to a reproduction of Our Lady of Czestochowa. He spent most of the night praying in front of the statue. It is clear that the pope, to whom the secrets of Fatima have been revealed, has established a link between these secrets and the events taking place in Poland and Russia.

Canonization of 103 martyrs in Asia

Meeting with Vasana Tara, head of the Thai Buddhists, in Bangkok.

Bangkok, May 12
The pope's ten-day visit to Asia and the Pacific finished in Thailand, where King Bhumibol Adulyadej greeted him. The highlight of this trip, which has also taken the pope to New Guinea and the Solomon Islands, was his time in South Korea, where he stayed from May 3 to 7. The Korean Catholic Church has two million faithful. On May 6, in Youido Square, Seoul, John Paul II canonized 103 Korean Christian martyrs, victims of violent religious persecution in the 17th and 18th centuries. A clear reminder of the high price paid in human lives for the spreading of the Gospels.

His passion for all sports remains intact

Italy, July 17
John Paul II today fulfilled a dream he has had since becoming pope: going skiing. For him, it is all about "friendship, simplicity and true human values," thus justifying that there is nothing shocking about a pope on the ski slopes. He and the Italian president, Sandro Pertini, were deposited by helicopter on the Adamello glacier in the Dolomites. The pope skied three descents, one after the other, surrounded by security guards and monitors. Signor Pertini remarked admiringly: "You ski like a swallow!"

April 12: he poses with football players in the Olympic stadium in Rome.

Clerics must answer for their actions

Vatican, September 9

As head of the Congregation for the Doctrine of the Faith, Cardinal Ratzinger convoked two South American priests this morning. The Peruvian, Gustavo Gutierrez, and the Brazilian Franciscan, Leonardo Boff, are the two most important theoreticians of liberation theology. Six days ago Mgr. Ratzinger accused them of "serious deviations" and implied their betrayal of the very cause they were supposed to defend. It is now up to them to explain their actions to Rome.

Latin mass to be tolerated again

Vatican, October 15

Those members of the faithful who are still in favor of the Latin mass, have certainly made their cause known at the Vatican. Special permission has been given to depart from the norm, henceforth allowing all bishops to tolerate Latin mass within their dioceses under certain conditions. The mass must be said in a place designated by the episcopal authorities, and according to the 1962 Latin missal which uses Saint Pius V's 1570 liturgy.

Maybe Ali Agça did not act alone

Rome, October 26

Ilario Martella, the committing magistrate, charged Sergei Ivanov Antonov with complicity in the 1981 plot to assassinate the pope. Two other Bulgarians and four Turks were also indicted. The press has been writing about this connection with the Bulgarian secret services since May 1982. Ali Agça, who had already been sentenced to life, had implicated three members of the Bulgarian embassy in Rome and several well-known figures of the Turkish underground in the plot. Luigi Scricciolo, imprisoned for spying for Sofia, confirmed Agça's statements. But nobody thinks for a minute that Bulgaria was acting alone. The judge thinks there was a second gunman present.

Canadians offended at being treated like a Third World country

The Canadians put on a colorful show in full multi-cultural fashion.

Ottawa, September 20

Members of the establishment in Canada, her political and economic leaders, barely attempted to hide their irritation by the end of the Holy Father's eleven-day visit. They sensed a strong whiff of third-worldness in all of his speeches and did not appreciate the smell. The pope's tour had taken him right across this vast country, from east to west, from Quebec to Vancouver, via the immense plains of the interior. Everywhere he had delivered his message of tolerance to this "melting pot for civilizations." He particularly annoyed the country's elite with the labored homage he paid to the American Indians and the poor. To the first he addressed his "recognition of their role, not only in society's multicultural tradition, but also in Church life." To the second, he declared: "Poor people, poor nations, need their freedom as well as food."

Popieluszko's death shocks the world

Warsaw, October 30

The ministry of the Interior today officially admitted the involvement of Polish state security organizations in the kidnapping and murder of Father Popieluszko (b. Sept. 14, 1947) on October 19. The repercussions are staggering. Curate for the Warsaw parish of St. Stanislaw-Kostka, and chaplain at the capital's steelworks, Popieluszko had been a supporter of Solidarity from the outset. His fiery sermons against the Communists and his militancy in general, irritated the government to the point where Mgr. Glemp had been obliged to ask him to be more moderate. The pope had discreetly let Father Popieluszko know of his own support, which naturally did nothing to dampen the fire. After numerous intimidating comments and threats, using the press, the regime finally did away with him.

He was murdered by agents of the Communist government on October 19.

Vatican becomes World Heritage site

Vatican, November 2

In 1972, UNESCO set up a World Heritage Convention, for protecting historical, architectural, cultural and natural sites throughout the world. A committee was charged with the preparation of a list of special sites and places suitable for designation representative of man's heritage. Nearly two years ago, the Holy See signed the Convention. Last February, it asked for the Vatican City to be included in this list, in view of the number of art treasures in its possession. From St. Peter's basilica to the museums, via Raphael's loggia and the Sistine Chapel, there is no other similar concentration of masterpieces in the world. The Vatican's request has now been unanimously adopted.

The pope around the world
21. May 2 to 12:
Korea, Papua New Guinea, Solomon Islands, Thailand.
22. June 12 to 17: Switzerland.
23. September 9 to 20: Canada.
24. October 10 to 13:
Spain, Santo Domingo, Puerto Rico.

Age 64 Age 65

Vatican, January 25.
The pope announces the convocation of a synod to assess the effects of Vatican II, 20 years on.

Vatican, February 19.
The pope grants an audience to the Israeli prime minister, Shimon Peres.

Moscow, March 11.
Constantin Chernenko is succeeded by Mikhail Gorbachev as general secretary of the Communist party.

Vatican, March 30.
John Paul II's first international youth gathering.

Belgium, May 17.
The pope presides over a ceremony to honor the dead from World War I in Ypres, where, every evening at 7 pm, since 1928, the bells have tolled for the dead.

Malines, May 18.
John Paul II celebrates his 65th birthday in this important Belgian place of dialog between Catholics and Anglicans.

Vatican, June 24.
The Holy See publishes a document entitled: *Notes on the Correct Way to Present the Jews and Judaism in Preaching and Catechism in the Roman Catholic Church.*

Vatican, August 29.
John Paul II announces that the secret archives from the pontificates of Pius X (1903-1914) and Benedict XV (1914-1922) will be opened up to historians.

Vatican, December 20.
The pope institutes World Youth Day.

Outspoken against extremist ideologies preaching hatred

The Amazonian Indians tell the pope of their ordeals, of the pillage, murder, and rape inflicted upon their people.

Peru, February 6
The last speech by the pope on his South American trip, prior to a stopover in Trinidad and Tobago, was delivered to Amazonian Indians from sixty or so tribes. Just as he had done in Mexico and Canada, the Holy Father spent a long time listening to their grievances and their accounts of brutalities of which they always seem to be the victims. On January 31, at Latacunga in Ecuador, John Paul II spoke out against "extreme ideologies ... which preach hatred, vengeance, ... atheism, or ... which further the cause of despotism, power, or money." Concerned to hit the right balance, social and racial oppression were denounced but the revolution option was still refused.

Whiff of gunpowder at heart of Church

Vatican, April
In preparation for the next synod, questionnaires have been sent to the episcopal conferences in each country. The replies are already starting to come in and, as noted by certain observers, "a whiff of gunpowder is in the air." The replies from Canada, the Netherlands, Great Britain, and the United States, all dispute the centralization of the Vatican, the insignificant power of the synods and the far too great power of the Roman Curia. The English bishops have even gone as far as to make allusion to the shady conduct surrounding the Vatican bank, the Institute of Religious Works. Doctrinal rigidity is equally denounced, as are intrusions by the Apostolic Nuncios in the internal debates of each nation's Church. Despite somewhat guarded language, the criticisms remain fierce.

Two Communists discuss the pope

Warsaw, April 1
What should have lasted one hour, ended up lasting five hours. General Jaruzelski and Mikhail Gorbachev spent all that time in a face to face meeting, without an interpreter. The Polish leader was particularly struck by the broad-mindedness of the new Soviet Communist party general secretary, in stark contrast to the attitude of those he normally meets. They discussed the status quo, not just in Poland, but throughout the entire Soviet sphere of influence. What the General especially noticed was Gorbachev's glaring misinformation concerning the history and affairs of the Church, compensated for by his personal curiosity. They spoke a lot about the pope and the Vatican, and the importance of the Church in Poland, as well as the pope's own influence throughout the world.

Project for convent in Auschwitz

Belgium, May
Aid to the Church in Need is an association which helps pay for the "Silent Church", as the Churches in Communist countries have been called for decades. This association is responsible for the tract currently doing the rounds in Belgium and the Netherlands, to coincide with the pope's visit. The pamphlet reminds Christians of their generosity: "Your gift to the pope: a convent in Auschwitz." It also informs them that eight Polish Carmelite nuns are inhabiting the old theater of the concentration camp. The mayor of Oswiecim (Auschwitz in Polish) has given them permission to convert this building into a convent, in order that "the door to hell become the gate to heaven." This project had barely been made public before it provoked an outraged reaction from Europe's Jewish communities.

Gulf between society and Church provokes angry outbursts

Utrecht, May 11
The Vatican is aware of the anti-establishment reputation of the Dutch Catholic Church, but it did not expect to be greeted in quite such a way. There is little overlap between one of the most permissive societies in the world, and the pope, who ardently defends the Catholic view of marital fidelity. Anarchist demonstrators and punks angrily hurled abuse despite a strong police presence, while John Paul II was taken to task in mid speech, as a member of the laity shouted: "Are we really following the message of the Gospels honorably when, instead of offering welcome, we close our door to homosexuals and divorcees? ... Many of us obey Christ and disobey the Church."

The free-thinking Dutch show their anger at the pope's conservatism.

An encyclical for ecumenism

Vatican, July 2
In his fourth encyclical, *Slavorum Apostoli* (*Apostles of the Slavs*), the pope delivers a passionate plea in favor of Christian unity in Europe. With specific reference to Saints Cyril and Methodios, evangelists of the Slav world, the pope invited the Oriental and Orthodox Churches to take up discussion with Rome, to promote the cause of ecumenism. Now that the Soviet authorities seem prepared to loosen their grip on religious matters, the pope is paving the way for regular contact with the Orthodox world. In 1980, he had already made the 9th century Saints Cyril and Methodios Patron Saints of Europe.

Welcomed as his 'most illustrious friend'

Morocco, August 19
After a ten-day visit to black Africa, John Paul II is in Casablanca. This visit provides the opportunity to launch an appeal for dialog between Christianity and Islam – a historic gesture. The pope was welcomed by Hassan II, the king of Morocco, who referred to him as his "most holy and most illustrious friend." The Muslim sovereign is himself a religious leader, bearing the title of Commander of the Faithful. At the stadium in Casablanca, packed with 80,000 young Muslims – Moroccans and foreigners – here to participate in the Pan-Arab Games, the pope proclaimed: "We worship the same God ... Dialog between Christians and Muslims is more vital today than ever, ... in an increasingly secular world which is, on occasion, atheist." He insisted equally on the notion of reciprocity, asking the Muslim countries to accord the same rights and the same welcome to Christians as the latter reserve for Muslims in Christian countries.

80,000 young Muslims cheer the pope in Casablanca stadium.

Synod assesses effects of Vatican II

Twenty years on, the bishops are invited to an Extraordinary Synod.

Vatican, December 8
The Extraordinary Synod has just been concluded. It was inaugurated on October 24 with a grand array of bishops, archbishops, and cardinals processing towards St. Peter's Basilica for high mass. The purpose of the synod was to celebrate the 20th anniversary of the Vatican II Council, and to assess its results. The assembly tried again to plead the cause of greater delegation of responsibility and a lesser role for the Curia within the administration of the Church. In vain. As for its conclusions, they followed those of the Council, especially with regard to ecumenism. In his final speech, John Paul II emphasized the need to strengthen the moral teachings of Christ. The major confrontation predicted between the pope and the bishops did not occur.

25. January 26 to February 6: Venezuela, Ecuador, Peru, Trinidad and Tobago.
26. May 11 to 21: Netherlands, Luxemburg, Belgium.
27. August 8 to 19: Togo, Ivory Coast, Cameroon, Central African Republic, Zaire, Kenya, Morocco.
28. September 9: Switzerland, Liechtenstein.

1986

Age 65   Age 66

New Delhi, February 1.
The pope prays on Mahatma Gandhi's tomb.

Vatican, April 27.
John Paul II grants a special audience to the representatives of the Albanian diaspora: "There is no worse injustice than to kill a man for his faith."

Vatican, May 30.
Publication of John Paul II's 5th encyclical *Dominum et Vivificantem*, evoking the presence of the Holy Spirit as the heart of the world.

Vatican, June 11.
The pope appoints the members of the council, led by Mgr. Ratzinger, which will draw up a universal catechism to replace national catechisms.

Miami, September 10.
Met by Ronald Reagan, the pope says: "I come as a friend of America, and of all Americans ... I come as a friend of the poor, the sick, the dying ..."

Poland, September 11.
General Jaruzelski announces a general amnesty for political prisoners.

France, October 6.
The pope visits the ecumenical community at Taizé, before revisiting the sanctuary at Ars.

Tashkent, November.
In Uzbekistan, Mikhail Gorbachev states the need to "improve the resolute and ruthless fight against religious revelations."

London, November 13.
The Anglican Church defines the pope's role as that of "a universal prelate."

In Gandhi's footsteps, John Paul II witnesses India's suffering

India, February 5
John Paul II's visit to India is only half way through, but he is already able to grasp the religious and social complexity of this ancient culture. In Madras, he meditated beside the grave of St. Thomas, one of the apostles. In New Delhi, he was greeted by Rajiv Gandhi, the prime minister. He celebrated his first mass in the Indira Gandhi Stadium, before a congregation made up of all the major Indian religions. The pope declared: "All here, Hindus, Muslims, Buddhists, Jains ... and Christians, we have all come together in fraternal love." The pope visited the Nirmal Hriday Ashram, the Pure Heart home for the dying, in Calcutta, where Mother Teresa welcomes the sick.

Mother Teresa is his guide in Calcutta where she shares the people's misery.

The Bulgarian lead draws a blank

Rome, March 29
The ever widening web of theories and accusations has led to nothing. This was the gist of the verdict returned by the Assize Court judging the alleged accomplices of Ali Agça. Unable to establish their guilt, it has acquitted them all; the Bulgarian trail has proved to be a dead end. Only one of the accused Turks, Omar Baggi, has been condemned to two years two months in prison. It was he who brought Ali Agça's gun from Italy. No news of the second gunman.

His position has seemingly softened

Vatican, April 5
Mgr. Ratzinger's renewed efforts to make the most progressive and the most politically engaged theologians see reason, do not seem to have prevented the latter from bending the pope's ear. He recently sent an unusually conciliatory message to the episcopal conference in Brazil, previously the recipient of vigorous papal warnings and reprimands. The Holy Father said: "As pastors, you are ... extraordinarily close to your people. Liberation theology is not only timely, but [it is] useful and necessary."

Pope visits synagogue

Rome, April 13
In terms of symbolic importance, the pope's visit to the synagogue in Rome is quite without precedent. John Paul II is the first pope to go inside a synagogue. Situated in the Trastevere district, not far from the Vatican, the Holy Father entered the building at precisely 5 pm. He was welcomed by the Chief Rabbi, Elio Toaff, and by Giacomo Saban, president of the Jewish community in Rome, the oldest of the diaspora.

Rabbi Toaff and John Paul II prayed together on some texts from Genesis. The pope recalled the Holy See's condemnation of anti-Semitism back in 1965, and asked for the Judeo-Christian dialog to be continued. He said: "With Judaism, we have a relationship which we have with no other religion." Recalling the phrase of his history teacher, he added: "You are our favorite brothers, and, in this sense, our older brothers."

Elio Toaff is the first rabbi to welcome a pope into a synagogue.

American curate stripped of position

Washington, August

Father Charles Curran can no longer teach theology at the Catholic University. A letter from the Congregation for the Doctrine of the Faith recently relieved him of his functions. Unlike the South American theologians, it is not political issues which are at stake here, but questions touching on sexual morality and private behavior. Last March, Curran was ordered to Rome to explain himself after stating that divorce and contraception should be accepted by the Church under certain circumstances, together with stable homosexual relationships. Ratzinger asked him to retract. He refused.

Nostradamus is still taken seriously

No exceptions are allowed by the security forces: everyone is frisked.

Lyon, October 4

One wonders if the high security presence would have been the same without Nostradamus! For the past few days, the world has talked of nothing but the predictions of the famous astrologer (1503-1566). One of his prophecies foretold of the assassination of the pope at the confluence of two rivers. Everybody was naturally thinking of the confluence of the Saône and Rhône, from where John Paul II today called on the world's armies and leaders to declare a universal truce on October 27. He also referred to one of his major concerns, sexual ethics, saying: "Moral permissiveness does not make man happy." With that, he left, alive and well!

September 7: restoring body and soul on Mont Blanc.

The world's religions gather in Assisi

Italy, October 27

For the World Day of Prayer for Peace presided over by the pope, sixty-three religious leaders and two hundred members of twelve major religions, have all come to Assisi, in central Italy, in order to pray side by side. Between them, they represent three billion human beings. Zoroastrians have lit a fire, Indian chiefs are smoking their peace pipes, Buddhist monks are sounding their gongs. The Holy Father has taken advantage of this communal prayer, which is not a common prayer, to make an act of contrition in the name of the Catholic Church: "This has taught us once again to be aware of the shared origin and the shared destiny of mankind ... I am now willing to recognize that we others, Catholics, have not always been the builders of peace."

The pope around the world
29. Jan. 31 to Feb. 10: India.
30. July 1 to 8:
Colombia, St. Lucia.
31. October 4 to 7: France.
32. Nov. 18 to Dec. 1:
Bangladesh, Singapore, Fiji,
New Zealand, Australia,
Seychelles.

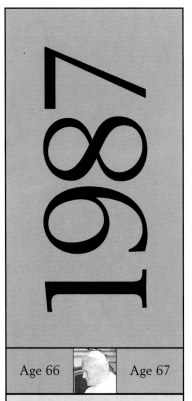

Age 66   Age 67

Vatican, January 1.
For the 20th World Day of Peace, John Paul II proclaimed: "Development and solidarity: the keys to peace!"

Monte Magnola, February.
The Holy Father goes skiing in the Abruzzi in Italy.

Vatican, February 20.
John Paul II receives Ali Agça's mother, who has come to ask pardon for her son. He blesses her and gives her an icon of the Virgin.

Santiago, April 2.
The pope asks the young: "Will you renounce the idolatry of wealth?" "Yes!" "Will you renounce the idolatry of power?" "Yes!" "Will you renounce the idolatry of sex?" "No!"

Buenos Aires, April 12.
The pope celebrates the 2nd World Youth Day. To the bishops he says: "I know that your involvement has saved human lives."

Augsburg, May 3.
In this Lutheran sanctuary, the pope declares: "We may dare to ask ourselves whether the Schism was not in fact necessary in order for the Church to be led along the path of renewal and reflection."

Rome, June 7.
The pope officially opens the Marian Year at Santa Maria Maggiore.

Vatican, October 4.
The pope beatifies Marcel Callo (1921-1945), a militant French Catholic worker, who died in Mauthausen.

John Paul II accords audience to head of Polish Communist party

Vatican, January 13
General Wojciech Jaruzelski, leader of the Polish government and the Communist party, received a special audience from the pope. They were together for an hour and a half. Jaruzelski confided to the pope the contents of his recent meetings with Gorbachev: according to him, the USSR is quite clear in its desire for reform. It remains to be seen exactly what concessions it is prepared to make over the political future of Poland. The Holy Father and the General agreed on future negotiations between the State, the Church and the opposition. The terms are yet to be decided. Before leaving, Jaruzelski added bitterly: "We have lost, there's no future for the Party."

The meeting concluded with Jaruzelski's admission of the Party's failure.

The pope loses his mentor Zacher

Wadowice, February 13
When the Holy Father learned of the death of Father Edward Zacher (b. 1900), he confided to those close to him: "He was one of the few to penetrate the depths of my soul and to determine the course of my life. My vocation of priest was born in the spiritual atmosphere created by Father Zacher in the life of our family parish." Father Figlewicz and he looked after the Church of Our Lady in Wadowice. He would have had the pleasure of seeing his model choirboy ascend the pontifical throne.

The role of the Virgin in the Church

Vatican, March 25
John Paul II has announced the Marian Year with the publication of his sixth encyclical. *Redemptoris Mater* (*Mother of the Redeemer*), evokes the place of the Virgin Mary within the doctrine and life of the Church. In explaining his own long-held deep devotion to the Virgin Mary, he wishes to give an example to others, especially with his obeisance to his Faith. Mother of man, symbol of the Incarnation, he feels it is crucial for her suffering and the mysteries of her life to remain a source of meditation and adoration.

Nuns given two years to quit

Geneva, February 22
After lengthy negotiations between the Vatican, the Polish Church and the Jewish authorities, a compromise has been reached concerning the highly contentious issue of the convent at Auschwitz. It has been agreed that a center for meditation and prayer, and for information on the Polish martyrdom and the holocaust, is to be built outside the camp perimeter. An official communiqué stated that "The Carmelite project will find its place within this new context." The nuns have been granted two years to move out.

Human embryos are human beings

Vatican, March 13
Cardinal Ratzinger is yet again the voice of the Vatican, publishing an "instruction" which recalls the Church's opposition to genetic manipulation and *in vitro* fertilization. The Holy See considers every fertilized ovum to be a human being which must be respected as such. The new reproduction techniques and especially *in vitro* fertilization inevitably lead to the destruction of embryos. The Catholic faculties of medicine at the universities of Lille and Louvain have announced that they will not respect this directive.

From July 8 to 14, the Holy Father took a few days' holiday in the Dolomites. What better occasion for the peasants to meet him!

Chile's bloody riots continue while the pope celebrates mass

Santiago, April 3
While John Paul II was celebrating mass in Plaza O'Higgins, Santiago, violent confrontations were taking place just a few hundred yards away, between militant Communists and the forces of order. So far there have been several hundred wounded. The regime's opponents are using the pope's visit to Chile as an opportunity to express their rejection of the dictatorship. The latter, meanwhile, wants to turn the visit into a moral approbation of it by the Holy See. The pope referred to the junta as "dictatorial but transitory," and he called upon them to start the process of democratization, and to respect the rights of the individual – a popular message with the crowds.

Young Communists confront Chile's forces of order, leaving 600 wounded.

Triumphal arrival of the Polish hero

Poland, June 14
Yet again the Holy Father's visit to Poland, the third of his pontificate, was a huge success with the people. In Gdansk, where John Paul II was able to meet Lech Walesa, this time beaming with confidence and hope, he celebrated a mass before 750,000 people. In Gdynia, he told the crowd: "The word Solidarity is known throughout the world." On his last day in Warsaw, he went to Father Popieluszko's former parish church, to pray at his grave. Several hours later, General Jaruzelski reproached him for this action.

Criticized for receiving Waldheim

Vatican, June 25
Kurt Waldheim was today given an audience by the pope. The Austrian president has been cast aside by the international community since the recent revelations about his past as a Nazi officer and of his implication in war crimes. In Italy, the Jewish community actively demonstrated its anger. The Israeli government and the Knesset have also protested vehemently. The Vatican replied that an audience had never been refused to any head of state who has requested one, and that nothing should interfere with this.

September 17: during his stop in San Francisco, John Paul II embraces Brendan Rourke, the young four-year-old who has contracted the AIDS virus as a result of a contaminated blood transfusion. In his speech beforehand, the pope proclaimed: "God loves all of you ... He loves the sick and those who are suffering from AIDS."

Jews annoyed by Stein's beatification

Cologne, May 1
Chancellor Helmut Kohl was present today in the Rhine town for the beatification mass for Sister Theresa Benedict of the Cross, the name taken by Edith Stein when she took holy vows. The pope delivered the homily. Edith Stein was a Jewish German philosopher who converted to Christianity. She entered the convent and was then deported to Auschwitz where she died in 1942. Many Jews consider the Catholics to have appropriated her death for their own cause: for them she died because she was a Jew. The Church, however, insists that she died because of her Christian faith.

Dimitrios I is John Paul II's guest

Vatican, December 6
This Sunday, the mass in St. Peter's was somewhat special. John Paul II was celebrating it in the presence of the Patriarch Dimitrios I, who has been the pope's guest for the past three days. The Holy Father and the patriarch of Constantinople have had talks on the reconciliation of their Churches and on the future of Christianity in the Orient.

An Arab Patriarch for Jerusalem

Jerusalem, December 28
Michael Sabbah has been appointed to the head of the ancient and highly prestigious patriarchy of Jerusalem. This move by the pope is seen as a real snub to the Israeli authorities as well as to tradition. It is the first time since the Crusades, that an Arab, a Palestinian too, has occupied this position, normally given to Italian prelates. The Arab Christians are highly appreciative of this gesture.

> **The pope around the world**
> **33.** March 31 to April 13: Uruguay, Chile, Argentina.
> **34.** April 30 to May 4: FRG.
> **35.** June 8 to 14: Poland.
> **36.** September 10 to 21: United States, Canada.

1988

Age 67 | Age 68

Vatican, January 1.
The pope's message for the 21st World Day of Peace: "Religious freedom is a condition of peace."

Vatican, January 25.
Before the Roman Catholic rota, John Paul II defends the Christian view of marriage and the sacred ties between spouses.

Ecône, June 2.
In a letter sent to the pope, Mgr. Lefebvre declares: "Modern Rome is infested with modernity."

Moscow, June 5.
The Kremlin organizes a gala evening for the millennium of Russian Christianity.

Vatican, June 19.
John Paul II announces the beatification of 117 Catholic martyrs, tortured in Vietnam in the 18th and 19th centuries.

Austria, June 24.
The Holy Father visits Mauthausen concentration camp. His lengthy homily examines the suffering of man.

Vatican, June 28.
John Paul II's 4th consistory. He nominates 25 cardinals.

Castel Gandolfo, July 27.
The *Comédie Française* perform *Le Mystère de la charité de Jeanne d'Arc* (1910), by Charles Péguy, for the pope.

Vatican, August 15.
End of the Marian Year.

Vatican, November 19.
20 days after a police raid on Czechoslovak Catholics, the pope receives Alexander Dubcek, the Communist party first secretary at the time of the 1968 Prague Spring.

Encyclical tackles social matters

Vatican, February 19
Two decades after the encyclical *Popularum Progressio*, published by Paul VI, John Paul II has made public *Sollicitudo Rei Socialis* (*On Social Concerns*), the seventh of his encyclicals. It assesses and outlines new departures concerning the Church's social doctrine – arguments well-known to the pope. He is equally critical of Communist and Capitalist ideologies, the first for the illusions it nurtures and for its false promises of freedom, and the second for its frenetic cult of money, as well as for its purely materialistic approach, which has led to man's total enslavement.

Peter's pence continues to rise

Vatican, March 3
A desire to achieve more openness and to crush all rumors, has led the Holy See to publish its accounts for 1986 and its provisional budget for 1988. In the mid-nineteenth century, the Catholics in France re-introduced Peter's pence, in order to overcome the structural financial deficit of the papacy. It is added to by collections made by the national episcopates. Until 1978 it had declined annually, but the popularity of John Paul II has increased the donations. In 1988, the revenue from Peter's pence was $53 million.

Gorbachev receives papal delegation

Moscow, June 13
As an illustration of the improved relations between the Vatican and Moscow, Mikhail Gorbachev has received a delegation led by the Vatican secretary of State, Mgr. Agostino Casaroli. Its mission is to discuss the thousandth anniversary of Russia's adoption of the Christian Faith, and to find out to what extent the Soviet authorities will allow the event to be celebrated. Gorbachev confided: "Man should be at the center of international relations. That is the starting point of our 'new way of thinking'."

Lefebvre goes too far

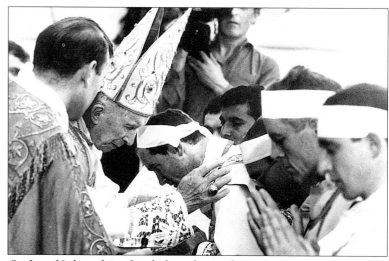

On June 30, he ordains four bishops despite the Vatican's interdiction.

Vatican, July 2
A *Motu Proprio* (decree made at the pope's own initiative) *Ecclesia Dei* has been published, pronouncing the *de facto* excommunication of Mgr. Marcel Lefebvre. In spite of the Vatican's exhortations, in spite of all the concessions and compromises granted by the Holy See, in spite of the highly understanding emissaries sent to the traditionalists, Mgr. Lefebvre went ahead with the ordination of four bishops two days ago. Done without the endorsement of the pope, this act is an open breach with the Church. The service took place in Switzerland, at the headquarters of the Society of St. Pius X. Thousands of faithful were present. It is for the sake of these faithful that the Church has decided to put in place various structures designed to welcome Catholics torn between their loyalty to the Roman Church and their attachment to the traditions defended by Mgr. Lefebvre. As for the latter, convinced that he was in the right, he refused to compromise with a Rome "in the shadow of error and [which] no longer listens to the voice of truth."

On July 13, the pope sets off into the Cadore mountains, between Venice and the Austrian border, for a few days' rest.

Gorbachev visits pope's publisher

Cracow, July 13
Having arrived in Poland two days ago, Mikhail Gorbachev made a private visit to No. 12 Wislna St. It was here that his father recuperated, when wounded at the end of the Second World War, serving with the Red Army. The building still stands, but instead of being an army hospital, it now houses Znak Publishers, who publish the works of John Paul II, among others! The coincidence adds an amusing note to this personal pilgrimage. Gorbachev left a dedication written on an edition of *Tygodnik Powszechny*, the Catholic weekly also housed in the same building.

Recognition given to Zairean mass

Vatican, September
After many years of debate, the Congregation for Divine Worship and the Discipline of the Sacraments has granted recognition to the "Zairean mass." Mgr. Joseph-Albert Malula, the archbishop of Kinshasa, instituted this ritual in the 1970s, mixing African dances and songs with the Roman rite. If Christianity is to be Africanized, the mass must be founded in local traditions. The Vatican's belated acceptance of this is another step toward the goal of rooting Catholicism in a non-European cultural environment.

John Paul II's address to women

Vatican, September 30
The Holy Father's Apostolic Letter, *Mulieris Dignitatem* (*The Dignity and Vocation of Women*), is the first important papal document to be addressed solely to women. Contrary to the ancient discourses preached to Catholics on the subject of women, the pope denounces the suffering to which women are still subject. He continues by saying that, far from being misogynist, the Bible states, as early on as Genesis, that "man and woman are called ... to exist side by side or together, but also ... one for the other."

Mitterrand welcomes the 'Father of Europe' to Strasbourg

Alsace, October 11
John Paul II brought his three-day visit to Alsace-Lorraine to a close, with a tribute to the construction of Europe. To those anxious at seeing the Church meddle in the management of this future political unity, the pope firmly replied: "No project of society can ever establish the Kingdom of God ... on earth." John Paul II was met by President Mitterrand, who greeted him saying: "Welcome to Strasbourg, father of Europe, Holy Father." He also met various important representatives of the Jewish and Protestant faiths, present in this land of concordats. To the Community's institutions, the Council of Europe and the Parliament, he spoke of the Christian Democrats, their founding fathers.

Turin Shroud's authenticity questioned

The shroud remains a mystery.

Turin, October 13
The Turin Shroud cannot have wrapped Christ's body, for it did not exist at that time. This is the conclusion reached by laboratories in Zurich, Oxford, and Tucson to whom the pope, guardian of the relic, entrusted it for further tests. Thanks to Carbon-14 dating, they confirmed that the cloth held in San Giovanni Cathedral was woven between 1260 and 1390. Both the geographical origin of this material and the visible human impression on it in negative remain a mystery. The anatomy is clearly that of a victim of torture. An object of great veneration, and a frequent embarrassment to the Church, the Shroud continues to intrigue: the analyses have already been contested.

Tackling the void is high on the agenda

Vatican, November 5
At the bishops' symposium the pope yet again explained the bases for the moral and spiritual reconquest that the Church must carry out in Europe. After "the ideological twilight and nihilism," he wants to breathe "a soul into modern society." A huge task.

The pope around the world
37. May 7 to 19: Uruguay, Bolivia, Paraguay, Peru.
38. June 23 to 27: Austria.
39. September 10 to 20: Zimbabwe, Botswana, Lesotho, Mozambique, Swaziland.
40. October 8 to 11: France.

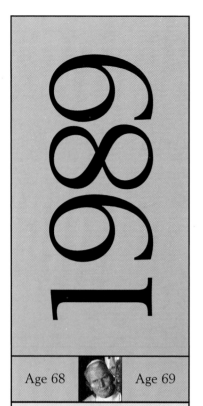

1989

| Age 68 | | Age 69 |

Vatican, January 1.
The pope's message for the 22nd World Day of Peace: "To build peace, we must respect minorities."

Bucharest, January 1.
President Ceausescu mocks "the return of bigotry."

Moscow, January 27.
Pravda runs a positive article on the Holy See, entitled *The Gardens of the Vatican*.

Vatican, February 6.
John Paul II receives the Soviet dissident Andrei Sakharov.

Poland, May 17.
The legal statutes of the Church are officially recognized.

Poland, June 17.
Diplomatic relations with the Vatican are re-established.

Albania, August 14.
Mother Teresa is permitted to pray at her mother's and sister's graves.

Vatican, September 19.
The Holy See confirms that it will enforce its agreement concerning the departure of the nuns from Auschwitz.

Seoul, October 8.
John Paul II invokes the Virgin to bring about a reconciliation and re-unification of the Koreans.

Rome, November.
In San Luigi dei Francesi, the pope denounces "the philosophers of the Enlightenment who threw doubt on God, on his Christ, on his Church. ... In emptying the heavens, the earth was not enriched."

Moscow, December 14.
Death of Andrei Sakharov (b. May 21, 1921).

Vatican criticised for overcentralization

Cologne, January 25
The *Declaration of Cologne* has just been signed by fourteen German-speaking theologians. In December, without consulting the German episcopate, the Vatican appointed Mgr. Joachim Meisner archbishop of Cologne. The manifesto expresses the anger of the Catholic hierarchy in Germany, denouncing the centralization of the Vatican, its refusal of any theological discussion and its close supervision of local Churches which "gradually reduces them to silence." In fact it is the whole of the Church's organization which is under question.

Solidarity is no longer clandestine

Warsaw, April 17
Solidarity has at last gained official status, after seven years of illegality. Lech Walesa and the minister of the Interior, Czeslaw Kiszczak, signed the agreement in the Radziwill Palace. Twelve days ago, trade union pluralism was re-established in a first agreement, and the holding of the first truly free elections was decided upon. The government have thus ended up recognizing Walesa as the leader of the opposition. Democracy is on the move. For many, it is the end of countless years of clandestine existence.

Letter of support to Jerzy Kluger

Wadowice, May 9
Survivors and relatives of the Jewish community were reunited for the inauguration of a commemorative plaque in memory of the Jews of Wadowice who were murdered by the Germans. Emotions ran high as Jerzy Kluger, a childhood friend of Karol Wojtyla, read out a letter from the pope. The latter had confided to his "dear Jurek" the task of relaying his constant concern for, and thoughts to, "all those who had been killed as citizens and Jews," and to all their "contemporaries of whatever creed [who] were friends at primary school and high school."

The Swiss Guards, formed in 1505, is the oldest and the last of the pontifical guards. Their uniform may have been designed by Michelangelo.

A voyage to Lutheran lands

Stockholm, June 10
At the end of his Scandinavian trip, John Paul II may well be satisfied by the warm reception afforded him by the Lutheran clergy and rulers of the five nations he visited. Catholicism in these countries represents a very small minority: 0.48% in Norway, 0.1% in Finland, 1.14% in Sweden and 0.6% in Denmark. The pope called for ecumenical unity.

Renewed anger over Auschwitz

Poland, July 14
The reciprocal tension and exasperation concerning the convent at Auschwitz has degenerated to blows. Led by Abraham Weiss, a New York rabbi, Jews invaded the site to protest against the continued presence of the nuns. After prayers and slogans, things hotted up: punches were exchanged with the workers on site.

Hungary, July 30: Billy Graham, the American preacher, goes on tour, just like a showbiz star. The Eastern bloc countries, starved of all spiritual input, are the perfect fertile ground for all manner of preachers.

Communism overthrown by people power

Opposition takes control in Poland

Warsaw, August 24

For the first time in many years an Eastern bloc country has a non-Communist PM. The Polish Diet elected Tadeusz Mazowiecki by 378 to 4, with 41 abstentions. Responding to this vote, President Jaruzelski then appointed him as head of government. Parliamentary elections on June 18, stipulated in last April's agreement, predicted a massive and inevitable victory for Solidarity. Transformed into a real political party, the union ended up taking 99 of the 100 seats in the Senate, and all 161 of the opposition seats in the Diet. The Polish United Workers' party (PZPR) reserved 299 seats for themselves, most of which went to Communist reformers. In the face of this sweeping electoral victory, Solidarity, who, at the outset, had only envisaged a role in opposition, declared itself ready to participate in a broad coalition, in order to get the country out of its current crisis. Despite initial reluctance, the PZPR finally agreed to take a minority role in the government. Mazowiecki, a Catholic intellectual and advisor to Walesa, sees the return of Poland to a market economy and to a state of law as the main priorities of his government. Moscow merely notes the Polish Parliament's decision.

Relentless pressure from protesters brings down Honecker and the Wall.

Berlin Wall comes tumbling down

Berlin, November 10

Never has a wall which came down so quickly made such a loud noise. The momentous event took place last night and will undoubtedly be remembered as one of the most important and historic dates of the late 20th century. Referred to as the wall of shame by westerners, the Berlin Wall was built in 1961 and was the single most powerful symbol of the Iron Curtain. The contagion that brought it down came from Poland. Thousands of East Germans had, for months, been flowing into Poland and Hungary, in particular. Keen to get out, and mostly heading for West Germany, they were encouraged by the liberalization taking place in both these countries. On September 10, Hungary made a first and decisive breach in the Iron Curtain by permitting all those refugees who wanted to, to cross into Austria without any formalities. The floodgates were opened. In East Berlin, the Communist authorities decided to replace the intransigent old guardian of orthodoxy, Erich Honecker, with Egon Krenz. Then yesterday, in a most casual manner, the authorities finally announced the abolition of visas and all the formalities for crossing into the West. The rush was immediate.

First Soviet leader to visit the Vatican

Vatican, December 1

At 11 o'clock this morning, Mikhail Gorbachev became the first Soviet leader to step inside the Vatican by invitation. St. Peter's Square was filled with thousands of people keen to witness this historic moment. Gorbachev was received by the pope in his private library. The two men met for over an hour, speaking in Russian, with the aid of an interpreter to smoothe out any wrinkles in the pope's use of the language. They discussed the crisis in Lebanon, as well as the upheavals currently taking place in Eastern Europe. The Soviet leader went on to announce the imminent law guaranteeing freedom of religion and freedom of conscience in the USSR. As he was leaving, the Holy Father handed him a gift: a naïve mosaic of Christ, made by a Vatican craftsman.

The pope around the world
41. April 28 to May 6: Madagascar, Reunion, Zambia, Malawi.
42. June 1 to 10: Norway, Iceland, Finland, Denmark, Sweden.
43. August 19 to 21: Santiago de Compostela, Asturias (Spain).
44. October 6 to 10: South Korea, Indonesia, Mauritius.

From August 19 to 21, John Paul II visits Santiago de Compostela, in northern Spain, one of the world's most renowned places of pilgrimage.

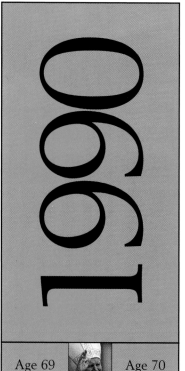

1990

Age 69 Age 70

Africa, January 25.
In the plane to Cape Verde, John Paul II confides: "Gorbachev told me that prayer is a manifestation of the spiritual values which his country so badly needs."

Auschwitz, February 19.
The foundation stone is laid for the new center which will replace the controversial convent.

Vatican, February 21.
The Holy Father declares: "It is God who has won in Eastern Europe!"

Moscow, April 13.
The Tass news agency admits that the Katyn massacre was perpetrated by the Soviet secret service (NKVD).

Prague, April 21.
The pope says: "If Europe's historical memory does not put down roots beyond the ideals of the Enlightenment, its new unity will rest on superficial foundations."

Vatican, August 24.
During his Angelus message, the Holy Father calls for a return to peace in the Gulf region.

Oslo, October 15.
The Nobel peace prize is awarded to Mikhail Gorbachev.

Rome, November 28.
Death of Mgr. Wladyslaw Rubin (b. September 20, 1917).

Rome, December 6.
For the 25th anniversary of the conciliatory declaration *Nostra Aetete*, Catholics and Jews take part in a colloquium at the Lateran University. John Paul II becomes the first pontiff to quote the Talmud.

Burt Lancaster stars in a film based on one of Wojtyla's plays

United States, 1990
The Jeweller's Shop, a film based on a play of the same name, written by Karol Wojtyla in 1960, has just gone on general release throughout much of the world. The director is the American Michael Anderson, and the film stars Burt Lancaster in the leading role. This long, dramatic poem, reminiscent of the work of the French Catholic playwright Paul Claudel, links the destinies and quests of three couples seeking to give love and meaning to their lives. Amusing and tender, the story is also a serious reflection on mankind and marriage. The theme music which accompanies the six characters on their search is by the French composer, Michel Legrand.

Olivia Hussey and Ben Cross in The Jeweller's Shop.

John Paul II inherits his aunts' house

Cracow, 1990
John Paul II was recently told that he had inherited his aunts' house in Tyniecka Street. Lengthy searches had been carried out to try to trace any of his aunts' immediate family members, but to no avail. The administration had therefore decided to inform the pope. Some of the lodgers in the house are related to Bogumila Gradowska, the woman who lived there at the same time as him in the 1930s. The pope has refused the house: it goes to the city.

Symbolic gesture for lepers

Guinea-Bissau, January 28
After the Cape Verde Islands, the pope is now visiting the former Portuguese colony of Guinea in West Africa. For the 37th World Day for Leprosy, the Pope planted a tree in the Cumura leper colony, run by Italian Franciscans. In his speech he reminded the world of the relatively modest cost of treating this terrible disease. The tree symbolizes hope, which can take root and grow even in those places marked by great suffering.

A diplomatic start for the Soviets

Holy See, March 15
The Soviets and the Vatican have been kept apart by 73 years of mutual incomprehension and hostility. But no more, for the two parties have finally established full diplomatic relations. The presentation and exchange of representatives of both States took place officially in the Vatican. An Apostolic Nuncio will shortly be sent to the Soviet capital, and a USSR special ambassador to the Vatican will come to Rome soon.

John Paul II tells the Czechs: 'You have conquered fear!'

Prague, April 21
Two days after diplomatic relations were re-established between the Vatican and Czechoslovakia, and four months after Vaclav Havel's election as president, the pope has arrived in the Czechoslovak capital. The former dissident and hero of the velvet revolution greeted him, saying: "In a country ravaged by the ideology of hatred, the messenger of love arrives; in a country ravaged by the power of the ignorant, ... the living symbol of culture arrives." Standing in the very place where Hitler had declared Czechoslovakia to be a German protectorate, the pope told the crowd: "You have conquered fear!" He then welcomed the rebirth of Europe.

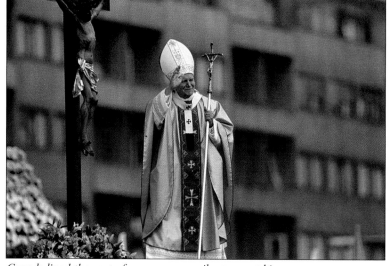

Crowds lined the route for over seven miles to greet him.

Ivory Coast replica of St. Peter's causes great indignation

Yamoussoukro, September 10
The Cathedral of Our Lady of Peace is a source of heated controversy. This vast building, inspired by St. Peter's in Rome, is the brainchild of President Houphouët-Boigny and is built in his home town. The question being asked is whether the Church can justify such extravagance in a continent ravaged by poverty. John Paul II's response to such questions was to visit the Ivory Coast in order to consecrate the new cathedral, where he declared that its immense size said more about the vigor of Catholicism in Africa than about the megalomania of its ruler. Over the past few days in Rwanda, Burundi and Tanzania, the pope has spoken out on behalf of refugees and AIDS victims. He had nothing but praise for the African family, so firmly anchored in faith and tradition despite the terrible, omnipresent scourges of disease and war.

The Cathedral in Yamoussoukro shocks by its ostentatious luxury.

Eastern Churches have laws codified

Vatican, October 18
For the very first time in their long history, the laws and canons of the twenty-one Catholic Churches of the Orient have been codified: the pope has promulgated the constitution *Sacri Canones*. Since the Great Schism between Constantinople and Rome in 1054 – which gave rise to the Orthodox Church – the Catholic Churches in the Orient have not been in an easy position.

Cardinal Casaroli is set to retire

Vatican, December 1
John Paul II will reluctantly accept the retirement of one of his most active diplomats, Mgr. Agostino Casaroli. The cardinal has just celebrated his 76th birthday, and is therefore over the official retirement age for cardinals. He has held the much sought-after post of secretary of State for eleven years. Small and lively, he became the main specialist on relations with the Eastern bloc and other sensitive areas. The pope has appointed Archbishop Angelo Sodano as his successor.

The commercialization of all sorts of goods bearing the pope's image is as much a sign of the liveliness of merchandising as of his popularity.

Lech Walesa is elected president

Poland, December 9
When, in the middle of August 1980, an unemployed electrician with a big mustache climbed onto a mechanical shovel and rallied the shipyard workers to continue their strike and to form a free union, no one could have imagined how quickly he would become part of History. Having won the Nobel prize for Peace in 1983, Walesa has now won the jackpot by defying a Communist party overly convinced of its right to represent the working class. Walesa has just been elected president of Poland with 74.7% of the vote in the second round. The rate of abstentions was surprisingly high: 47%. This is perhaps due to the weariness of the electorate and to their feeling that their victory over the Communists has already been achieved. Walesa crushed his rival, Stanislaw Tyminski, who only got 25.3% of the vote. He now succeeds Wojciech Jaruzelski, who is as much the "father" of the state of war as Walesa is, involuntarily, of the transition to democracy.

Father Aristide is Haiti's president

Port-au-Prince, December 17
Since Jean-Claude Duvalier quit Haiti four years ago, this country, one of the poorest in the world, has undergone a series of coup d'états, each civil election provoking a military reaction. It now remains to be seen whether Father Jean-Bertrand Aristide, democratically elected to the presidency with the support of the poor, will manage to retain his post. Expelled from the Salesian Order in 1988 for his involvement in politics, this priest cannot count on the support of the hierarchy.

The pope around the world
45. January 25 to February 1: Cape Verde, Guinea-Bissau, Mali, Burkina Faso, Chad.
46. April 21: Czechoslovakia.
47. May 6 to 14: Mexico, Curaçao.
48. May 25: Malta.
49. Sept. 1 to 10: Tanzania, Burundi, Rwanda, Ivory Coast.

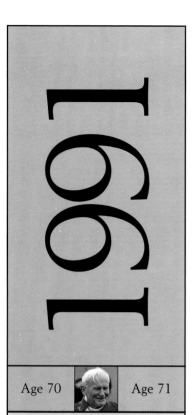

| Age 70 | | Age 71 |

Vatican, January 22.
Publication of the pope's 8th encyclical, *Redemptoris Missio*, "on the permanent validity of the Church's Missionary Mandate."

Vatican, February 24.
There were 401,479 Catholic priests worldwide on December 31, 1990, 471 less than in 1988.

Soviet Union, April 13.
Official reorganization of the Roman Catholic Church in Russia, Belorussia and Kazakhstan.

Vatican, June.
Document of the Congregation for the Doctrine of the Faith affirms that the communion of all the Churches can only occur around the pope, for his power is "supreme, plenary and universal."

Vatican, June 28.
Addressing the Consistory of cardinals, the Pope says: "To serve and give your life, pledging your blood: that is the assignment which you are solemnly given."

Vatican, June 28.
The Vatican reveals the nomination *in pectore* in 1979 of the Chinese cardinal, Ignatius Kung Pin-Mei.

Haiti, September 30.
President Aristide is ousted by a coup.

Germany, October 8.
Eugen Drewermann is relieved of his Chair at Paderborn Faculty of Theology.

London, October 30.
Alexis II, patriarch of Moscow, accuses Rome of "religious poaching."

Vatican opposition to Gulf War

Vatican, January 15
Since last summer, the rumble of war has been heard all along the Iraqi frontier. A coalition, based in Saudi Arabia and led by the United States, is ready for an offensive. Just a few hours before the expiry of the ultimatum given to Baghdad by Washington, John Paul II sent a message to George Bush. In the name of the defense of peace, the pope opposes the Americans' arguments for this war: "Problems are not resolved with weapons but ... new and greater tensions between peoples are created." The American administration has paid him not the slightest attention.

Vatican intervenes over 'black pope'

Vatican, February 5
Traditionally, the head of the Jesuits is called the "black pope." The man who once occupied this post for sixteen years, Father Pedro Arrupe (b. November 14, 1907), died earlier today. Renowned for their intellectual brilliance and their social involvement, the Jesuits have often been in the line of fire from the guardians of orthodoxy. In 1983, against the wishes of Father Arrupe, the pope ensured that the Dutchman Hans Peter Kolvenbach succeeded as the head of the Order.

Mgr. Lefebvre dies unrepentant

Martigny, Switzerland, March 25
Mgr. Lefebvre (b. Nov. 29, 1905) is no more. Former archbishop of Dakar and bishop of Tulle, in 1969 he founded the Society of St. Pius X, which he subsequently led from his seminary in Ecône, in the Valais. He was hostile to the reforms undertaken after Vatican II, and was a firm defender of the liturgical tradition and the Latin mass. In 1976, he was suspended *a divinis* and, in 1988, he was excommunicated for having ordained four bishops without the pope's permission. Right up to the end, the pope tried, in vain, to find a compromise with him.

No beatification for Isabella of Castille

Vatican, March 26
It has been decided to suspend *sine die* the beatification process of the former queen of Spain, Isabella "the Catholic" of Castille. For two decades, Spanish Catholics have been campaigning hard to promote the cause of their queen. However, the process had barely opened last year before there was a great outcry. The Jewish community, and various important historians, theologians and high-placed Church dignitaries, recalled that Isabella gave her full support to the Inquisition (1478) and signed the decree to expel the Jews from Spain. The case has been abandoned, in the name of Judeo-Christian relations, and in memory of the persecutions.

Threat from sects reunites cardinals

Vatican, April 4
For two days, the presidents of all the Episcopal Conferences and the College of Cardinals have debated the theme of: "The Church facing the threat against human life and the challenge of the sects." The Vatican is only too aware, as it nears the end of the 20th century, that the spiritual needs of human beings, particularly in the developed nations, far from decreasing, are being attracted to structures other than the Church. The Church accuses these sects, apart from their doctrinal errors, of alienating and of endangering their followers. The threat is real, be it from highly active cults in South America, apocalyptic sects, or syncretic guru-based groups. Eastern Europe is also a fertile ground for such organizations.

Solidarity for the poor: 9th encyclical

Vatican, May 1
With the publication of *Centesimus Annus*, John Paul II's 9th encyclical, the pope is clearly commemorating the centenary of a former encyclical, *Rerum novarum*. Published by Leo XIII, the latter was the first to take a serious interest in the fate of the working class and to present a real social doctrine. *Centesimus Annus* reaffirms the Church's support for the poor. Modern society, it states, generates new forms of poverty, no longer purely economic, but also cultural and religious. The pope also denounces the havoc being wreaked by liberalism and materialism in former Communist countries and in Latin America. In the name of "public good," he writes: "As history demonstrates, a democracy without values easily turns into open or thinly disguised totalitarianism."

Poland's World Youth Day gathers over a million followers

They flocked from all corners of the world, one in ten from the Soviet Union.

Czestochowa, August 14
After stopovers in Cracow, where he prayed by his parents' tomb, and Wadowice, his hometown, the pope is now in Czestochowa, the religious heart of Poland. The city is host to the 6th World Youth Day. Instituted by John Paul II in 1985, these gatherings are becoming increasingly popular. More than a million young Catholics have made the journey to the famous sanctuary of Jasna Gora. A sign of the geographical and political changes taking place in Europe at the moment, are the 100,000 young Soviets who have chosen to ignore all warnings and have crossed the border with no other possessions than their fervor. The Holy Father is convinced that it is the Black Virgin, central to his own private devotion, who has changed the face of the Old Continent. This is the message he wants to give to Hungary, his next stop.

'I am indebted to the Virgin!'

Fatima, May 13
A decade after the assassination attempt on John Paul II's life, he is in Fatima to thank the Virgin Mary. The pope is convinced that it was she who protected him: "A hand fired a shot, another hand deviated the bullet ... I am ever indebted to the Virgin." This conviction has strengthened his already strong devotion to the Mother of Christ. In every country he visits, he ensures that the sanctuaries dedicated to the Virgin Mary are on his itinerary, and there are many of them.

Catholics on Orthodox territory

Poland, June 3
In Lubaczow, near to the Soviet border, John Paul II replied to the accusation by the Orthodox hierarchy that the Catholics are being too active in "their" territory. The pope was most explicit on the matter: "We are amazed to see bishops in Moscow and Kazakhstan; but if there are bishops, that means there are people, and they expect bishops just as they expect priests!"

Lutherans' first Vatican visit

Vatican, October 5
Not since the Reformation have there been Lutheran bishops inside St. Peter's basilica. Today, however, the primates of the Churches of Sweden and Finland have come to pray with the pope, along with the Catholic bishops from Stockholm and Helsinki. They are celebrating the 6th centenary of St. Bridget of Sweden's canonization.

Touched by plight of Brazil's children

Salvador de Bahia, October 20
Before his imminent return to the Vatican, John Paul II has gone to meet Brazil's children. He offers his support and love to those who he says are even more vulnerable than the indigenous population or the peasants. Abandoned and left to cope on their own, these children must no longer be exploited "to immoral ends," he says.

The pope's 4th Polish trip: he is bitter for he feels that his people are becoming resistant to the Church's authority. Walesa supports him.

No regrets over Gorbachev leaving

Moscow, December 31
Red Square, the very place where the defunct Soviet regime used to flaunt its power, is tonight thronged with crowds of deliriously happy, drunk people. They are celebrating the end of the Soviet Union, which has not lived to see the New Year. On December 8, the Commonwealth of Independent States replaced the Union of Soviet Socialist Republics. After six years and nine months of *perestroïka*, Mikhail Gorbachev chose to depart on Christmas Day, leaving the way clear for the new president, Boris Yeltsin. The break-up of the USSR accelerated after the failed coup d'état last August. Gorbachev had understood what the present pope has known from the very beginning; that to try to re-build the Soviet Union, land of triumphalist Communism, was a truly impossible and suicidal task.

The pope around the world
50. May 10 to 13: Portugal.
51. June 1 to 9: Poland.
52. August 13 to 20: Czestochowa (Poland), Hungary.
53. October 12 to 21: Brazil.

1992

Age 71 Age 72

Vatican, January 12.
The Holy See recognizes the sovereignty and independence of Slovenia and Croatia.

Haiti, January 15.
The Vatican is the only State to send an ambassador (the Apostolic Nuncio, Mgr. Lorenzo Baldassari) to Port-au-Prince, where Father Aristide, the elected president, has been overthrown by a coup d'état.

Vatican, March 7.
Promulgation of the Roman Curia's new rules.

Vatican, May 13.
John Paul II institutes the World Day for the Sick, to take place every year on February 11.

Vatican, May 17.
The Holy Father beatifies Sister Giuseppina Bakhita, a Sudanese slave.

Brazil, May 26.
The Franciscan Leonardo Boff announces he is leaving the order and the Roman Catholic Church.

Vatican, July 29.
Start of official negotiations between the Vatican and Israel to reach a reciprocal, *de jure* acknowledgement of both States.

Holy See, August 22.
John Paul II launches an appeal for peace in the Balkans.

Vatican, October 23.
The pope receives Shimon Peres, the Israeli foreign minister, who in turn, officially invites him to visit Israel.

Great Britain, December.
The Anglican Church seriously considers ordaining women.

Mgr. Gaillot is told to step back in line

Vatican, January 22
Mgr. Jacques Gaillot, bishop of Evreux, has been granted an audience by John Paul II, along with all the other bishops from his region of France, who are on a visit to Rome. Mgr. Gaillot has been in the public eye since 1983. He has been rocking the Church's traditional discretion with his public stands on such varied issues as nuclear deterrence, celibacy of priests, the ordination of women and the place of homosexuals within the Church. The Holy Father has warned him quite firmly: he must "sing within the choir, not outside the choir."

Trip to Gorée, the slave island

Senegal, February 22
John Paul II visited the island of Gorée, which used to be the transit point for millions of slaves en route for the Americas. He made no attempt to hide his emotion and pain, as he denounced "the shameful commerce undertaken by those who had been baptized but who did not live by their faith." He recalled that slavery, this appalling aberration, had resurfaced in this century, and he took care to add: "It is time that this sin of man against man, this sin of man against God, was confessed in all sincerity and humility."

The Vatican recalls Rome's authority

Holy See, June 15
The Congregation for the Doctrine of the Faith has published a very important *Letter to the Bishops of the Catholic Church on some aspects of the Church understood as communion*. Those in favor of collegiality see this text as yet another attempt to question certain changes enacted by Vatican II, namely with regard to ecclesiastical prerogatives and decision-making. The document itself merely seems to reiterate an eternal truth, one of the very foundations of the papacy itself: the primacy of Rome's authority over national and local Churches.

The founder of Opus Dei is beatified

Vatican, May 17
It is extremely rare that anyone is beatified within less than fifty years of their death. Josemaria Escriva de Balaguer, the founder of Opus Dei, only had to wait sixteen years. The speed of this decision came as a surprise to many, some of whom immediately expressed their feeling that favoritism had been at play. Certainly, since long before he was elected pope, John Paul II was close to the Opus Dei order, with its unswerving tenets of fidelity to the pope, doctrinal conformity and duty to the Church.

The liberalization of the Church is a delicate matter: on the one hand, those in favor of abortion and contraception, on the other, the conservatives.

Operation to remove colon tumor

Rome, July 27
John Paul II is already back at work, having only left the Gemelli Clinic yesterday. Twelve days ago he had an operation to remove a tumor of the colon. According to his doctors, it was not cancerous, but from now on the pope must undergo regular and rigorous health checks. Indeed, routine examinations which had not been done would have detected this growth, which was the size of an orange. The "radical and curative" surgery was performed urgently. In spite of their reassuring words, the doctors nevertheless referred to the possibility of a "dysplasia," which implies that the tumor was on the point of turning malignant. Before going into hospital, the Holy Father had asked to be prayed for.

Even when weak, the pope always finds comfort to give to others.

Truth about Katyn confirmed at last

Warsaw, October 14
Lech Walesa has just received some horrifying documents from Boris Yeltsin, his Soviet counterpart. They are the official papers, kept secret until now, which reveal that it was Stalin in person who ordered the NKVD to liquidate all the Polish officers, whose mass grave was discovered by the Nazis at Katyn in 1943. Another document gives the gruesome statistics of this appalling crime: 21,857 dead.

Galileo's belated rehabilitation

Vatican, October 31
Obliged to retract his statements, condemned to silence and then placed under house surveillance, the Italian scientist Galileo must have felt immense sorrow on hearing the verdict of the Inquisition. The Church refuted his proof of the validity of Copernicus' view of the Universe and the untenability of that of Ptolemy putting the Earth at the center of the Universe. All this took place in 1633. Nearly 360 years later, Galileo, who was the symbolic victim of this blind opposition to reform, has belatedly had his reputation restored by the Church.

Santo Domingo welcomes the pope

Santo Domingo, October 12
John Paul II is in the Dominican Republic to celebrate the 5th centenary of the discovery of America by Europeans and the beginning of its evangelisation. He said mass in front of Christopher Columbus' lighthouse-mausoleum. The Latin-American bishops are holding their General Conference here at the same time. In his address, aimed equally at the Indians, John Paul II recalled that this conquest had led to the most terrible abuse of the indigenous peoples after "the cross had been planted there." Faced with extreme poverty and the proselytism of alternative religions, the pope called for renewed energy to be put into winning Christian souls.

New catechism out at last

Vatican, December 7
The Church has a new catechism. Such a thing has not happened since 1566. Today, John Paul II officially promulgated the text which has been in bookshops since November 16. This catechism has nothing to do with what is normally understood by the word, that is to say a succinct résumé aimed at teaching the rudiments of religion to children. On the contrary, it is a complete synthesis of Catholic doctrine, of the fundamentals of the Faith and of the views of the Church on every aspect of human activity. It is man, his dignity and his honesty which are very much at the centre of this new universal catechism. Back in 1986, it was the challenges and upheavals of the modern world which led to the decision to undertake this vast enterprise. A first version was ready in 1989, but it was completely reworked in the light of the 25,000 amendments sent in from bishops all around the world!

The pope around the world
54. February 19 to 26: Senegal, Gambia, Guinea.
55. June 4 to 10: Angola, Sao Tomé and Principe.
56. October 9 to 14: Santo Domingo.

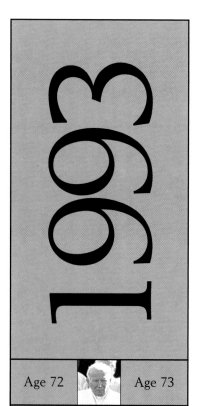
Holy See, January 1.
The Vatican recognizes the recently separated Czech and Slovak Republics.

Assisi, January 9.
John Paul II takes part in the Day of Prayer for Peace in Europe and the Balkans.

Uganda, February 6.
The Holy Father says: "Without the ties of marriage, sexual relationships are a lie."

Vatican, February 11.
First World Day for the Sick.

Vatican, March 10.
The pope says: "It would be a bad day for the pope if he was afraid of criticism and of being misunderstood!"

Mexico, May 26.
Assassination of Cardinal Campo, archbishop of Guadalajara.

Holy See, June 11.
The pope receives Abouna Paulos, patriarch of the Ethiopian Orthodox Church, and says to him: "We share the same Faith handed down to us by the Apostles, the same sacraments and the same ministry rooted in the Apostolic succession.

Paris, November 2.
In an interview given to several European newspapers, John Paul II denounces the "degenerative aspects" of "rampant" Capitalism. He even states that there are some "grains of truth" in Socialism.

Vatican, November 5.
The Lebanese president, Elias Hraoui, a Maronite Christian, visits the pope.

15 years on: decline less severe

Holy See, 1993
The recent statistics reviewing the state of the Catholic clergy, 15 years into this pontificate, show definite improvements. The average age is still increasing, but the crisis in vocations seems to have abated. In 1978, there were 62,670 seminarists; today there are 103,709. However, the overall figure hides considerable disparities between countries. In 1978, the Church had 416,329 working priests; in 1993, their number was 404,570. During this same period, 19,085 priests chose to leave the priesthood. These figures show that there is still a crisis within the clergy, which John Paul II's action and popularity have considerably abated, but have not halted.

Letter to put an end to convent dispute

Poland, April 14
The pope has just sent a letter to Mgr. Rakoczy, bishop of Bielsko-Biela, whose diocese has included the Auschwitz camp since 1991, and to the mother superior of the Carmelite nuns, in the hope of putting an end to this ten-year dispute. He informs them both of "the Church's desire" to see the nuns leave the camp. The pope does, however, pay homage to the spirit of atonement shown by the 15 nuns, a sign of true, noble spirituality.

Mafia will face Divine Judgement

Sicily, May 9
The mass celebrated in the famous Valley of the Temples of Agrigento ended with John Paul II's response to the sorely-tried Sicilians' wish that he take a stand on the blight that afflicts the daily life of the island: the Mafia. Addressing the assassins of judges, the murderers of entire families, the drug dealers and all those who profit from crime, he pronounced a scathing and totally unambiguous warning: "I say it to those responsible: Repent! One day you will come face to face with the judgement of God!"

The pope calls for chastity to fight AIDS

The virus is spreading like wildfire.

Khartoum, February 10
Controversy surrounds the last stage of John Paul II's African trip, his stopover in Khartoum: should the pope visit a country whose regime oppresses the Christian minority? The Holy Father had the courage to ask the right questions and to put respect and tolerance above all else. The most memorable speech of the tour was given in Kampala, the Ugandan capital. Before a crowd of 70,000 young men and women he discussed the problems linked to AIDS which are ravaging East Africa. He called for a "moral revolution." After praising the institution of marriage, he declared that "self-control and chastity are the only safe and virtuous ways of putting an end to the threat of AIDS which is claiming so many victims."

Visit to the world's most atheist country

Tirana, April 25
Mother Teresa was at the airport to greet the pope. "The servant of the poor" is without doubt the best-known Albanian in the world. The Communist dictatorship prides itself on making Albania "the world's only truly atheist State." However, in spite of the terror, the prisons and the endless propaganda, the failure is evident. The pope talked of "the rampart of the Faith" and of religious freedom, "God's precious gift." He met 30 Albanian priests who had all experienced years of detention. Afterwards, he ordained four bishops. In reply to President Sali Berisha's greeting, the pope made a fine exhortation to hope: creating a democratic society would be difficult, especially in the face of such extreme poverty, but the Church, he promised, would give its full support.

Mother Teresa has already shown the way to her people.

Outspoken against taking life from the unborn and the old

Denver, August 14
The capital of Colorado, Denver, is host to this year's World Youth Day. The Holy Father warned the young Catholics, who have come from all over the world, against the attacks made on life itself. Referring to the issues of abortion and euthanasia, the pope condemned "a mentality which militates against life – an attitude of hostility towards life in the mother's womb and life in its last phases." This "massacre of the innocents" is made no less sinful for its accomplishment in "a legal and scientific manner." He opposes the Western world's tendency to make of life "a commodity to be controlled, marketed and manipulated at will," with the words of Christ himself: "I came that they may have life, and have it abundantly."

The image of the Church in America is far from how he wishes it to be.

Fundamentals of moral teaching

Vatican, October 5
The pope's 10th encyclical, *Veritatis Splendor*, reminds the faithful of the moral foundations of the Catholic Church. It stresses the damage done to modern democratic societies by blind, materialistic individualism. Given the same status as freedom – that of a universal truth – it leads to the rapid moral decline of communities. The text points out that both Church and Gospels offer an ethic which does not separate reason and Faith. It is only necessary for reason to accord with natural law and with the revealed Truth. For the pope, there is a standard of morality above and beyond that of the individual, which has wrongfully placed itself at the center of all human actions.

After Communism, beware Capitalism

Riga, September 9
The pope has never hidden his fear of seeing Communism in Eastern European countries replaced with values that have nothing to do with the Gospels, namely indifference, hedonism and consumerism. Nevertheless, in the midst of this Baltic tour – the first by a pontiff to the region – the pope surprised the faithful who had come to greet him when he claimed that Marxism's "kernel of truth" was its recognition of the "situation of exploitation to which an inhumane capitalism had subjected the proletariat." Despite his attacks on dissident theologians tempted by Socialism, John Paul II, who has lived with the reality of Communism, knows that rampant Capitalism conceals almost as many dangers. He warned those people, who have just tasted of the fruits of liberty, to beware not to spoil them.

In Lithuania's capital, Vilnius, the pope climbs the Hill of Crosses.

Fall casts doubt on pope's health

Vatican, November 11
It was at the end of an audience that the Holy Father slipped and fell backwards onto the floor, landing on his shoulder. The first X-rays from the Gemelli Clinic showed that his shoulder had a slight fracture and was dislocated. It must not be moved for a month. Various eyewitnesses talk of having seen the pope faint, but Vatican sources only refer to him missing his step. The film of the audience has still not been made public. This confusion can only add to speculation about the health of John Paul II.

Talk of the pope contracting AIDS

Italy, December 1
Taking up a news item released by a television journalist, the daily *La Repubblica* leads with the article: "The pope has been infected." It naturally refers to the AIDS virus. At the end of the 1980s, an identical rumor created a scandal. In exactly the same way as now, the Vatican lost no time in denying the rumor. Its origin is known: at the time of a blood transfusion, John Paul II was infected by a cytomegalovirus, which was cured by antibiotics.

Mutual recognition after 45 years

Vatican, December 30
Mgr. Claudio Celli, the Assistant Secretary of State for the Vatican, has signed a crucial agreement with his Israeli counterpart. It is the first step in the official reconciliation between the two countries, more than 45 years after the creation of the Jewish State. The document sets out the precise stages for putting in place diplomatic relations in both States. The agreement also marks the normalization of relations between Judaism and Catholicism, two religions born in the same land and issuing from the same holy book, the Bible. The Vatican has agreed to solemnly undertake to combat all forms of Christian anti-Semitism. For its part, the Israeli government has promised to respect the *status quo* of the Christian Holy Places. The Vatican is, however, less than happy about the status of the Holy Places and of Jerusalem.

The pope around the world
57. February 3 to 10: Benin, Uganda, Khartoum (Sudan).
58: April 25: Albania.
59: June 12 to 17: Spain.
60: August 9 to 16: Jamaica, Denver (United States).
61: September 4 to 10: Lithuania, Latvia, Estonia.

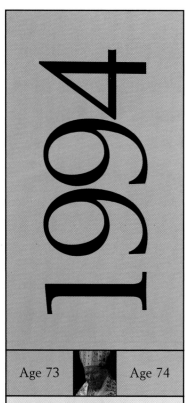

1994

Holy See, January 6.
The pope says: "We find ourselves faced with a new paganism: the deification of the nation."

Vatican, February 11.
Creation of the Pontifical Academy for Life.

Abruzzi, April.
The pope falls while skiing. His secretary breaks his own arm trying to cushion the fall.

Rome, May.
While in the Gemelli Clinic, John Paul II says: "I shall accomplish Peter's task for as long as Providence allows."

Vatican, May 10.
John Paul II creates a nun's cloister within the Vatican, so that they can pray for him permanently.

Castel Gandolfo, August.
The pope only uses the swimming pool for physical therapy sessions. He admits to being a *biedaczek*, a "doddery old man."

Vatican, September 29.
Israel's first ambassador to the Vatican, Schamouel Hadas, is received by the pope.

Haiti, October 17.
At Rome's request, Father Aristide, back in power two days ago, renounces the priesthood.

World, October 20.
Crossing the Threshold of Hope, a book of interviews with the pope, is published in 25 languages in 35 countries.

Vatican, December 13.
The pope's *Letter to Children* is published, telling them: "Christmas is the feast day of a child, of a newborn baby. So it is your feast day too!"

Women ordained in Anglican Church

Great Britain, March 31
Over the past month, the Anglican Church has ordained its first female vicars, in London and Bristol. The decision to open up the priesthood to women was taken two years ago, after much heated debate and threats of schism. At the time, the Holy See reacted very promptly. It stated that, in the light of the Church of England's decision, the ordination of women could only serve as a "serious obstacle to the ecumenical reconciliation" of the two Churches. That remains the case.

St. Peter's resounds to African music

Vatican, April 10
The inaugural mass for the Special Assembly of the Synod of African Bishops set the tone for the ensuing debates: for the first time, drums and other African instruments resounded beneath the vaults of St. Peter's, and the Credo was sung in Swahili. The Synod's theme is *The Church in Africa and her Evangelizing Mission toward the Year 2000*. The bishops will certainly debate long and hard on the issue of Africanization, which some people see as the only possible way for the Church to stand up to the threat posed by Islam and by various sects.

Hip replacement for pope's right leg

Rome, April 29
Last night, around 11 pm, the pope slipped while getting out of his shower, and broke his right femur when he fell to the floor. He has just undergone a hip replacement at the Gemelli Clinic – a frequent and straightforward operation. Doctors expect his convalescence to take about a month. However, they have already indicated that from now on, the pope will almost certainly have to use a stick to help him walk. This new fall once again brings to the fore all manner of speculation about the real state of health of a man who was once an accomplished sportsman.

Michelangelo's masterpiece is restored

Extensive restoration has shed new light on the Sistine Chapel's frescoes.

Vatican, April 8
For those lucky enough to be present at the mass celebrated by John Paul II in the Sistine Chapel, there was plenty to feast the eyes on. After fourteen years, the restoration of Michelangelo's frescoes is finally complete, including his masterpiece *The Last Judgement*. The work was undertaken by Italian restorers, and financed with Japanese funds. There were the usual arguments over the authenticity of the colors found. Having been obscured by centuries of dirt, the freshness of the present colors means that many of the existing theories on the great master's art will have to be revised.

Ordination of women priests rejected

Vatican, May 22
Ordinatio Sacerdotis is the pope's Apostolic Letter defining, once and for all, his position and that of the Roman Catholic Church on the ordination of women. John Paul II writes: "I declare that the Church has no authority whatsoever to confer priestly ordination on women and that this judgement is to be definitively held by all the Church's faithful." It could not be clearer. For all those hoping for change on this question, especially those in the Western world, the debate appears to be well and truly closed.

On August 26, John Paul II was in visible pain while celebrating mass in Combes, in the Italian Alps. Yet his published checkups say he is fine.

The pope is dead! The faithful pray

Vatican, September 4
Those attending the early morning mass in St. Peter's listened, stunned and confused, as the officiating priest prayed for the repose of the Holy Father's soul. John Paul II is not, however, dead, he is just resting at Castel Gandolfo. The priest was the victim of a particularly macabre joke. Around 6.30 am, only a few minutes before the mass began, he received a telephone call informing him of the pope's death. The voice was steady, the diction and words most official. There are rumors that other similar calls have taken place. The Vatican prefers to quietly forget the whole unpleasant incident.

John Paul II is too weak to kiss the ground upon arrival

John Paul II's face cannot hide his physical pain and suffering.

Croatia, September 10
As the Holy Father descended the steps from his plane, all the world's cameras were able to record his visible pain. For the first time in his pontificate, he did not kneel down to kiss the ground of the host nation. Instead, two young Croats brought a bowl containing some Croatian earth for him to kiss. The pope then addressed the million faithful awaiting him. His voice was tired and weak. He referred with great bitterness to the cancellation of his trip to Sarajevo: "To put an end to this bloody war, I have tried everything, I have knocked at every door. It was with this same aim in view that I had planned my visit for last Thursday."

Papal fury over UN project

Cairo, September 5
For eight days, the Egyptian capital is host to the United Nations International Conference on Population and Development. A delegation from the Vatican is participating in the working sessions. Referring to a United Nations family planning project, the pope, who stayed in Rome, lost his temper, something he rarely does: "Tell them no! They must reconsider the project. Let them convert! The family is not an institution to be changed around at will. ... It is part of the most sacred heritage of humanity."

Still no communion for divorcees

Vatican, October 14
In response to a motion put forward by three German bishops, the Congregation for the Doctrine of the Faith has replied that the Eucharist must continue to be refused to all divorcees, remarried or otherwise. This reply is not a case of moral cruelty on behalf of the pope or the Church, but quite simply a reminder that the indissolubility of marriage is a divine precept and that even if he wanted to, the Holy Father cannot contradict this rule. The faithful concerned, nonetheless, still have the right to their priests' mercy.

Yet more cardinals: a new record reached

Today's ordinations bring the total number of cardinals to 165.

Sarajevo visit is too dangerous

Vatican, September 6
John Paul II will not be flying to the Bosnian capital. The Holy Father was well aware of the risks his visit to Sarajevo entailed, devastated as it is by civil war. He was not worried about his own suffering or the risk to his own life in the face of such appalling suffering in others. The Croatian and Bosnian Catholics were already awaiting his visit. But his security advisors were not at all keen to let him go. Earlier in the year, in Rome, the Holy Father had said to the Bosnians: " We are with you. We will not abandon you."

The year 2000 will unite the Church

Vatican, November 10
Today John Paul II sent a letter, *Tertio Millenio Adveniente*, to all the clergy and all the faithful, intended to help prepare for the Jubilee in the year 2000. The text lays down the conditions for celebrating the event and calls for an end to all differences. Recalling the importance of Christianity for mankind as a whole over the past two thousand years, John Paul II also requested the Church to ask forgiveness for the errors, the violence and the acts of intolerance which have been carried out in its name.

Holy See, November 26
For his sixth consistory, the Pope has created 30 new cardinals from 24 countries. The total has now reached 165, more than ever before in the entire history of the papacy. 120 of them – the limit set by the papal electoral process – under the age of 80, form the Sacred College. 90 of the 120 owe their nominations to John Paul II. Since his election, he has in fact created 137 cardinals. The other electors were chosen by Paul VI. The cardinals originate from 57 different countries. Within the Sacred College there are only 55 European cardinals left. 12 cardinals are from North America, 28 from Latin America, 13 from Asia and 15 from Africa. The Italians make up no more than 15.8 per cent of the electoral body, whereas at the beginning of the century they formed 61 per cent. Never before has the Curia been so weakly represented within the heart of the Sacred College.

The pope around the world
62. September 10 to 11:
Zagreb (Croatia).

Sierra Leone, March.
Liberation of 7 nuns held in captivity for two months. During this time they had converted their captors!

Evry, April 11.
Mgr. Guy Herbulot inaugurates the new cathedral, the only one built in France this century.

China, April 16.
In Jiangxi province, 40 Catholics are arrested for having celebrated Easter without permission.

Yaoundé, April 24.
The Jesuit Father Engelbert Mveng is assassinated in Cameroon.

India, May 1.
A nun is assassinated in Assam. Earlier in the year, another nun, Maria Rani, was killed near Indore.

Vatican, May 8.
On the 50th anniversary of the end of the Second World War, the pope castigates "the worship of the cult of the nation."

Brussels, June 3.
The Holy Father pays homage to King Baudouin who died on July 31, 1993. In the presence of his son, King Albert II, he says: "He knew how to serve his fellow countrymen with an evangelical devotion."

Yaoundé, September 15.
John Paul II signs a papal exhortation, *Ecclesia in Africa*, the first document of such importance signed outside Rome.

Vatican, November 22.
Universi Dominici Gregis, confirms that only 120 cardinals can elect the pope.

Mgr. Gaillot is revoked by the Vatican

Vatican, January 13
The Congregation of Bishops has today taken the decision to relieve Mgr. Gaillot of his functions as bishop of the diocese of Evreux. He has been transferred to the titular Episcopal See of Partenia. This was an ancient archbishopric, which no longer exists, in the Setif region of Algeria. Over the past few years, the French bishop has made a popular name for himself with the media. His punishment has provoked a general outcry in France, forcing the Vatican to explain itself: despite numerous warnings and an undertaking by Mgr. Gaillot himself to abide by the discipline and authority of the Holy See, he has not done so. Sanctions were therefore inevitable.

He already has the media's support.

Encyclical continues moral crusade

Vatican, March 30
Evangelicum Vitae (*The Gospel of Life*), the pope's eleventh encyclical, pursues his moral crusade and his denunciation of what he calls "the culture of death." The text attacks abortion, contraception, euthanasia, artificial insemination, and lastly experimentation on human embryos. The pope considers all of these to be in the same category as AIDS, terrorism, warfare, the arms race and drug addiction. Defending the supremacy of moral law over civil law, the pope urges doctors to take a stand by becoming conscientious objectors.

Setting an example for the faithful

Vatican, April 4
The two Italian women beatified by John Paul II, Gianna Beretta Molla and Elisabetta Mora, are both described by him as true "models of Christian perfection." The first, pregnant and stricken with cancer, refused an abortion which might have saved her life. The second demonstrated her "absolute fidelity to the sacrament of marriage," when her unfaithful and unworthy husband abandoned her and her children. The models offered by these beatifications run counter to the current of development in Western societies. The pope knows this.

Colombo gives him a cold welcome

Sri Lanka, January 20
Dialog between different religions is rarely straightforward, as the pope's visit to Sri Lanka showed. Having been greeted by the crowds on the route from the airport, he found only a few Hindu and Muslim dignitaries waiting to welcome him at the Bandaranaike Centre. The reason for the Buddhist boycott is found in his book *Crossing the Threshold of Hope*. In it he defines Buddhism as an "atheist system," a philosophy of salvation which is "almost entirely negative," and he reproaches it for refusing "divine transcendence." These comments shocked and upset the Buddhists, and they showed it.

The truth emerges with latest poll

Italy, 1995
Respect for the moral precepts of the Church is declining fast. This is particularly true in Europe. In Italy, where the Vatican's influence used to be strongest and most direct, and in Poland, the change in habits is staggering. Over the past year an opinion poll undertaken for the Conference of Italian bishops showed that only 23% of Italians still attend mass regularly; 60% of Catholics never go to confession; over half accept divorce and homosexuality; 70% are in favor of the pill; and only 14% are against abortion.

John Paul II is not expected to step down after his 75th birthday

Vatican, May 18
John Paul II is today celebrating his 75th birthday. It is the age at which all bishops must offer their resignation to the pope, who can choose to accept it or not. In reply to rumors of his own resignation, put about more for reasons of his physical weakness than for his age, he replied: "I give thanks to God for being born and for having been called to this mission ... which is mine. I renew before Christ the offer of my readiness to serve the Church as long as He wishes. I leave Him to decide ... how and when He wishes to relieve me of this service."

'I ask forgiveness for the wrongs inflicted on non-Catholics'

Olomouc, May 21
Having had a rather poor turnout in Prague, John Paul II has made the journey to this small town in Moravia, in the Czech Republic, to celebrate the canonization of Jan Sarkander, martyr of the Wars of Religion in the 17th century. The pope criticized the manifest intolerance of Christians which is found today in the developed nations, and then he declared with the utmost solemnity: "In the name of all Catholics, I ask forgiveness for the wrongs inflicted on non-Catholics during the turbulent history of these peoples; at the same time I pledge the Catholic Church's forgiveness for whatever harm her sons and daughters suffered."

The new gestures inspired by Vatican II are now commonplace.

New encyclical to unite the Churches

Vatican, May 30
Christianity in all its guises must recover its lost unity. This message is the essence of the twelfth encyclical, *Ut Unum Sint* (*That They May Be One*). In it, John Paul II states that "every factor of division can be transcended and overcome in the total gift of self for the sake of the Gospel." For the "necessary purification of past memories" to come about, Christians must "re-examine together their painful past." The Catholic Church recognizes and confesses "the weaknesses of her members." Finally, he says that the question of the primacy of the pope may be open to discussion.

Pope speaks out for liberation of women

Vatican, July 10
On the eve of the Peking conference on women, John Paul II has published a *Letter to Women* in which he recognizes the "incalculable debt" humanity owes them. He thanks in turn mothers, wives, daughters, sisters, workers, nuns – the list is far from exhaustive – for the simple fact of being women. Yet again, the Holy Father condemns violence, sexual, domestic or economic, and all forms of slavery to which women have been and still continue to be subjected, victims of the "numerous sons of the Church."

He says that the latter clearly forgot that "Jesus treated women with openness, respect, acceptance and tenderness." The Holy Father spoke up in favor of women's liberation becoming a reality, and for equality between men and women to become more than illusory. He took issue with a "hedonistic and commercial" culture which treated women as mere objects. By way of conclusion, he made a point of recognizing and praising the "genius of women," saying that "the Church sees in Mary the highest expression of the 'feminine genius'."

Yet another alert for the pope's health

He did not finish his speech...

Vatican, December 25
Unfortunately, John Paul II's health is yet again great cause for concern among the faithful. Pale and with a heaving stomach, the Holy Father was forced to interrupt his traditional Christmas address given from the balcony of his Vatican office. While all the world's cameras were focused on him delivering his speech, he suddenly withdrew from the window, leaving the crowd of faithful below, bewildered and worried, until a member of the Vatican personnel announced that the pope was suffering from gastric flu.

Mary Ann Glendon led the Vatican delegation at the Peking conference.

Even Ireland and Poland are no longer his

Europe, December 31
The Church's ability to influence the behavior and decisions of individuals is no longer what it was, not even in the two countries considered to be bastions of Catholicism, Ireland and Poland. On November 24, the Irish voted for the liberalization of divorce. In spite of the Catholic Church's campaign against it, and in spite of all the clergy's pleas to the faithful, the motion was carried. Two days later, the Vatican suffered a new affront in Poland. The second round of the presidential election saw the outgoing president, Lech Walesa, defeated by Alexander Kwasniewski, the neo-Communist candidate transformed into Social Democratic leader. Yet again, the

Church had brought all its weight to bear, openly supporting Walesa. In his description of the second ballot, Mgr. Glemp, the Polish primate, called it a fight between "Christian and neo-pagan values."

The pope around the world
63. January 11 to 21: Manila, Papua New Guinea, Australia, Sri Lanka.
64. May 20 to 22: Czech Republic.
65. June 3 to 4: Belgium.
66. June 30 to July 3: Slovakia.
67. September 14 to 20: Kenya, Cameroon, South Africa.
68. October 4 to 9: America.

1996

Age 75  Age 76

Vatican, January.
The pope evokes the fate of Sarajevo, "a city which symbolizes the tragedies of 20th century Europe," calling it "the Jerusalem of Europe" where all three monotheisms are found.

Port-au-Prince, January 20.
Jean-Bertrand Aristide marries an American lawyer.

Tunisia, April 14.
No news yet of the seven French monks kidnapped from the monastery of Tibehirine in Algeria on March 26. The pope calls Islam to a "proper respect for the differences" of the "small fragile flock" of Christians.

Vatican, April 27.
The pope pays homage to Raoul Follereau and to all clergy who dedicate their lives to caring for lepers.

Algeria, May 23.
A communiqué from the Armed Islamic Group announces: "We have slit the throats of the seven monks."

Sainte-Anne-d'Auray, September 20.
In Brittany, the Holy Father recalls the importance of the family to Christian life. The previous evening, he had prayed by the tomb of Saint Louis-Marie Grignion de Montfort, to whom he owes his motto "Totus Tuus."

Stockholm, October 3.
The Nobel prize for literature goes to the Polish poetess Wislawa Szymborska.

Vatican, November 19.
Fidel Castro is received in a private audience by the pope.

Caracas is the last stop on a grueling Latin American trip

Venezuela, February 11
Nearly 700,000 faithful took part in the closing mass of John Paul II's week-long visit to four Central and South American countries. In the airplane en route for Guatemala, the Holy Father confided to journalists: "With the fall of Communism, Liberation Theology has also fallen!" In countries marked by guerilla warfare and poverty, the pope was pleased to note the progress that had been made toward democracy and peace. In Managua, in particular, he rejoiced to see that Nicaragua had refound its "Christian identity" and was no longer a battlefield for the superpowers. He did however go on to deplore the encroachment of "sensualism and hedonism."

The pope weaves his way to the center of San Salvador to celebrate mass.

French Church takes the middle road

France, March 9
Since the appearance of AIDS as a worldwide epidemic, the Church has been questioned and condemned incessantly for its views on the use of condoms. Considered until recently solely as an artificial method of contraception, they have never received papal approval; the pope has preferred to emphasize the primacy of chastity and fidelity. The French bishops have just opted for a middle road. In a society where sexual freedom is well established, they have issued a statement declaring that, though the condom may sometimes be necessary, it should only be used in circumstances where the sexual act is both fulfilling and dignified.

More concern over pope's health

Vatican, March 25
After twelve days of speculation and worry, the pope was this morning allowed to take up his normal round of engagements. On March 13, an audience with some pilgrims was cancelled, due apparently to the pope's sudden fever. Four days later, weak with exhaustion, he cut short the beatification ceremony over which he was presiding. All his engagements for the following week were subsequently suspended.

Invitation to go on a television-free diet

Vatican, February 21
The Holy Father has chosen Ash Wednesday to launch an initiative which may seem like a penance for many young Catholics: no television for the duration of Lent. In fact the reasoning behind this appeal is far from punitive. In John Paul II's mind, it is a question of freeing people from an alienating force: the hypnotic power of the small screen. He sees this fast from the media as a magnificent opportunity for reunion: with God, with one's family and with oneself. It is not a question of condemning television but of trying out a new sort of spiritual retreat for a period of forty days.

On March 30, John Paul II visits Colle di Val d'Elsa and Sienna. Three days ago, seven French Trappist monks were kidnapped by a commando of the Armed Islamic Group in Algeria. They were from the Monastery of Notre-Dame-de-l'Atlas. "No-one can kill in God's name" the pope says.

The pope takes issue with the new 'radical capitalist ideology'

Berlin, June 22
In front of a crowd 100,000 strong, in Berlin's old Olympic stadium, John Paul II criticized the unbridled materialism of the West and its "radical capitalist ideology," too willing to deny the Truth and the dignity of human life. This speech was the last on a trip characterized by endless polemic between the pope and German Catholics, known to be among the most outspoken in Europe. Last year, over one and a half million people signed a virulent petition demanding more dialog at the center of the Church. Beside the Brandenburg Gate, the pope reminded the faithful: "He who takes liberty to latitudinarian extremes delivers its coup de grâce."

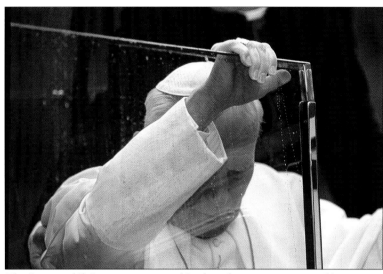
The "popemobile" serves to protect him but also, now, to support him.

The Bishop of Oran is assassinated

Algeria, August 1
The pope has just been informed of the murder of Mgr. Pierre Claverie, bishop of Oran. Together with his Muslim chauffeur, he was killed by a bomb exploding outside the front of his residence. Born in Algeria in 1938, Mgr. Claverie was nominated to Oran in 1981. He was mortified by the horrors of the Algerian civil war. He was also well aware of the Islamic terrorist threats on his life, for he urged intransigence towards them. He had helped promote an Islam ready for dialog with the Christians, an enlightened Islam. This may have encouraged the fundamentalists to silence him.

Angry French Catholics deny their baptism

France, August 11
The Holy Father's presence in Reims on September 22 to celebrate the fifteenth centenary of Clovis's baptism aroused the anger of certain groups of laity. They have not forgotten the pope's exhortation on his first visit to Paris: "France ... are you faithful to your baptismal promises?" After stern criticism over the use of French public funds for this religious event, these anti-papist groups are making their stand by denying their baptism. Several hundred Catholics have sent letters, some as printed forms, to their parishes or archbishoprics to ask to be struck off the baptismal registers. These renunciations or apostasies as yet remain marginal but, as the debate has grown over the past few months, so has their number. The clergy has reminded the faithful that, like all the sacraments, baptism lasts for eternity. Nonetheless, the desire to renounce will be recorded alongside each name in the margin of the baptismal registers.

In Amiens, a patchwork is being prepared for the arrival of the Holy Father.

Never too old for appendicitis

Rome, October 15
Having been operated on on October 6 for appendicitis, John Paul II has just left the Gemelli Clinic. This is the Holy Father's sixth operation since the start of his pontificate. The rooms which the pope occupies, on the tenth floor of the Clinic, are now more like an apartment. A room next to his has just been transformed into a private chapel for him. All through this latest stay in hospital, Stanislaw Dziwisz, John Paul II's private secretary, and a small group of nuns, remained constantly at the pope's side.

Multimedia and the mystery of Christ

France, November
The Son of God has made his debut in the world of multimedia. Several publishers have produced the CD-ROM *Jesus, Gospels and Paintings*, which offers an "interactive voyage in the footsteps of Jesus." The voice of the actor Jean Rochefort guides the user. The last time the pope was in France, he was shown the new Internet site for the Conference of the Bishops of France (www.cef.fr), which started on September 6. By the end of September, 16,000 visits had already been recorded. Net-surfers pop up in unexpected places!

John Paul II's vocation and mission

Vatican, November 1
To celebrate the 50th anniversary of his ordination, John Paul II has published *Gift and Mystery*, in which he explains his personal mission as a priest. Subtitled *My Priestly Ordination*, the work is a mixture of his thoughts and memories. One such example is that which has guided his every action at the head of the Catholic Church: that "the Council [Vatican II] illustrated the possibility and need for renewal, while remaining faithful to the word of God and the Church's tradition." The book is written in the name of John Paul II, but Karol Wojtyla's voice comes across very clearly. As, for instance, when he confides all the "gratitude" he feels toward his father, or when he expresses the "immense cordiality" and "great wisdom of life" that he discovered in sharing the daily existence of the Solvay factory workers. Never has a pope spoken so openly.

The pope around the world
69. February 5 to 12: Guatemala, Nicaragua, Salvador, Venezuela.
70. April 14: Tunisia.
71. May 17 to 19: Slovenia.
72. June 21 to 23: Germany.
73. September 6 to 7: Hungary.
74. September 19 to 25: France.

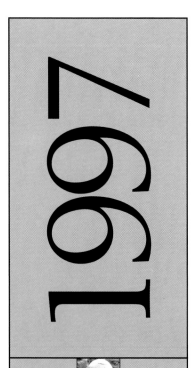

Age 76   Age 77

Albania, January 28.
Death of Cardinal Mikel Koliqi (born September 29, 1902). He had spent forty years in prison under the Communist regime. Freed in 1986, he was made a cardinal in 1994.

Calcutta, March 18.
The Missionary Sisters of Charity choose Sister Nirmala as Mother Teresa's successor. This Indian nun, of Nepalese Hindu origin, converted at the age of 24.

Paris, April 21.
France-Soir publishes an interview with Mehmet Ali Ağca, in which he presents himself as "the material and spiritual reincarnation of Christ."

Vatican, May.
On the eve of the European Congress of Vocations, the Holy See reveals that, since 1978, there has been a 13% decline in priests and monks in Europe. This fall is strongest in the Netherlands, Belgium, and France.

Poznan, June 3.
The pope urges the young to avoid becoming "slaves to worldly goods, to the economic system, to technology, ... to easy money."

Paris, August 21.
John Paul II celebrates World Youth Day and pays homage to Father Joseph Wrezinski, founder of ATD Fourth World.

Drancy, September 30.
The French Church expresses contrition for the attitude of some of its members during the German occupation.

Papal bullet encased in gold

Fatima, 1997
Highly venerated by John Paul II, the sanctuary at Fatima now houses an unusual *ex voto*. The bullet which went straight through his abdomen has been set into a gold crown that the pope himself placed on the head of the statue of the Virgin. The belt he was wearing that same day has already been placed in Jasna Gora, in Poland. The pope is convinced that "a maternal hand guided the trajectory of the bullet and saved me ... at death's door."

Netanyahu invites the pope to Israel

Holy See, February 3
Benyamin Netanyahu, the Israeli prime minister, and his wife, Sarah, were received by the pope earlier today. After discussing the progress in Judeo-Christian relations, the two men discussed the difficult question of the status of the Holy Places. The Israeli prime minister reiterated his invitation for the pope to visit Jerusalem. John Paul II's dream is to celebrate the Christian Jubilee there in the year 2000.

Turin Shroud saved from flames

Turin, April 12
At 11.15 last night, a fire broke out in Turin Cathedral. Firemen were quickly on the scene. One of them, Mario Trematore, had only one idea in mind: to save the Holy Shroud, even at risk to his own life. Using an axe, he managed to break the glass protecting the relic, seized it and made his way back outside to be greeted by cheers. Overcome with emotion, he fainted!

The pope around the world
75. April 12 to 13 Sarajevo.
76. April 26 to 27: Czech Republic.
77. May 10 to 11: Lebanon.
78. May 31 to June 10: Poland.
79. August 21 to 24: France.
80. October 2 to 6: Brazil.

Top security for pope's visit to Sarajevo

Ex-Yugoslavia: scenes of the appalling destruction are all around.

Bosnia, April 13
The surveillance measures for the Holy Father's visit to Sarajevo are being highly publicized, for security reasons. In this war-torn city, there was soon confirmation of the necessity for such measures. The police uncovered twenty-three landmines linked to a detonator, buried a few yards from the pope's planned route. Furthermore, a man claiming to want to kill the Holy Father has been arrested. John Paul II finally arrived yesterday, in freezing weather, to be greeted by Cardinal Vinco Puljic. The city's Catholics, 20,000 out of a population of 360,000, are Croats. Large numbers of Muslims had also come to greet the messenger of peace. Today, before leaving, the pope celebrated mass in the old Olympic stadium.

New assassination plot – or hoax?

Rome, May 9
The daily newspaper, *Il Giornale*, has confirmed that the security forces have succeeded in thwarting an assassination attempt on the pope's life. However, neither the police nor the Vatican have made any comment on this disturbing news. Eighteen terrorists from Iran, Bosnia and Turkey had intended to park a car, packed with explosives, near the esplanade in St. Peter's, timed to explode as the Popemobile drove past. There is no firm confirmation of this information, which may well be a hoax.

La Croix counts its true followers

France, May 11
The Catholic daily, *La Croix*, has published a vast survey on the state of the Church in France. Written by Bruno Chenu, the editorial confirms that France is in the same situation as other Catholic nations: it is living through a "delicate process of change, of becoming a minority religion." This is partly due to the arrival of other religions and to conversions to Buddhism and Islam; but more importantly, to a loss of spirituality within French society. Traditions live on, such as baptisms and communions, but faith is receding.

John Paul II finally makes it to Lebanon

Beirut, May 11

Nearly 20,000 soldiers and policemen were drafted in to ensure the safety of the Holy Father for his 32-hour visit to the Lebanon. The country is no longer at war, but the tension between the religious communities and the different political camps remains high. This is the first visit by a pope to the Near East since Paul VI's trip to Jerusalem in 1964. Having been cancelled three times, this trip is the conclusion of the 1995 Synod on the Lebanon. Virtually the entire Christian population came to welcome him: 40% of the 3.3 million Lebanese. In the Square of Martyrs, the pope called for "the sovereignty of Lebanon to be restored" – a remark aimed at both Syria and Israel.

His return to Poland has all the appearances of a pilgrimage

On June 9, he goes to pray at the grave of his parents in Cracow.

Poland, June 10

This eleven-day trip to Poland, the 7th of John Paul II's pontificate, was more of a return to his roots, a pilgrimage down memory lane. In Gniezno, the pope celebrated the millennium of St. Adalbert, the first Polish saint, before a crowd which included seven heads of European States. It was to these seven that he addressed this warning: "May no European nation, not even the smallest power, be left out of the organizations that are currently taking shape in Europe." On June 5, the pope's day of rest, he stopped beside Lake Morskie Oko, at a spot where he often used to go as a young man. He then visited the Ursuline Convent, where he found a pair of his own skis, last used in 1978. After a stop in Zakopane, he met up with old friends in Ksiezowska. While in Cracow, he saw again the site of the Solvay factory, as well as friends from Jagiellonian University, and he said a celebratory mass in honor of the canonization of Queen Edwige (1374-1399). A service in the crypt of Wawel Cathedral reminded him of his first mass there in 1946. Lastly, he prayed at the graves of his parents and his brother.

Euphoric reception for World Youth Day

France, August 24

This year's World Youth Day, the twelfth, was held in France, and, despite the country's reputation for being religiously skeptic and upset periodically by bouts of anticlericalism, it was a spectacular success. This was largely due to the enormous popularity of John Paul II among young Catholics, who came in vast numbers from all over the world to greet him, behaving like true "fans" for the entire duration of his four-day visit to Paris. 300,000 young people assisted at the mass in the Champ-de-Mars. The ceremony held on 22 August, celebrating the beatification of Frédéric Ozanam (1813-1853), who dedicated his life to the poor, also paid homage to the social action of the Church. After visits to Place Sainte Geneviève and Evry Cathedral, it was today's mass at Longchamp that was perhaps the most moving, not least due to the sheer number of people attending. It was the closing mass of the trip, a ceremony of hope, celebrated in front of one million people, the vast majority of whom were French.

Mother Teresa gave her all to the poor

Calcutta, September 13

From the most humble, who called her "Our Mother," to the most powerful, the whole of India is weeping for Mother Teresa, buried today in Calcutta. Born as Agnes Gonxha Bojaxhiu on August 27 1910 in Macedonia, she chose the name Teresa when she joined the Church. She died on September 5. Cardinal Angelo Sodano, Secretary of State to the Vatican, represented the pope at her funeral in the Netaji Stadium. John Paul II's message summed up everyone's grief: "The entire Church thanks you for your luminous example, and promises to make it our heritage." After this, representatives of India's major religions paid their homage to her.

September 27: at the Italian Eucharistic Congress in Bologna, Bob Dylan, a Jew converted to Catholicism and back again, sings for the pope.

The albs were designed by the French couturier Jean-Charles de Castelbajac.

1998

Age 77 — Age 78

The Church is not afraid of the truth

Vatican, January 1
From today, the archives of the Congregation of the Holy Office are open to researchers, upon written request. This is a personal decision by John Paul II, who wishes to show that the Church is not afraid of the truth. The archives in question contain 4,500 volumes, testimony to the controversies that have beset the Church since 1542. While the minutes of the most famous trials, those of Giordano Bruno, Galileo, and Savonarola, have already been seen, researchers will now be able to study the workings of the Inquisition in detail, an issue which still divides many historians.

Will the Vatican adopt the euro?

Holy See, January
The Italian lira has been the legal tender of the Vatican since 1929. The only difference is that Vatican coins are stamped with the pontifical symbols. Now that the lira has been accepted into the euro camp, the question arises as to whether the Vatican will follow suit. Nothing has been decided yet. If it opts for the euro, the Vatican will have to deal with Brussels and Frankfurt.

No Poles for Italian song contest

San Remo, February 24
The prestigious Italian song festival has opened amidst a raging polemic: the group *I Cugini di Campagna* and its leader, Ivano Michelli, have been banned from singing a song entitled *La Nostra Terra*, whose text is by a certain Karol Wojtyla. Although the Vatican had given permission for its use, the festival's jury have refused it on the grounds that its author is not Italian. The group pointed out that Karol Wojtyla is in fact John Paul II, the bishop of Rome; to which the jury replied that his fame would disadvantage all the other song candidates. Outraged, Ivano Michelli retorted: "That's as if one said that Brazil should not play football!"

Mass is celebrated in Revolution Square!

Keen to project a peace-loving image, Castro greets the pope in civilian clothes.

Havana, January 25
Beneath portraits of Che Guevara and Christ, half a million Cubans attended this morning's mass which was celebrated by John Paul II at his last engagement in Cuba. Having been rather reserved on the previous days, this morning's crowd let themselves go, singing and swaying to the pope's words, especially when he quoted from St. Luke's Gospel: "The Spirit of the Lord has sent me to proclaim release to the captives, to set at liberty those who are oppressed." To the crowd, who were chanting: "The pope wants to see us all free," the Holy Father replied: "That word ... today it shall be accomplished." In the face of such a challenge, Fidel Castro remained uncompromising on the "principles of the Revolution," although he had the satisfaction of hearing the pope condemn the American embargo.

Russian Orthodox Church resents Catholics

Vatican, February 10
John Paul II has just received the Russian president, Boris Yeltsin. Central to their discussions is the question of the relations between the Catholic and Orthodox Churches. According to Alexis II, patriarch of Moscow, the Catholics have been "proselytizing excessively" in Eastern Europe, which, it is true, the Pope does view as potentially good "territory for missionaries."

Before embarking on the Way of the Cross to the Coliseum, in Rome, the pope performs the ritual kissing of the feet in Santa Maria Maggiore.

The Church repents toward the Jews

Holy See, March 16

We Remember: A Reflection on the Shoah is the title of the thirteen-page document published by the Vatican on the Church of Rome's repentence for its attitude during the last war. It has been keenly awaited for the past decade. In it, the pope says that the Shoah "remains an indelible stain on the history of the century that is coming to a close." The text defends Pius XII and recalls that numerous Christians helped save Jews. *Reflection* concludes that: "the Catholic Church desires to express her deep sorrow for the failures of her sons and daughters in every age. This is an act of repentance, since, as members of the Church, we are linked to the sins as well as the merits of all her children." This goes some way to satisfying the rabbis.

The head of the Swiss Guards and his wife murdered in Rome

Aloïs Estermann had been with the Swiss Guards since 1980.

Vatican, May 4

"It is with great pain that I learned of the unbearable news of the violent death of your son ... and his dear wife." These were the words which John Paul II used to address Commandant Aloïs Estermann's parents. This forty-four-year-old man from Lucerne had just been promoted to the head of the Swiss Guards. It was he who, back in May 1981 when Ali Agça fired at the pope, leapt toward the Popemobile in order to shield him with his own body. Today's tragedy has shocked the highly insulated world of the Vatican. The assassination took place in the officer's lodgings, which overlook the private apartments of the pope. Estermann and his wife were killed by a jealous corporal who reckoned he had been unjustly overlooked for the job of commandant. He then committed suicide.

Our God's Brother on the silver screen

Vatican, March 27

In a private viewing today, the pope saw what the film maker Krzysztof Zanussi had made of his play *Our God's Brother*, which he wrote nearly half a century ago. The film stars Scott Wilson as Father Adam Chmielowski, the painter-cum-priest beatified by John Paul II. Zanussi is no novice in this field. He has already made a film on the life of Karol Wojtyla, and he is the author of a dramatic adaptation of another of Wojtyla's plays, *Job*, into which he has integrated the assassination of Aldo Moro and that of Father Jerzy Popieluszko!

Fake or not, the Turin Shroud still brings in the crowds

The pace of his travels is slowing down, but he still likes crowd contact.

Turin, May 24

After he had knelt and prayed in front of the Holy Shroud of Turin, John Paul II read out a short address. He has always refused to get involved in the debate on the dating of the Shroud, explaining that it is not a "problem of faith" but a scientific question. Referring to it as an "icon of suffering," he spoke of an "image of silence ... a tragic silence of incommunicability, which finds its greatest expression in death." The doubt cast on the authenticity of the Shroud has not prevented tens of thousands of people coming to pray before the glass case in which it has been exhibited since mid-April.

China remains hostile to the Vatican

Holy See, May 2

There are about 10 million Catholics in China. The "patriotic" Church is recognized by the regime, but the clandestine Church is not. The Synod of Bishops which opened on April 19, had invited two Chinese bishops, members of the clandestine Church. They were unable to obtain exit visas. This clearly illustrates Peking's refusal to renew links with the Vatican. Relations between the two States were broken 41 years ago. This morning, before the whole Synod, the message from one of the two invited prelates, Mgr. Matthias Duan Yin-Ming, was read out. It deplored not being able to participate in the sessions "for political reasons," and particularly not being able to see "the Holy Father for once in my life." Mgr. Duan is 91. Peking's intransigent position is sure to hold back the long-awaited and necessary reconciliation between the two Churches in China.

John Paul II beatifies a Croat bishop

Marija Bistrica, October 3

400,000 people were present at the beatification ceremony near Zagreb of Cardinal Alojzije Stepinac (1898-1960), primate of Croatia during the Second World War. John Paul II did not care to reply to those who accuse the Cardinal of dragging his feet over his condemnation of the pro-German regime which was installed in Croatia in 1941 by Ante Pavlic's *ustachis*. Instead, the pope preferred to recall the primate's instructions to his clergy in 1943: "Welcome [the Jews and the Serbs] in order to save their lives. ... The Orthodox faithful are Christian, and the Jewish faith is the fount of Christianity."

The pope around the world
81. January 21 to 25: Cuba.
82. March 21 to 23: Nigeria.
83. June 19 to 21: Algeria.
84. October 2 to 4: Croatia.

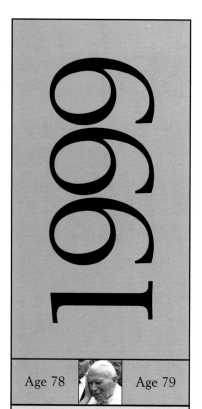

Age 78		Age 79

Vatican, January 13.
John Paul II receives a delegation from the World Union of Progressive Judaism. "The time has come", declares the Holy Father, "to develop fully the dialog between Jews and Catholics."

St Louis, January 26.
Receiving John Paul II, President Bill Clinton pays tribute to his actions with regard to Eastern Europe: "May you live to be a hundred or more!" "Slowly, slowly," the pope replied.

Vatican, January 26.
The Holy See is modernizing the ritual of exorcism, still subject to rules dating from the 16th century Council of Trent.

Vatican, March 11.
Making the first European visit of an Iranian head of state since the Islamic revolution, Mohammad Khatami is granted a private audience with the pope, who considers this meeting promising.

Vatican, April 18.
Marcellin Champagnat (1789-1840), founder of the Order of the Brothers of Mary, is to be canonized.

Vatican, April 23.
In a *Letter from John Paul II to artists*, he urges them to "rediscover the depth of the spiritual and religious dimension" of their craft.

Vatican, October 1.
Opening of the Synod of Bishops of Europe, devoted to "radical dechristianisation".

Vatican, October 10.
John Paul II's trip to Ur, the city of Abraham in Iraq, is cancelled.

136

The pope in Mexico: "No more exploitation of the oppressed!"

Mexico, January 25
At the last stop of his trip to Mexico, "Juan Pablo," as he is known here, was cheered by a huge crowd as he repeated Christ's words: "I am with you every day till the end of the world." In a 90% Catholic country, where one inhabitant out of two suffers from malnutrition, the pope two days ago signed an apostolic exhortation concerning the Church in America, the resonance of which carried far beyond Mexico's boundaries. "The time has come," he said, "to banish once and for all from the continent all assaults against life. No more violence, no terrorism, no drug dealing! No more torture! No more exploitation of the oppressed, no racial discrimination, no more ghettoes! Never again!"

A diverse crowd of over 130,000 people cheer the pope at the Aztec stadium.

John Paul II saves a man from execution

St Louis (Missouri), January 28
Darrell Mease, aged 42, will not be executed. Mel Carnahan, governor of Missouri State, has commuted the triple murderer's death sentence. He will remain in prison for the rest of his days. Mease owes his life to the Holy Father who, having described the death sentence as "cruel and useless" had asked, upon his arrival in St Louis two days ago, for his sentence to be reduced. "Out of deep respect for the pope and for everything he represents, I have decided to grant his request," the governor stated. John Paul II considers that modern society should be able to protect itself "without denying criminals the right to make amends." Last year, 68 people were executed in the US.

Papal plea to NATO remains unanswered

Vatican, April 4
Contrary to John Paul II's wishes, the conflict in Kosovo, begun on March 24, has not had the benefit of an Easter truce. The pope's Maundy Thursday plea remained unanswered. Today, Easter Day, the Holy Father has made clear his wish to see a humanitarian corridor set up to help the refugees.

Catholics and Orthodox united in Bucharest

Bucharest, May 9
John Paul II's often-expressed dream of reconciling the "two lungs" of Christianity, the Orthodox and the Catholic Churches, has reached a new threshold. This visit, ending tonight, is the first ever made by a pope to a country with an Orthodox majority. At the close of these three days in Bucharest, the Holy Father celebrated mass this afternoon in front of a crowd chanting: "Unity! Unity!" as two giant portraits of Christ floated from the palace of the former Communist dictator Ceausescu. There is, however, still a long way to go: the Holy Father was not authorized to go to Transylvania and Moldavia, the two regions where the faith of the Uniates (Catholics using the Greek rite but attached to Rome) is strongest.

The Orthodox patriarch Teoctist accompanied him throughout the three days.

His longest trip is for his native country

Poland, June 17

The pope's 13-day trip to Poland is not only the longest he has made in a single country, but has also proved to be the most trying. Due to his Parkinson's disease, and to the medication designed to combat it, the pope now walks only with difficulty. No doubt as a result of this, on June 12 he fell and injured his forehead. Three days later, a sudden high fever prevented him from celebrating mass in Cracow where two million people waited for him in pouring rain. Cardinal Macharski, the archbishop of Cracow, officiated in his place. Because of accumulated stress the pope was forced to cancel a trip to Armenia. On his way back to Rome, the Supreme Pontiff had intended to go to the bedside of the seriously ill head of the Apostolic Armenian Church. Instead, he will pray for him. In his native country, where his stay had begun on June 5, the Poles' fervor is as strong as ever. Among other places, John Paul II

The Holy Father bears the mark of his fall at the Warsaw nunciature.

visited Gdansk, stronghold of the fight against Communism, and the port of Elblag, where he had gone kayaking "I don't know how many years ago." He also went to Warsaw, where for the first time he spoke before the national parliament. In Wadowice, his native town, confident and moved, the pope took time out to speak to the people: "It is here that it all began for me." In Cracow, which is celebrating the millennium of its diocese, he prayed for his parents and, his voice a little weak, sang with some youths, *Mary, queen of Poland*, an ancient national song. Though not alluding to the political issues stirring the country, John Paul II made two appeals: first to the deputies and the citizens, telling them to make sure that ethics are respected, and then to the Polish clergy, asking them to pay heed to the teachings of the Second Vatican Council and to increase their awareness of modernity on the eve of the year 2000.

A historic agreement on "justification"

Augsburg, October 31

The ground had been prepared for thirty years. John Paul II himself recognised that the disagreement on justification was outdated. Behind the term "justification" lies not only the question of the paths to humanity's salvation, but also the central historical breach between Catholics and Lutherans. In contrast to "justification through works and merit", symbolised by the notorious practice of indulgences, Luther advocated salvation exclusively through faith and divine grace. This principle sums up the Reformation. For the first time since the 16th century, the two Churches have agreed that remaining theological differences between them should be considered legitimate expressions of the truth, not causes for division.

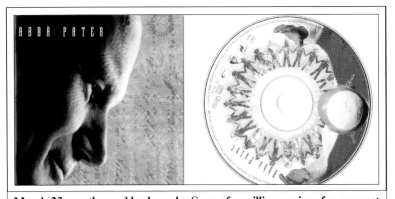

March 23 saw the world release by Sony of a million copies of a compact disc titled *Abba Pater* (abba means father in Aramaic, the language in which much of the New Testament was originally written). The eleven tunes composed and arranged by two Italian musicians, Leonardo de Amicis and Stefano Mainetti, are a background to prayers, homilies, and psalms recited or sung by John Paul II between 1978 and 1998.

Revered English Catholic leader dies

London, June 17

Cardinal Basil Hume OM, archbishop of Westminster and leader of the Catholics of England and Wales, died of cancer today (b. March 2, 1923). In the period since he was plucked in 1976 from the relative obscurity of Abbot of Ampleforth Abbey he succeeded in reintegrating Catholicism into English life after centuries of suspicion. This gentle, diffident monk developed an increasingly powerful, yet always spiritual, influence. The key to his leadership was his determination to heal the disunity in the Church resulting from the Second Vatican Council. He decided that "what united people has to be very deep. It is the life of prayer. Get that right and much else falls into place." Although his manner persuaded Catholic liberals that he was one of them, he was always prepared in the end to defend papal authority. The fact that he sometimes gave the impression that, left to himself, he might have handled matters differently, was wisely accepted by Rome! The ordination of women was the greatest single test of his leadership, when in 1991-92 it threatened to tear the Anglican church apart. While managing to reassure his fellow Catholics that no doctrinal concessions were being made, he negotiated a compromise that did not alienate the Anglican authorities. Several hundred Anglican priests joined the Catholic church, and cardinal Hume ensured that, through special arrangements agreed with Rome, even the many married priests among them could be accepted. He has for long been viewed by people of all denominations as one of the most spiritual religious leaders the country has seen. Not long before his death Queen Elizabeth – the head of the Anglican Church – conferred on him the Order of Merit as a demonstration of her own personal admiration.

The pope around the world	
85. January 22 to 28: Mexico, United States (Missouri).	**87.** June 5 to 17: Poland (the longest trip)
86. May 7 to 9: Romania	**88.** September 19: Slovenia.
	89. November 4 to 7: India.

Jubilee Year

'THOU SHALT SANCTIFY THE FIFTIETH YEAR,' God says in the Book of Leviticus, 'and shalt proclaim remission to all the inhabitants of thy land, for it is the year of Jubilee'. In obedience to this command the Jewish people observe every fiftieth year as a special year: land is allowed to lie fallow, quarrels are resolved, and outstanding debts are remitted. Jewish priests initiate each such year by blowing a ram's horn, the Hebrew term for which is yobel. *This word eventually passed into English as* jubilee.

John Paul, watched by Jordan's King Abdullah, blesses well-wishers at the start of his Jubilee Year trip to the Holy Land.

In a papal bull, *Antiquorum Habet Fida Relatio*, published in February, 1300, Pope Boniface VIII instituted the first Christian Jubilee Year, inviting Christians from all over the world to make a pilgrimage to Rome. The city, he observed, was rich in memories of the early martyrs – not least St Peter and St Paul, who had died during Nero's persecution around AD 65. Boniface decreed that anyone making a Jubilee Year pilgrimage to Rome to venerate the tombs of the martyrs would gain a special indulgence, the remission of their sins.

The bull fell on receptive ears. Not only was this the heyday of pilgrimages – Santiago in Spain, Canterbury in England, Jerusalem in the Holy Land were centers of pilgrimage and devotion – but Rome was especially popular since it was the abode of the pope, Peter's successor. There was a long tradition of pilgrims making the arduous journey to Rome to receive the pope's blessing and gain an indulgence. When, therefore, Boniface issued his bull the effect was dramatic: pilgrims flocked to Rome from all around the shores of the Mediterranean and from every corner of Europe.

The success of the first Jubilee Year encouraged future popes to make the event a regular feature of the Church's calendar. Although the frequency was originally intended to be once every hundred years, as early as 1350 Pope Clement VI reduced the interval to fifty years. In 1470 Pope Paul II made a further reduction to twenty-five years, which gave more people the opportunity of making a

Jubilee pilgrimage to Rome at least once in their lifetime. In the runup to each Jubilee the pope would prepare the city for the influx of visitors. New churches would be commissioned from famous architects, existing churches embellished with magnificent works of art, and the finest composers of the day invited to compose music worthy of the solemn ceremonies of the Holy Year.

Although Holy Years have continued to be celebrated more or less every twenty-five years ever since Paul II's time, political complications led to the tradition faltering during the nineteenth century, only for it to be reestablished with renewed vigor in the course of the twentieth.

On Christmas Eve, 1999, Pope John Paul II presided over the opening of the Holy Doors at St Peter's Basilica. This ceremony, with which a Jubilee Year officially begins, dates back to 1500, when Pope Alexander VI knocked on the doors with a hammer and repeated, in Latin, the words of the Jewish psalm, 'This is the door of the Lord. The just will enter through it. I will enter your house, O Lord. I will kneel in your holy temple with adoration'. For John Paul – who eschewed the use of a hammer in favor of a symbolic push – it was an emotional moment, one to which he had looked forward for many years. As the great bronze doors were swung slowly open before him, ushering in the third millennium, he felt a great rush of history in his heart. He had invited people from all five continents to decorate the Holy Doors, as a sign of the universality of the Catholic Church. The doors' lintel was perfumed with precious oil and garlanded with exotic tropical flowers whose fragrance mingled with that of the incense rising in plumes before the doors.

No Jubilee Year just happens. For years John Paul has been perfecting plans to make a vast multitude of pilgrims as welcome as possible. They will come from every corner of the globe, from every country in the world. All will pass through the Holy Doors, reminded of the words of Jesus, who likened himself to a door that would open to anyone who knocked upon it. Poor or rich, sick or well, disheartened or content – all will come seeking something, some blessing, some solace. Ever practical, the pope has arranged special Jubilee Days when he will welcome particular groups so that he can celebrate with them their special gifts. There will be, among others, days for children, the sick, artists, the elderly, and the military. He is preparing with great interest for the World Day of Youth in August. 'You are the hope of the future,' he wrote in the letter inviting the young people of the world to participate. 'You are the hope of the world.'

In February John Paul traveled to Egypt, a land steeped in biblical tradition. The goal of his journey was Mount Sinai, where God spoke to Moses and gave him the Ten Commandments. This place, observed the pope, was where the three great monotheistic religions of the world – Judaism, Christianity, and Islam – all had their birth. At the foot of the mountain he made an impassioned plea for tolerance and respect for all, begging God's forgiveness for the suffering caused throughout the world by religion.

The next month saw him in Palestine, Jordan, and Israel, his pilgrimage following in the footsteps of Jesus. In the twilight of his own earthly life, and two thousand years after Christ's birth, John Paul prayed fervently for the peace and advancement of humanity, constantly repeating Jesus' own prayer, 'Father, may they all be one.'

The pope, during his Holy Land pilgrimage, looks toward Jerusalem from Mount Nebo in Jordan. Tradition has it that it was from this mountain that Moses first saw the land promised by God to the Israelites.

Complete List of Popes and Antipopes

Although popes are considered to be the successors of the Apostle Peter, Peter himself is not generally reckoned as a pope. The dates for four of the first five popes are unknown. An antipope is a man whose election has not been recognized by the Church as canonically valid. In the list the names of antipopes are given in *italics* and have been omitted from the official numbering system.

St Peter

John XXI 1276–1277

Clement V 1305–1314

CLEMENS V. *Bertrand. de Gotho,*
Burdegalensis, creat *die s.Iunij an.1305,*
Sedit an.8.mens.10 *dies 16. Obijt die 20*
Aprilis an.1319.Vac. *Sed.an.2.mens.3.di7.*

#	Name	Dates
1	St Linus	
2	St Anacletus	
3	St Clement	c.96
4	St Evaristus	
5	St Alexander I	
6	St Sixtus I	c.116 – c.125
7	St Telesophorus	c.125 – c.136
8	St Hyginus	c.138 – c.142
9	St Pius I	c.142 – c.155
10	St Anicetus	c.155 – c.166
11	St Soter	c.166 – c.174
12	St Eleutherius	c.175 – c.189
13	St Victor	c.189 – c.199
14	St Zephyrinus	c.199 – c.217
15	St Callistus	c.217 – 222
	St Hippolytus	*217 – c.235*
16	St Urban I	c.222 – 230
17	St Pontian	230 – 235
18	St Anterus	235 – 236
19	St Fabian	236 – 250
20	St Cornelius	251 – 253
	Novatian	*251 – 258*
21	St Lucius I	253 – 254
22	St Stephen I	254 – 257
23	St Sixtus II	257 – 258
24	St Dionysius	260 – 268
25	St Felix I	269 – 274
26	St Eutychian	275 – 283
27	St Gaius (Caius)	283 – 296
28	St Marcellinus	296 – ?
29	St Marcellus	c.308 – 309
30	St Eusebius	310
31	St Miltiades	311 – 314
32	St Sylvester I	314 – 335
33	St Mark	336
34	St Julius I	337 – 352
35	Liberius	352 – 366
	St Felix II	*355 – 365*
36	St Damasus I	366 – 384
	Ursinus	*366 – 367*
37	St Siricius	384 – 399
38	St Anastasius I	399 – 401
39	St Innocent I	401 – 417
40	St Zosimus	417 – 418
	Eulalius	*418*
41	St Boniface	418 – 422
42	St Celestine I	422 – 432
43	St Sixtus III	432 – 440
44	St Leo I (the Great)	440 – 461
45	St Hilarus (Hilary)	461 – 468
46	St Simplicius	468 – 483
47	St Felix III (II)	483 – 492
48	St Gelasius I	492 – 496
49	Anastasius II	496 – 498
50	St Symmachus	498 – 514
	Laurence	*498 – 499*
		501 – 506
51	St Hormisdas	514 – 523
52	St John I	523 – 526
53	St Felix IV (III)	526 – 530
	Dioscorus	*530*
54	Boniface II	530 – 532
55	John II	533 – 535
56	St Agapitus I	535 – 536
57	St Silverius	536 – 537
58	Vigilius	537 – 555
59	Pelagius I	556 – 561
60	John III	561 – 574
61	Benedict I	575 – 579
62	Pelagius II	579 – 590
63	St Gregory I (the Great)	590 – 604
64	Sabinian	604 – 606
65	Boniface III	607
66	St Boniface IV	608 – 615
67	St Deusdedit I (Adeodatus)	615 – 618
68	Boniface V	619 – 625
69	Honorius I	625 – 638
70	Severinus	640
71	John IV	640 – 642
72	Theodore I	642 – 649
73	St Martin I	649 – 653
74	St Eugenius I	654 – 657
75	St Vitalian	657 – 672
76	Adeodatus II	672 – 676
77	Donus	676 – 678
78	St Agatho	678 – 681
79	St Leo II	682 – 683
80	St Benedict II	684 – 685
81	John V	685 – 686
82	Conon	686 – 687
	Theodore	*687*
	Paschal	*687*
83	St Sergius I	687 – 701
84	John VI	701 – 705
85	John VII	705 – 707
86	Sisinnius	708
87	Constantine I	708 – 715
88	St Gregory II	715 – 731
89	St Gregory III	731 – 741
90	St Zacharius	741 – 752
91	Stephen II (III)	752 – 757

(In 752 another Stephen, a presbyter, had been elected pope but he died before he could be ordained bishop. He is considered by some to be the true Stephen II.)

#	Name	Dates
92	St Paul I	757 – 767
	Constantine	*767 – 768*
	Philip	*768*
93	Stephen III (IV)	768 – 772
94	Hadrian I	772 – 795
95	St Leo III	795 – 816
96	Stephen IV (V)	816 – 817
97	St Paschal I	817 – 824
98	Eugenius II	824 – 827
99	Valentine	827
100	Gregory IV	827 – 844
	John	*844*
101	Sergius II	844 – 847
102	St Leo IV	847 – 855
103	Benedict III	855 – 858
	Anastasius Bibliotecharius	*855*
104	St Nicholas I (the Great)	858 – 867
105	Hadrian II	867 – 872
106	John VIII	872 – 882
107	Marinus I (Martin II)	882 – 884

108	St Hadrian III	884 – 885
109	Stephen V (VI)	885 – 891
110	Formosus	891 – 896
111	Boniface VI	896
112	Stephen VI (VII)	896 – 897
113	Romanus	897
114	Theodore II	897
115	John IX	898 – 900
116	Benedict IV	900 – 903
117	Leo V	903
	Christopher	*903 – 904*
118	Sergius III	904 – 911
119	Anastasius III	911 – 913
120	Lando	913 – 914
121	John X	914 – 928
122	Leo VI	928
123	Stephen VII (VIII)	928 – 931
124	John XI	931 – 936
125	Leo VII	936 – 939
126	Stephen VIII (IX)	939 – 942
127	Marinus II (Martin III)	942 – 946
128	Agapitus II	946 – 955
129	John XII	955 – 964
130	Leo VIII	963 – 965
131	Benedict V	964
132	John XIII	965 – 972
133	Benedict VI	973 – 974
	Boniface VII	*974*
		984 – 985
134	Benedict VII	974 – 983
135	John XIV	983 – 984
136	John XV	985 – 996
137	Gregory V	996 – 999
	John XVI	*997 – 998*
138	Sylvester II	999 – 1003
139	John XVII	1003
140	John XVIII	1003 – 1009
141	Sergius IV	1009 – 1012
	Gregory VI	*1012*
142	Benedict VIII	1012 – 1024
143	John XIX	1024 – 1032
144	Benedict IX	1032 – 1044
		1045
		1047 – 1048
145	Sylvester III	1045
146	Gregory VI	1045 – 1046
147	Clement II	1046 – 1047
148	Damasus II	1048
149	St Leo IX	1049 – 1054
150	Victor II	1055 – 1057
151	Stephen IX (X)	1057 – 1058
	Benedict X	*1058 – 1059*
152	Nicholas II	1058 – 1061
153	Alexander II	1061 – 1073
	Honorius (II)	*1061 – 1064*
154	St Gregory VII	1073 – 1085
	Clement III	*1080*
		1084 – 1100
155	Bl. Victor III	1086 – 1087
156	Bl. Urban II	1088 – 1099
157	Paschal II	1099 – 1118
	Theodoric	*1100 – 1101*

	Albert	*1102*
	Sylvester IV	*1105 – 1111*
158	Gelasius II	1118 – 1119
	Gregory (IX)	*1118 – 1121*
159	Callistus II	1119 – 1124
160	Honorius II	1124 – 1130
	Celestine II	*1124*
161	Innocent II	1130 – 1143
	Anacletus II	*1130 – 1138*
	Victor IV	*1138*
162	Celestine II	1143 – 1144
163	Lucius II	1144 – 1145
164	Bl. Eugenius III	1145 – 1153
165	Anastasius IV	1153 – 1154
166	Hadrian IV	1154 – 1159
167	Alexander III	1159 – 1181
	Victor IV	*1159 – 1164*
	Paschal III	*1164 – 1168*
	Callistus III	*1168 – 1178*
	Innocent III	*1179 – 1180*
168	Lucius III	1181 – 1185
169	Urban III	1185 – 1187
170	Gregory VIII	1187
171	Clement III	1187 – 1191
172	Celestine III	1191 – 1198
173	Innocent III	1198 – 1216
174	Honorius III	1216 – 1227
175	Gregory IX	1227 – 1241
176	Celestine IV	1241
177	Innocent IV	1243 – 1254
178	Alexander IV	1254 – 1261
179	Urban IV	1261 – 1264
180	Clement IV	1265 – 1268
181	Bl. Gregory X	1271 – 1276
182	Bl. Innocent V	1276
183	Hadrian V	1276
184	John XXI	1276 – 1277

(Calling him 'XXI' was a contemporary error: there had never been a John XX.)

185	Nicholas III	1277 – 1280
186	Martin IV	1281 – 1285
187	Honorius IV	1285 – 1287
188	Nicholas IV	1288 – 1292
189	St Celestine V	1294
190	Boniface VIII	1294 – 1303
191	Bl. Benedict XI	1303 – 1304
192	Clement V	1305 – 1314
193	John XXII	1316 – 1334
	Nicholas (V)	*1328 – 1330*
194	Benedict XII	1334 – 1342
195	Clement VI	1342 – 1352
196	Innocent VI	1352 – 1362
197	Bl. Urban V	1362 – 1370
198	Gregory XI	1370 – 1378
199	Urban VI	1378 – 1389
	Clement VII	*1378 – 1394*
200	Boniface IX	1389 – 1404
	Benedict XIII	*1394 – 1417*
201	Innocent VII	1404 – 1406
202	Gregory XII	1406 – 1415
	Alexander V	*1409 – 1410*

	John XXIII	*1410 – 1415*
203	Martin V	1417 – 1431
	Clement VIII	*1423 – 1429*
	Benedict (XIV)	*1425 – ?*
204	Eugenius IV	1431 – 1447
	Felix V	*1439 – 1449*
205	Nicholas V	1447 – 1455
206	Callistus III	1455 – 1458
207	Pius II	1458 – 1464
208	Paul II	1464 – 1471
209	Sixtus IV	1471 – 1484
210	Innocent VIII	1484 – 1492
211	Alexander VI	1492 – 1503
212	Pius III	1503
213	Julius II	1503 – 1513
214	Leo X	1513 – 1521
215	Hadrian VI	1522 – 1523
216	Clement VII	1523 – 1534
217	Paul III	1534 – 1549
218	Julius III	1550 – 1555
219	Marcellus II	1555
220	Paul IV	1555 – 1559
221	Pius IV	1559 – 1565
222	St Pius V	1566 – 1572
223	Gregory XIII	1572 – 1585
224	Sixtus V	1585 – 1590
225	Urban VII	1590
226	Gregory XIV	1590 – 1591
227	Innocent IX	1591
228	Clement VIII	1592 – 1605
229	Leo XI	1605
230	Paul V	1605 – 1621
231	Gregory XV	1621 – 1623
232	Urban VIII	1623 – 1644
233	Innocent X	1644 – 1655
234	Alexander VII	1655 – 1667
235	Clement IX	1667 – 1669
236	Clement X	1670 – 1676
237	Bl. Innocent XI	1676 – 1689
238	Alexander VIII	1689 – 1691
239	Innocent XII	1691 – 1700
240	Clement XI	1700 – 1721
241	Innocent XIII	1721 – 1724
242	Benedict XIII	1724 – 1730
243	Clement XII	1730 – 1740
244	Benedict XIV	1740 – 1758
245	Clement XIII	1758 – 1769
246	Clement XIV	1769 – 1774
247	Pius VI	1775 – 1799
248	Pius VII	1800 – 1823
249	Leo XII	1823 – 1829
250	Pius VIII	1829 – 1830
251	Gregory XVI	1831 – 1846
252	Bl. Pius IX	1846 – 1878
253	Leo XIII	1878 – 1903
254	St Pius X	1903 – 1914
255	Benedict XV	1914 – 1922
256	Pius XI	1922 – 1939
257	Pius XII	1939 – 1958
258	Bl. John XXIII	1958 – 1963
259	Paul VI	1963 – 1978
260	John Paul I	1978
261	John Paul II	1978 –

Gregory XIII 1572–1585

Bl. Pius IX 1846–1878

Pius XII 1939–1958

Index

Crucitti, Professor
– Operates on John Paul II's wounds *May 13, 1981*
– Cautious about the pope's health *May 14, 1981*
– Advises the pope to lose weight *September 1981*

Cuba
– Excommunication of Castro *January 3, 1962*
– Pope's visit: to defy the "lider maximo" *January 25, 1998*
– Political prisoners are freed *February 12, 1998*

Curaçao
– Visit of John Paul II *May 1990*

Curie, Marie (née Sklodowska)
– Birth in Warsaw *November 7, 1867*
– Dies in Sallanches (France) *July 4, 1934*

Curran, Charles (theologian)
– Dismissed from Washington University *August 1986*

Cyrankiewicz, Jozef
– Polish prime minister *February 8, 1947*
– Warns the Church *November 28, 1947*
– Threatens agitators with reprisals *June 29, 1956*

Czech Republic (See also Czechoslovakia)
– Recognized by the Vatican *January 1, 1993*
– John Paul II canonizes Jan Sarkander at Olomouc *May 21, 1995*
– New visit of the pope *April 1997*

Czechoslovakia
– Signs Warsaw Pact *May 14, 1955*
– Soviet repression during Prague Spring *August 21, 1968*
– Police raid on Catholics *October 31, 1988*
– Diplomatic relations with the Vatican *April 19, 1990*
– Pope's speech in Prague *April 21, 1990*
– Split of the country (See Czech and Slovak Republics) *December 31, 1992*

Czestochowa (Poland)
– Pilgrimage of Father Wojtyla *April 6, 1953*
– Mass to a million pilgrims *June 26, 1956*
– Militia storms monastery and seizes publications *July 21, 1958*
– 1,000 years of Christianity in Poland *May 3, 1966*
– Communist demonstrators stop the Black Virgin procession *September 4, 1966*
– John Paul II goes to the Marian sanctuary *June 4, 1979*
– Pope's *ex-voto* to the virgin *June 19, 1983*
– Pope's visit for World Youth Day *August 14, 1991*

D

Dalbor, Edmund (primate of the Polish Church)
– Supports election of Cardinal Ratti *February 6, 1922*

Delbos, Yvon
– Birth in France *May 7, 1885*
– Minister of foreign affairs *June 4, 1936*
– Polish visit fails *December 1937*
– Dies in Paris *November 15, 1956*

Della Chiesa, Giacomo See Benedict XV

Denmark
– Diplomatic relations with the Vatican *August 2, 1982*
– Visit of John Paul II *June 1989*

Deskur, Andrzej Maria
– Consecrated bishop by Paul VI *June 21, 1974*
– Celebrates his friend Karol's 58th birthday *May 18, 1978*
– In charge of Karol's "campaign" *October 13, 1978*
– Hospitalized following a heart attack *October 13, 1978*
– Karol visits him before the conclave *October 14, 1978*
– Karol is elected pope *October 16, 1978*
– John Paul II visits him *October 17, 1978*

Dimitrios I, patriarch of Constantinople
– Celebrates orthodox mass in presence of John Paul II *November 30, 1979*
– Visits the Vatican *December 3, 1987*

Dos Santos, Lucia
– Appearance of the Virgin Mary at Fatima *May 13, 1917*
– Joins the Carmelite Order (Sister Maria Lucia)
– The Virgin appears to her in the convent *June 13, 1929*
– Reveals the Virgin's secrets to John Paul II *February 13, 1982*

Drewermann, Eugen (German theologian)
– Dismissed from Paderborn University *October 8, 1991*

Duan Yin-Ming, Matthias
– Prevented from traveling to Rome *May 2, 1998*

Dubcek, Alexander
– Received by John Paul II *November 19, 1988*

Duvalier, Jean-Claude
– Greets John Paul II in Haiti *March 10, 1983*

Dylan, Bob
– Sings for the pope in Bologna *September 27, 1997*

Dziwisz, Stanislaw
– Birth at Raba Wyzna *April 27, 1939*
– Ordained priest *June 23, 1963*
– Cardinal Wojtyla's secretary *1966*
– Accompanies Mgr. Wojtyla to the United States *July 27, 1976*
– Mgr. Wojtyla is elected pope *October 16, 1978*
– John Paul II's personal secretary *June 18, 1979*
– Supports the pope when he is wounded *May 13, 1981*
– Sits by the pope's bedside in hospital *May 18, 1981*
– Breaks the pope's fall *April 1994*
– Sits by the pope's bedside in hospital *October 15, 1996*
– Calls the pope to order *February 1998*
– Appointed archbishop *March 19, 1998*

EF

Ecuador
– John Paul II's speech against extremist ideologies *January 31, 1985*

Edith Stein (saint)
– Birth at Breslau *October 12, 1891*
– Joins the Carmelite Order in Cologne *October 13, 1933*
– Arrested by the Germans *August 2, 1942*
– Dies in Auschwitz *August 9, 1942*
– Beatified in Cologne *May 1, 1987*
– Canonized in Rome *October 11, 1998*

Edwige (saint) [1374-1399]
– Canonized in Cracow *June 8, 1997*

Egypt
– Visit of John Paul II (Jubilee Year) *February 2000*

Elizabeth II, queen of England
– Official visit to the Vatican *October 17, 1980*
– Receives John Paul II *May 28, 1982*

El Salvador
– Assassination of Mgr. Romero *March 24, 1980*
– Shooting during the funeral *March 30, 1980*
– Visit of John Paul II *March 1983*
– Pope's second visit *February 1996*

Emmaüs, Les Chiffoniers d'
– Founded by Abbé Pierre *November 25, 1949*

Escriva de Balaguer, Josemaria
– Birth *January 9, 1902*
– Creates Opus Dei *October 2, 1928*
– Dies in Rome *June 26, 1975*
– Beatified by John Paul II *May 17, 1992*

Estermann, Commandant Aloïs
– Assassination of the head of the Swiss Guards *May 4, 1998*

Estonia
– Visit of John Paul II *September 10, 1993*

Etchegaray, Roger (archbishop of Marseilles)
– Organizes meeting of Catholics and Jews in Paris *December 16, 1971*

Ethiopia
– Patriarch Paulos visits the Vatican *June 11, 1993*

Eufrosyna (Polish sister)
– In charge of the pope's private correspondence *November 1978*

Fatima (Portugal)
– The Virgin Mary appears to three children *May 13, 1917*
– Second appearance and promise of a great miracle *July 13, 1917*
– "Danse of the sun" before 70,000 people *October 13, 1917*
– New apparition *June 13, 1929*
– Assassination attempt against John Paul II *May 12, 1982*

– The pope meets Sister Maria Lucia *May 13, 1982*
– Statue of the Virgin is transferred to the Vatican *March 24, 1984*
– Pope's new visit *May 13, 1991*
– Pope leaves an *ex-voto* to the Virgin *1997*

Faulhaber, Michael von (archbishop of Munich)
– Helps Pius XI write the encyclical *Mit brennender Sorge* *March 14, 1937*

Felici, Pericle
– Announces Mgr. Wojtyla's election *October 16, 1978*
– Places the pallium around John Paul II's neck *October 22, 1978*

Fernand (Polish sister)
– In charge of the shopping for John Paul II *November 1978*

Figlewicz, Kazimierz (vicar of Wadowice)
– Karol's spiritual leader *1931*
– Leaves Wadowice for Cracow *August 1933*
– Meets up with Karol in Cracow *August 1938*
– Celebrates mass during the German invasion *September 1, 1939*
– Assists Father Wojtyla at Wawel Cathedral *November 2, 1946*
– Dies in Cracow *September 23, 1983*

Fiji
– Visit of John Paul II *November 1986*

Finland
– Helsinki conference for Security and Cooperation in Europe *July 31, 1975*
– Visit of John Paul II *June 1989*

Follereau, Raoul
– Creates leprosy foundation in Paris *1966*
– Death *December 6, 1977*
– John Paul II's tribute *April 27, 1996*

France
– Creation of a Polish army *June 4, 1917*
– Joan of Arc is canonized *May 16, 1920*
– Poland asks for aid *May 28, 1920*
– Delegation sent to Warsaw *July 21, 1920*
– Creation of the Communist party *December 30, 1920*
– Alliance treaty with Poland *February 1, 1921*
– Diplomatic relations with Rome *May 16, 1921*
– Theresa of Lisieux is canonized *May 23, 1925*
– Jean-Marie Vianney is canonized *May 1925*
– Bernadette Soubirous is beatified *June 14, 1925*
– *Action Française* is inscribed on the index of banned books *December 29, 1926*
– Ashes of Polish poet Slowacki are transferred *June 26, 1927*
– Pius XI condemns *Action Française* *March 25, 1928*
– Primate of Spain seeks refuge *May 10, 1931*
– Bernadette Soubirous is canonized *December 8, 1933*
– Creation of a Polish government in exile *September 3, 1939*
– Ecumenical community at Taizé *August 20, 1940*
– Jean Rodhain founds the Secours Catholique *September 8, 1946*
– Father Wojtyla stops in Paris on his way to Rome *November 1946*
– Father Wojtyla stops in Lourdes and Marseilles *August 5, 1947*
– Father Wojtyla visits Ars *October 1947*
– Abbé Pierre founds the Emmaüs organization *November 25, 1949*
– Death of Yvon Delbos *November 15, 1956*
– Mgr. Wojtyla visits Taizé *September 1965*
– Contraception is made legal *December 19, 1967*
– Father Barreau announces his marriage in *Le Monde* *September 2, 1971*
– Committee for Liaison meeting between Jews and Catholics *December 16, 1971*
– Cardinal Wojtyla's visit *November 11, 1973*
– Abortion is made legal *January 17, 1975*
– Death of Mgr. Rodhain *February 1, 1977*
– Mgr. Lefebvre's followers occupy St. Nicolas church in Paris *February 27, 1977*
– Polish Catholics' meeting at Osny *July 1, 1977*
– Giscard d'Estaing visits John Paul II *October 26, 1978*
– *The Jeweller's Shop* is published *June 1979*
– Pope's homily on baptism *June 1, 1980*
– Holy Father's speech at UNESCO *June 2, 1980*

- Mgr. Lustiger is named archbishop of Paris *February 2, 1981*
- Reaction of the chief rabbi of France *February 24, 1981*
- Pope's pilgrimage to Lourdes *August 14, 1983*
- John Paul II's speech in Lyon *October 4, 1986*
- Pope visits Taizé *October 5, 1986*
- John Paul II visits Ars sanctuary *October 6, 1986*
- Marcel Callo is beatified in Rome *October 4, 1987*
- John Paul II arrives in Strasbourg *October 8, 1988*
- Pope pays tribute to the construction of Europe *October 11, 1988*
- Mgr. Gaillot is granted an audience at the Vatican *January 22, 1992*
- Pope's interview in newspaper *Libération November 2, 1993*
- Mgr. Gaillot is dismissed *January 13, 1995*
- Inaugural mass at Evry Cathedral *April 11, 1995*
- Bishops' texts on the use of condoms *March 9, 1996*
- Seven Trappist monks are kidnapped in Algeria *March 27, 1996*
- Assassination of Mgr. Claverie in Oran (Algeria) *August 1, 1996*
- The French deny their baptism *August 11, 1996*
- The Church in France on Internet *September 6, 1996*
- Pope stops in the Vendée *September 19, 1996*
- Pope's speech in Brittany on the family *September 20, 1996*
- 15th centenary of Clovis' baptism *September 22, 1996*
- CD-ROM on Jesus *November 1996*
- Ali Agça's interview in newspaper *France-Soir April 21, 1997*
- *La Croix* survey on the Church in France *May 11, 1997*
- Pope's visit for the World Youth Day (Paris) *August 18, 1997*
- Pontifical mass on the Champs-de-Mars (Paris) *August 21, 1997*
- Frédéric Ozanam is beatified *August 22, 1997*
- World Youth Day closing mass at Longchamp *August 24, 1997*
- The Church asks the Jews for forgiveness *September 30, 1997*

Frank, Hans
- Birth *May 23, 1900*
- Poland's German governor *September 1939*
- Decrees forced labor *October 26, 1939*
- Condemned to death at Nuremberg *October 1, 1946*
- Executed *October 16, 1946*

Freemasonry
- Masons are no longer excommunicated *November 26, 1983*

G

Gabon
- Visit of John Paul II: tribute to the wisdom of Black Africa *February 19, 1982*

Gagarin, Yuri
- Makes statement on his return to earth *April 12, 1961*

Gaillot, Jacques
- Birth in Saint-Dizier (France) *September 11, 1935*
- Ordained priest in Langres (France) *March 18, 1961*
- Bishop of Evreux (France) *June 20, 1982*
- Called to order by John Paul II *January 22, 1992*
- Dismissed by the Vatican *January 13, 1995*

Gajowniczek, Franciszek
- Saved by Father Kolbe's sacrifice *July 30, 1941*
- Attends Father Kolbe's canonization *October 10, 1982*

Galileo [1564-1642]
- Rehabilitated by the Vatican *October 31, 1992*

Gambia
- Visit of John Paul II *February 1992*

Gandhi, Rajiv
- Greets John Paul II in New Delhi *February 1, 1986*

Gasparri, Cardinal Pietro
- Signs Lateran agreements with Mussolini *February 11, 1929*

Gaulle, Charles de
- End of mission in Poland *January 10, 1921*
- Head of the provisional government of the Republic (GPRF) *June 3, 1944*
- Signs treaty of alliance with USSR *December 10, 1944*
- President of the Vth Republic *December 21, 1958*
- Official visit to Poland *September 8, 1967*

Germane (Polish sister)
- John Paul II's cook *November 1978*

Germany
- Takes Warsaw *August 8, 1915*
- Brest-Litovsk peace with Russia *March 3, 1918*
- Troops withdraw from Warsaw *November 11, 1918*
- Versailles Treaty *June 28, 1919*
- Concordat with the Church *July 9, 1933*
- Non-aggression pact with Poland *January 26, 1934*
- Goebbels visits Poland *June 13, 1934*
- Pius XI condemns Nazism *March 14, 1937*
- Pius XI's encyclical is read out in all the churches *March 21, 1937*
- Friendship treaty with Poland *November 5, 1937*
- Annexation of Austria *March 14, 1938*
- Munich agreements *September 30, 1938*
- German-Polish pact is revoked *April 28, 1939*
- Claims the Danzig corridor *July 30, 1939*
- Non-aggression pact with the USSR *August 23, 1939*
- Invades Poland *September 1, 1939*
- Cracow is occupied *September 6, 1939*
- Warsaw surrenders *September 27, 1939*
- Jews are deported to Warsaw *December 1, 1939*
- Invades USSR *June 22, 1941*
- Soviet counterattack before Moscow *December 6, 1941*
- Warsaw revolt is crushed *October 2, 1944*
- Soviet offensive in Poland *January 13, 1945*
- Loses Warsaw *January 17, 1945*
- Loses Cracow *January 18, 1945*
- Adolf Hitler commits suicide *April 30, 1945*
- Surrender of the Reich *May 8, 1945*
- Birth of the Federal Republic (FRG) *May 8, 1949*
- Creation of the Democratic Republic (GDR) *October 7, 1949*
- GDR signs Warsaw Pact *May 14, 1955*
- Letters of Polish bishops *November 18, 1965*
- Mgr. Wojtyla visits Mainz *June 23, 1977*
- Visit of the Polish episcopate *September 25, 1978*
- John Paul II visits FRG *November 1980*
- John Paul II beatifies Edith Stein *May 1, 1987*
- Pope's speech at Augsburg *May 3, 1987*
- Tensions between the Church and the Vatican *January 25, 1989*
- Destruction of the Berlin Wall *November 10, 1989*
- Dismissal of theologian Drewermann *October 8, 1991*
- Pope's controversial visit *June 22, 1996*

Ghana
- Visit of John Paul II *May 1980*

Gierek, Edward
- Succeeds Gomulka *December 20, 1970*
- Calls for Polish Church to cooperate with government *September 9, 1976*
- Greets John Paul II *June 2, 1979*

Glemp, Jozef
- Birth in Inowroclaw *December 18, 1929*
- Polish primate *July 7, 1981*
- Meeting with John Paul II *October 18, 1981*
- Named cardinal *February 2, 1983*
- Supports Walesa at the presidential elections *November 26, 1995*

Goebbels, Joseph Paul
- Hitler's propaganda minister *January 30, 1933*
- End of his visit to Poland *June 15, 1934*

Goering, Hermann
- Negotiates friendship treaty with Poland *November 5, 1937*

Gomulka, Wladyslaw
- Birth *February 6, 1905*
- Secretary of the Polish Communist party *December 1943*
- Sacked *September 5, 1948*
- Becomes first secretary of the Party's Central Committee *October 21, 1956*
- Demands the return of order *October 26, 1957*

- Appeases Moscow *October 20, 1964*
- Revives anti-Semitism *June 19, 1967*
- Supports the Communist intervention in Prague *August 21, 1968*
- Resigns *December 20, 1970*
- Dies in Warsaw *September 1, 1982*

Gorbachev, Mikhail
- Birth in Privolnoie (the Caucasus) *March 2, 1931*
- Secretary general of the Communist party *March 11, 1985*
- Lengthy meeting with Jaruzelski *April 1985*
- Speech on religion in Uzbekistan *November 1986*
- Receives delegation from the Vatican *June 13, 1988*
- Private visit to Cracow *July 13, 1988*
- Received by John Paul II *December 1, 1989*
- Nobel Prize for Peace *October 15, 1990*

Graham, Billy
- Tours the countries of eastern Europe *July 30, 1989*

Grant, Steve
- Author of comic book on John Paul II's life *March 23, 1983*

Great Britain
- Defense agreement with Poland *April 6, 1939*
- Polish government in exile in London *June 18, 1940*
- Yalta agreements *February 11, 1945*
- End of Potsdam conference *August 2, 1945*
- Creation of an Anglican-Catholic commission *March 24, 1966*
- Queen Elizabeth is granted an audience at the Vatican *October 17, 1980*
- Visit of John Paul II: revival of Anglican-Catholic dialog *May 28, 1982*
- Anglican Church recognizes the pope as "universal prelate" *November 13, 1986*
- Priesthood open to women *December 1992*
- First women priests are ordained *April 1994*

Grignion de Montfort, Louis-Marie
- See Louis-Marie Grignion de Montfort (saint)

Grouès, Henri See Pierre (l'Abbé)

Guam
- Visit of John Paul II *February 28, 1981*

Guatemala
- John Paul II meets Maya Indians *March 7, 1983*
- Pope's second visit *February 1996*

Guinea
- Visit of John Paul II *February 1982*
- Pope's second visit *February 1992*

Guinea-Bissau
- Pope's symbolic gesture at Cumura *January 28, 1990*

Guitton, Jean
- Obtains audience for Mgr. Lefebvre from Paul VI *September 11, 1976*

Gutierrez, Gustavo (theoretician of liberation theology)
- Summoned to the Vatican *September 9, 1984*

H

Hadas, Schamouel
- First ambassador of Israel to the Vatican *September 29, 1994*

Hall, Rose
- Wounded in the assassination attempt against the pope *May 13, 1981*

Hassan II, king of Morocco
- Greets John Paul II in Casablanca *August 19, 1985*

Havel, Vaclav
- President of Czechoslovakia *December 29, 1989*
- Greets John Paul II in Prague *April 21, 1990*

Haiti
- Visit of John Paul II *March 10, 1983*
- Father Aristide is president *December 17, 1990*
- Military coup *September 30, 1991*
- Arrival of an ambassador from the Vatican *January 15, 1992*
- Father Aristide returns to power *October 15, 1994*

Herbulot, Mgr. Guy
- Celebrates first mass in Evry Cathedral (France) *April 11, 1995*

Hertberg, Arthur (International Zionist movement)
- Organizes meeting of Jews and Catholics in Paris *December 16, 1971*

Himmler, Heinrich
– Orders building of Auschwitz concentration camp *March 24, 1940*

Hindenburg, Paul von (Field Marshal)
– Defeats the Russians at Tannenberg *August 31, 1914*
– Occupies Warsaw *August 8, 1915*

Hitler, Adolf
– Birth *April 20, 1889*
– President of the NSDAP *July 29, 1921*
– Reich chancellor *January 30, 1933*
– Pius XI denounces Nazism *March 14, 1937*
– Promises not to attack Poland *November 5, 1937*
– Annexes Austria *March 14, 1938*
– Revokes the German-Polish pact *April 28, 1939*
– Non-aggression pact with USSR *August 23, 1939*
– Invades Poland *September 1, 1939*
– Commits suicide *April 30, 1945*

Hlond, August
– Birth at Brzeckowice *July 5, 1881*
– Primate of Poland *October 12, 1926*
– Named cardinal *June 20, 1927*
– Exiled in France *September 4, 1939*
– Arrested and imprisoned in Germany *February 15, 1944*
– Heads the dioceses taken back from Germany *August 15, 1945*
– Dies in Warsaw *October 22, 1948*

Honduras
– Visit of John Paul II *March 1983*

Houthakker, Hendrick
– Presents Mgr. Wojtyla as the next pope *September 1, 1976*

Hoxha, Enver (president of Albania)
– Leads a "scientific battle" against believers *November 22, 1967*

Hraoui, Elias (president of Lebanon)
– Received by John Paul II *November 5, 1993*

Hungary
– Primate Mindszenty is arrested *December 23, 1948*
– Religious orders are dissolved *November 7, 1950*
– Signs Warsaw Pact *May 14, 1955*
– Budapest uprisings *October 23, 1956*
– Soviet intervention *November 4, 1956*
– Tour by Billy Graham *July 30, 1989*
– Visit of John Paul II *August 1991*
– Pope's new visit *September 1996*

Hussein, king of Jordan
– Greets Paul VI at Amman *January 4, 1964*

IJ

Iceland
– Visit of John Paul II *June 1989*

Index (of banned books)
– Inscription of journal *L'Action Française* *December 29, 1926*
– Inscription of Pax Movement's weekly review *June 8, 1955*
– Abolished *April 9, 1966*

India
– Mother Teresa founds the Missionary Sisters of Charity *1950*
– Mother Teresa awarded Nobel Prize for Peace *December 8, 1979*
– John Paul II prays on Gandhi's grave *February 1, 1986*
– Pope visits the Pure Heart home for the dying *February 4, 1986*
– Pope prays on St. Thomas' grave *February 5, 1986*
– A nun is assassinated in Assam *May 1, 1995*
– Death of Mother Teresa *September 5, 1997*
– Mother Teresa's funeral *September 13, 1997*

Indonesia
– Visit of John Paul II *October 1989*

Iran
– Postwar Poland's fate is decided upon in Tehran *November 28, 1943*
– Mohammad Khatami meets the pope in Rome *March 11, 1999*

Ireland
– Visit of John Paul II *September 1979*
– Divorce is made legal *November 24, 1995*

IRW (Institute of Religious Works)
– Created by Pius XII *July 27, 1942*

Israel
– Birth of the State *May 14, 1948*
– Joins UN *December 9, 1949*
– Mgr. Wojtyla visits the Holy Land *December 15, 1963*
– Paul VI's historic visit *January 5, 1964*
– Annexation of East Jerusalem *June 22, 1967*
– Free access to Holy Places *June 27, 1967*
– Golda Meir is granted an audience at the Vatican *January 16, 1973*
– Reacts to Arafat's visit to the Vatican *September 15, 1982*
– Vatican's first mention of the Jewish State in official text *April 20, 1984*
– Shimon Peres visits the Vatican *February 19, 1985*
– Pope names an Arab as patriarch of Jerusalem *December 28, 1987*
– Negotiations with the Holy See *July 29, 1992*
– Shimon Peres is granted an audience at the Vatican *October 23, 1992*
– Fundamental agreement with the Vatican *December 30, 1993*
– Exchanges ambassadors with the Vatican *September 29, 1994*
– Netanyahu is received by the pope *February 3, 1997*
– A Jewish delegation visits the pope *January 13, 1999*
– Visit of John Paul II (Jubilee Year) *February 2000*

Italy (See also Rome, Vatican and Castel Gandolfo)
– Signing of Lateran agreements with the Church *February 11, 1929*
– Monetary agreement with the Vatican *August 2, 1930*
– Pius XI denounces Fascism *June 29, 1931*
– Mussolini granted an audience at the Vatican *February 11, 1932*
– Joins anti-Comintern Pact *November 6, 1937*
– 7th centenary of the death of St. Thomas Aquinas *April 24, 1974*
– Passes divorce law *May 13, 1974*
– Murder of Aldo Moro, president of the Christian Democrats *May 9, 1978*
– Cardinal Wojtyla is elected pope *October 16, 1978*
– Article in *la Stampa* *October 17, 1978*
– John Paul II visits the Marian sanctuary of Mentorella *October 29, 1978*
– Unhealthy rumors about the new pope *December 9, 1978*
– Assassination attempt against John Paul II in Rome *May 13, 1981*
– Abortion is made legal *May 15, 1981*
– Ali Agça is sentenced to life imprisonment *July 22, 1981*
– Pope visits Solvay factory *March 19, 1982*
– Bulgarian lead in assassination attempt in May *November 25, 1982*
– Turin shroud is bequeathed to the pope *March 25, 1983*
– Lateran agreements are revised *February 18, 1984*
– Sergei Antonov is arrested *October 26, 1984*
– Bulgarian lead comes to a dead end *March 29, 1986*
– Ecumenical day in Assisi *October 27, 1986*
– Prayor for peace at Assisi *January 9, 1993*
– Fire in Turin cathedral *April 12, 1997*
– Rumors of a failed assassination attempt *May 9, 1997*
– Eucharistic Congress in Bologna *September 27, 1997*
– Dispute at San Remo song festival *February 24, 1998*
– Pope gives short speech in Turin *May 24, 1998*

Ivory Coast
– Visit of John Paul II *May 1980*
– Pope's second visit *August 31, 1985*
– John Paul II consecrates Yamoussoukro Cathedral *September 10, 1990*

Jakubowicz, Maciej
– Greets Mgr. Wojtyla at Kazimierz synagogue *February 28, 1969*

Jamaica
– Visit of John Paul II *August 9, 1993*

Jan Sarkander (saint)
– Canonized by John Paul II *May 21, 1995*

Jankowski, Father Henryk
– Received at the Vatican *January 15, 1981*

Japan
– John Paul II delivers speech at Hiroshima *February 25, 1981*

Jarlan, André (French priest)
– Assassinated in Chile *September 4, 1984*

Jaroszewicz, Piotr
– Prime minister of Poland *December 20, 1970*
– Makes positive overtures toward the Church *January 25, 1971*
– Meets Primate Wyszynski *March 3, 1971*

Jaruzelski, General Wojciech
– Birth in Kurow *July 6, 1923*
– Polish defense minister *April 11, 1968*
– Joins Party's official office *December 11, 1971*
– Prime minister *February 9, 1981*
– Warning from Brezhnev *April 1981*
– Secretary of the Party *October 18, 1981*
– Declares a state of war in Poland *December 13, 1981*
– Meeting with John Paul II in Warsaw *June 16, 1983*
– Lengthy meeting with Gorbachev *April 1985*
– Releases the political prisoners *September 11, 1986*
– Granted a special audience at the Vatican *January 13, 1987*
– Reproaches the pope for his visit to Popieluszko's grave *June 14, 1987*
– Defeated at the elections *June 18, 1989*
– Appoints Mazowiecki prime minister *August 24, 1989*
– Succeeded by Walesa *December 9, 1990*

Jawien, Andrzej
– Karol Wojtyla's pseudonym in *Tygodnik Powszechny*

Jean-Marie Vianney (saint) [1786-1859]
– Canonized by Pius XI *May 1925*

Joan of Arc (saint) [1412-1431]
– Beatified by Pius X *April 18, 1909*
– Canonized by Benedict XV *May 16, 1920*

John XXIII (Angelo Giuseppe Roncalli)
– Birth *November 25, 1881*
– Succeeds Pius XII *October 28, 1958*
– Announces intention to convoke a synod *January 25, 1959*
– Removes mention of "perfidious Jews" from the liturgy *March 1959*
– Creates a secretariat for the Promotion of Christian Unity *June 5, 1960*
– Inaugurates the Council of Vatican II *October 11, 1962*
– Encyclical *Pacem in Terris* *April 11, 1963*
– Death *June 3, 1963*
– Paul VI announces his beatification *November 18, 1965*

John Paul I (Albino Luciani)
– Birth *October 17, 1912*
– Would like to see Mgr. Wojtyla become pope *November 1972*
– Succeeds Paul VI *August 26, 1978*
– Receives Mgr. Wojtyla *August 30, 1978*
– Metropolitan Nikodim dies in his arms *September 5, 1978*
– Vision of the papal charge *September 17, 1978*
– Condemns Leninism *September 20, 1978*
– Reveals his state of health *September 27, 1978*
– Dies of a stroke *September 29, 1978*
– Funeral *October 4, 1978*

John Paul II See Wojtyla, Karol Jozef

Jordan
– Visit of John Paul II (Jubilee Year) *February 2000*

K

Kaczmarek, Czeslaw (bishop of Kielce)
– Sentenced to 12 years' hard labor *September 21, 1953*
– Released *December 12, 1956*

Kaczorowska, Anna See Sanak, Anna

Kaczorowska, Emilia See Wojtyla, Emilia

Kaczorowska, Maria Anna See Wiadrowska, Maria Anna

Kaczorowska, Maria-Anna (Karol's grandmother)
– Birth in 1853 or 1858
– Marries Feliks Kaczorowski *1875*
– Gives birth to Emilia *March 26, 1884*
– Death *April 12, 1897*

Kaczorowska, Rudolfina (Karol's aunt)
–Birth *March 31, 1889*
–Puts Karol up in Cracow *August 1938*
–Death *June 30, 1948*
Kaczorowski, Feliks (Karol's maternal grandfather)
–Birth in Biala *June 26, 1849*
–Marries Anna-Maria Scholz *1875*
–Death of his wife *April 12, 1897*
–His daughter marries Karol Wojtyla *1904*
–Birth of his grandson Edmund *August 27, 1906*
–Death *August 19, 1908*
Kaczorowski, Robert (Karol's uncle)
–Birth *April 26, 1887*
–Puts Karol up in Cracow *August 1938*
–Death *December 27, 1962*
Kakol, Kazimir (minister of religions)
–Limits the role of the Church in Poland *January 1974*
–Revives the Church-State conflict *May 19, 1976*
Kane, Sister Teresa
–Addresses the pope on the subject of ordination of women priests *October 7, 1979*
Kania, Stanislas
–Secretary general of the Polish Communist party *September 5, 1980*
–Warned by Brezhnev *April 1981*
–Succeeded by General Jaruzelski *October 18, 1981*
Kantor, Tadeusz (playwright)
–Birth *April 16, 1915*
–Death in Cracow *December 8, 1990*
Kaplan, Jacob (chief rabbi of France)
–Reacts to Mgr. Lustiger's nomination *February 24, 1981*
Kenya
–Speech by John Paul II *May 12, 1980*
–Pope's second visit *August 1985*
–Pope's third visit *September 14, 1995*
Kiszczak, Czeslaw
–Polish minister of the interior *July 31, 1981*
–Signs document legalizing Solidarnosc *April 17, 1989*
Kluger, Jerzy
–Karol's best friend *February 1928*
–Tells Karol that they are accepted in high school *June 30, 1930*
–Starts state high school in Wadowice with Karol *September 1, 1930*
–Goes on expeditions with his friend *1931*
–Karol allows him to copy his work during exams *April 25, 1938*
–Passes his exams *May 14, 1938*
–Arrested by the Germans *June 1940*
–Moves to Rome *1954*
–Meets up with his friend Karol *November 20, 1965*
–Karol is elected pope *October 16, 1978*
–Present when the pope goes to the synagogue in Rome *April 13, 1986*
–Reads a letter from the pope to Wadowice's Jewish community *May 9, 1989*
Koenig, Franz (primate of Austria)
–Considers Mgr. Wojtyla to be *papabile August 24, 1978*
–Supports Mgr. Wojtyla's candidacy *October 16, 1978*
Kohl, Helmut
–Attends Edith Stein's beatification *May 1, 1987*
Kolbe, Maximillian See Maximilian Kolbe (saint)
Koliqi, Mikel
–Birth *September 26, 1902*
–Released from the Albanian prisons *1986*
–Named cardinal *November 26, 1994*
–Death *January 28, 1997*
Kolvenbach, Hans Peter
–General of the Jesuit order *September 2, 1983*
Koman, Jozef
–Karol Wojtyla's first primary school teacher *September 15, 1926*
KOR (Committee for Defense of Workers)
–Founded in Poland *September 23, 1976*
–Assassination of student Pyjas *May 7, 1977*
–Raid of militia militants *May 14, 1977*
–Creation of a mobile university *November 1977*
Korea
–John Paul II canonizes 103 martyrs in Seoul *May 6, 1984*
–Pope's visit: calls for reconciliation *October 8, 1989*

Kotlarczyk, Mieczyslaw
–Birth *May 6, 1908*
–Becomes member of the youth theater group *1934*
–Creates the Rhapsodic Theater *August 22, 1941*
–Karol puts him up in Cracow *August 1941*
–Performance of *The King Spirit November 1941*
–Tries to dissuade Karol from becoming a priest *October 1942*
–Karol pays tribute to his work *April 7, 1957*
–Dies in Cracow *February 21, 1978*
Krenz, Egon
–President of the GDR *October 18, 1989*
–Opens border into the FGR *November 9, 1989*
Krohn, Juan Fernandez
–Aggresses John Paul II at Fatima *May 12, 1982*
Krol, John (archbishop of Philadelphia)
–Polish representative of the American "Polonia" *September 1, 1976*
Krolikiewicz, Halina See Kwiatkowska, Halina
Kuczmierczyk, Jozef
–Birth in Wilamowic *September 12, 1868*
–Karol Wojtyla's godfather *June 20, 1920*
–Death *April 11, 1944*
Kudlinski, Tadeusz
–Leads Cracow's literary group *December 1938*
–Convinces Karol to become a priest *October 1942*
Kung Pin-Mei, Ignatius
–Nominated cardinal "in pectore" *June 28, 1991*
Kuron, Jacek
–Jailed for "Zionist schemings" *1968*
–Founder of the KOR *September 23, 1976*
Kurowski, Tadeusz (Saint-Florian priest)
–Assisted by Father Wojtyla *1949*
–Father Wojtyla leaves *September 1, 1951*
Kwasniewski, Alexander
–Defeats Walesa at the presidential elections *November 26, 1995*
Kwiatkowska, Halina (née Krolikiewicz)
–Birth *April 25, 1921*
–Karol's partner at the theater *March 1936*
–Beats Karol at the high school poetry recitation contest *January 1937*
–Marries Karol in a play by Slowacki *May 14, 1937*
–Her father refuses to let her have an acting career *1937*
–Dances with Karol at the end-of-year ball *May 14, 1938*
–Participates in evening of poetry recitals *October 15, 1938*
–Goes to Cracow University with Karol *October 1938*
–Joins Julius Kydrinsky's theater group *1938*
–Member of the Rhapsodic Theater *August 22, 1941*
–Acts in Slowacki's *The King Spirit November 1941*
–Marries Tadeusz Kwiatkowski *October 28, 1945*
–Gives birth to Monika *October 20, 1946*
–Monika is christened by Father Wojtyla *November 11, 1946*
–Meets up with Karol for the 20-years graduation anniversary *September 14, 1958*
Kwiatkowska, Monika
–Birth *October 20, 1946*
–Christened by Father Wojtyla *November 11, 1946*
Kwiatkowski, Tadeusz
–Birth *May 6, 1920*
–Member of Kydrynski's theater group in Cracow *December 31, 1938*
–Marries Halina Krolikiewicz *October 28, 1945*
–Birth of his daughter Monika *October 20, 1946*
–Monika's christening *November 11, 1946*
Kydrynski, Juliusz
–Becomes friends with Karol in Cracow *1938*
–Works with Karol in the Solvay factory *February 1941*
–Puts Karol up after his father's death *March 1941*
Kydrynski, Maria
–Finds Karol's father dead in his home *February 18, 1941*
Küng, Hans (Swiss theologian)
–Condemned by the Vatican *December 18, 1979*

Lancaster, Burt
–Star of film *The Jeweller's Shop December 1990*
Latvia
–John Paul II delivers speech *September 9, 1993*
Laval, Pierre
–Attends Jozef Pilsudski's funeral *May 17, 1935*
Lebanon
–President Hraoui visits the Vatican *November 5, 1993*
–Pope's visit under close watch *May 11, 1997*
Lefebvre, Marcel
–Birth in Tourcoing (France) *November 29, 1905*
–Ordained priest in Lille (France) *September 21, 1929*
–Denounces Vatican II's decisions *December 8, 1965*
–Founds the Society of St. Pius X in Fribourg *June 6, 1969*
–Transfers the Society to Ecône (Switzerland) *June 6, 1971*
–Publishes manifesto against Vatican II *December 21, 1974*
–Suspended *a divinis July 22, 1976*
–Meeting with Paul VI fails *September 11, 1976*
–Letters of reproach to John Paul II *December 11, 1983*
–Denounces Rome's modernization *June 2, 1988*
–Consecrates four bishops without the pope's consent *June 30, 1988*
–Excommunicated *July 2, 1988*
–Dies in Martigny (Switzerland) *March 25, 1991*
Lenin, Vladimir Ilyich
–Birth *April 22, 1870*
–Rejects all religious concepts *November 14, 1913*
–Leads the Bolshevik coup *November 7, 1917*
–Dies in Gorki *January 21, 1924*
Leo XIII (Gioacchino Pecci)
–Birth *March 2, 1810*
–Beginning of his pontificate *February 20, 1878*
–Encyclical *Rerum Novarum May 15, 1891*
–Death *July 20, 1903*
Lesotho
–Visit of John Paul II *September 1988*
Liechtenstein
–Visit of John Paul II *September 9, 1985*
Lithuania
–John Paul II climbs the Hill of Crosses *September 7, 1993*
Lopez Portillo, José (president of Mexico)
–Gives cold welcome to John Paul II *January 26, 1979*
Louis-Marie Grignion de Montfort (saint) [1673-1716]
–Karol's spiritual model *October 1941*
–Canonized by Pius XII *July 20, 1947*
–Mgr. Wojtyla takes his motto *October 1958*
Lourdes (France)
–Bernadette Soubirous is beatified *June 14, 1925*
–Bernadette Soubirous is canonized *December 8, 1933*
–Jean Rodhain founds the Secours Catholique *September 8, 1946*
–Death of Mgr. Rodhain *February 1, 1977*
–Visit of John Paul II *August 14, 1983*
Lubac, Henri de
–Corresponds with Mgr. Wojtyla *February 1968*
Lublin
–Setting up of the Communist regime *July 22, 1944*
–Government transferred to Warsaw *January 18, 1945*
–Father Wojtyla given post at the Catholic University *July 19, 1954*
–Father Wojtyla takes up the Chair of Ethics *December 10, 1956*
Luciano, Albino See John Paul I
Lustiger, Jean-Marie
–Born a Jew (forename Aaron) *September 17, 1926*
–Converts to Catholicism (chooses names: John and Mary) *August 25, 1940*
–Bishop of Orléans *November 10, 1979*
–Named archbishop of Paris *February 2, 1981*
–Reaction of the chief rabbi of France *February 24, 1981*
–Named cardinal by John Paul II *February 2, 1983*
Luxemburg
–Visit of John Paul II *May 1985*

Macharski, Franciszek
- Named cardinal by John Paul II *June 30, 1979*

Madagascar
- Visit of John Paul II *April 1989*

Malawi
- Visit of John Paul II *May 1989*

Mali
- Visit of John Paul II *January 1990*

Malinski, Mieczyslaw
- Assists Father Wojtyla in his first mass *November 2, 1946*
- Gets lost in the mountains with Karol *1950*
- Accompanies Karol to Rome (Vatican II) *October 21, 1963*
- Accompanies Mgr. Wojtyla to the United States *July 27, 1976*
- Admires Karol's vigor *September 1978*
- Karol is elected pope *October 16, 1978*
- Helps in the writing of a comic book on John Paul II's life *March 23, 1983*
- Private visit to the Vatican *February 1998*

Malta
- Visit of John Paul II *May 25, 1990*

Marconi, Guglielmo
- Meets Pius XI to inaugurate Radio Vatican *February 12, 1931*

Marenches, Alexandre de
- Warns John Paul II of a plot *January 1981*

Maria Lucia (sister) See Dos Santos, Lucia

Martella, Ilario (judge)
- Makes new charges in the attempt against the pope's life *October 26, 1984*

Marto, Francisco and Vacunta
- The Virgin appears to them at Fatima *May 13, 1917*

Mathilda (Polish sister)
- In charge of John Paul II's wardrobe *November 30, 1978*

Matlak, Jozef
- Praises the seminarist Karol *December 12, 1945*

Mauritius
- Visit of John Paul II *October 1989*

Maximilian Kolbe (saint)
- Birth *January 8, 1894*
- Founds a monthly Catholic journal in Cracow *1921*
- Gives his life to save a father of young children *July 30, 1941*
- Executed in Auschwitz *August 14, 1941*
- Beatified by Paul VI *October 17, 1971*
- Canonized by John Paul II *October 10, 1982*

Mazowiecki, Tadeusz
- Birth in Plock *April 18, 1927*
- In charge of the Catholic review *Wiez February 1957*
- Polish prime minister *August 24, 1989*

Meir, Golda
- Received by John Paul II *January 16, 1973*

Meisner, Joachim
- Appointed archbishop of Poland *December 1988*

Mercier, Cardinal Désiré Joseph
- Birth in Braine-l'Alleud (Belgium) *November 22, 1851*
- Letter *Patriotisme et endurance December 26, 1914*
- Dies in Brussels *January 23, 1926*

Messori, Vittorio
- Writes *Crossing the Threshold of Hope* with John Paul II *October 20, 1994*

Mexico
- Papal legate is expelled *October 6, 1932*
- Visit of John Paul II: General Assembly of bishops in Puebla *January 26, 1979*
- Pope's second visit *May 1990*
- Assassination of Mgr. Campo *May 26, 1993*

Michelli, Ivano (singer)
- Polemic at San Remo song festival *February 24, 1998*

Mikolajczyk, Stanislaw
- Birth *November 18, 1901*
- Head of the Polish government in exile in London *July 14, 1943*
- Prevented from claiming the legitimate government *July 22, 1944*
- Defeated at the elections in Poland *January 19, 1947*
- Death *December 13, 1966*

Millerand, Alexandre
- Head of the French government *January 19, 1920*
- Agrees to come to aid of Poland against the Russians *July 21, 1920*

Milosz, Czeslaw
- Birth *June 30, 1911*
- Nobel Prize for Literature *October 1, 1980*

Mindszenty, Jozsef (primate of Hungary)
- Arrested by the Communists *December 16, 1948*
- Sentenced to hard labor for life *February 1, 1949*

Missionary Sisters of Charity
- Created in Calcutta by Mother Teresa *1950*
- Sister Nirmala succeeds Mother Teresa *March 18, 1997*
- Death of Mother Teresa *September 5, 1997*

Mitkowski, Jozef
- Praises Mgr. Wojtyla *February 1, 1963*

Mitterrand, François
- President of the French Republic *May 10, 1981*
- Greets John Paul II in Tarbes *August 14, 1983*
- Greets John Paul II in Lyons *October 4, 1986*
- Greets John Paul II in Strasbourg *October 8, 1988*

Molla, Gianna Beretta
- Beatified by John Paul II *April 4, 1995*

Molotov, Vyacheslav
- Signs Soviet-Polish nonaggression pact *January 25, 1932*

Montini, Giovanni Battista See Paul VI

Mora, Elisabetta
- Beatified by John Paul II *April 4, 1995*

Moro, Aldo (president of the Christian Democrats)
- Found murdered in Rome *May 9, 1978*

Morocco
- Visit of John Paul II: calls for Christian-Muslim dialog *August 19, 1985*

Moscicki, Ignacy
- President of the Polish Republic *June 2, 1926*
- Delivers funeral oration in praise of Marshal Pilsudski *May 17, 1935*

Mozambique
- Visit of John Paul II *September 1988*

Mussolini, Benito
- Signs Lateran agreements with the Church *February 11, 1929*
- Relations tense with Pius XI *June 29, 1931*
- Granted an audience at the Vatican *February 11, 1932*

Mvent, Engelbert (Jesuit father)
- Assassinated in Cameroon *April 24, 1995*

N

Narutowicz, Gabriel
- Birth *March 17, 1865*
- Succeeds Pilsudski who resigns *December 9, 1922*
- Assassinated in Warsaw *December 16, 1922*

Netanyahu, Benyamin
- Israeli prime minister *May 31, 1996*
- Invites the pope to Israel *February 3, 1997*

Netanyahu, Sarah
- Received at the Vatican *February 3, 1997*

Netherlands
- Ecumenical Council in Amsterdam *August 23, 1948*
- Bishops are summoned to the Vatican *January 14, 1980*
- Church called to order *January 31, 1980*
- Angry outbursts during pope's visit *May 11, 1985*

New Zealand
- Visit of John Paul II *November 1986*

Nicaragua
- Difficult visit for John Paul II *March 4, 1983*
- Pope goes to Managua *February 1996*

Nicholas (grand duke)
- Promises Poland's rebirth *August 5, 1914*

Niegowic
- Father Wojtyla is named assistant pastor *July 28, 1948*
- Departure of Father Wojtyla *August 17, 1949*
- Surge of religious fervor *1949*
- Father Wojtyla's secretary is kidnapped *1949*
- Mgr. Wojtyla consecrates the new church *September 25, 1966*

Nigeria
- Visit of John Paul II *February 1982*
- Pope's speech *March 23, 1998*

Nikodim (metropolitan of Leningrad)
- Dies in John Paul I's arms *September 5, 1978*

Nirmala (sister)
- Chosen to succeed Mother Teresa *March 18, 1997*

Nixon, Richard
- Official visit to Warsaw *August 1959*
- President of the United States *November 5, 1968*
- Receives warm welcome in Poland *June 1, 1972*

Norway
- Diplomatic relations with the Vatican *August 2, 1982*
- Visit of John Paul II *June 1989*

Novak, Tadeusz (chamberlain)
- Shares the unleavened bread with Mgr. Wojtyla *12.1972*

Nowa Huta
- Fight for the construction of a church *April 28, 1960*
- Laying of the foundation stone of the church *May 18, 1969*
- Mgr. Wojtyla celebrates midnight mass *December 25, 1971*
- Mgr. Wojtyla consecrates the church *May 15, 1977*
- Visit of John Paul II *June 9, 1979*

OP

Ochbad, Edward
- President of the Polish Council *August 12, 1964*
- Greets General de Gaulle *September 8, 1967*

Odre, Adam
- Wounded in the assassination attempt against the pope *May 13, 1981*

Opus Dei
- Created by Father Escriva de Balaguer *October 2, 1928*
- Death of Mgr. Escriva de Balaguer *June 26, 1975*
- Becomes the personal prelacy of the pope *November 28, 1982*
- Beatification of its founder *May 17, 1992*

Ortega, Daniel
- Greets John Paul II in Nicaragua *March 4, 1983*

Osservatore Romano
- Authorized in Poland *June 1, 1980*
- John Paul II is outraged *June 24, 1983*

Ottoni, Fernando Luis Benedicto
- Miraculous healing *February 2, 1926*

Ozanam, Frédéric (1813-1853)
- Start of beatification proceedings *March 15, 1925*
- Beatified by John Paul II *August 22, 1997*

Pacelli, Eugenio See Pius XII

Pakistan
- Visit of John Paul II *February 16, 1981*

Palestine
- Arafat is granted an audience at the Vatican *September 15, 1982*
- Visit of John Paul II (Jubilee Year) *February 2000*

Panama
- Visit of John Paul II *March 1983*

Papua New Guinea
- Visit of Cardinal Wojtyla *February 8, 1973*
- Pope's second visit *January 1984*
- Visit of John Paul II *May 1995*

Paraguay
- Visit of John Paul II *May 1988*

Paul VI (Giovanni Battista Montini)
- Birth in Brescia *September 26, 1897*
- Ordained priest *1920*
- Archbishop of Milan *1954*
- Named cardinal *1958*
- Succeeds John XXIII *June 21, 1963*
- First pope to go to the Holy Land *January 5, 1964*
- Names Mgr. Wojtyla archbishop of Cracow *January 13, 1964*
- Creates a Secretariat for Non-Christians *May 19, 1964*
- Condemns the use of the pill *June 23, 1964*
- Receives Mgr. Wojtyla in private *November 30, 1964*
- Speech at UN *October 5, 1965*
- Proceedings for beatification of Pius XII and John XXIII *November 18, 1965*

- Establishes the Congregation for the Doctrine of the Faith *December 7, 1965*
- Puts an end to the Great Schism of the Church (1054) *December 7, 1965*
- Closing mass of Vatican II *December 8, 1965*
- Mgr. Wojtyla becomes the pope's trusted man in Poland *1965*
- Receives the head of the Anglican Church *March 24, 1966*
- Stopped from going to Poland *May 3, 1966*
- Wants to rejuvenate the clergy *August 12, 1966*
- Encyclical *Populorum Progressio March 26, 1967*
- Names Mgr. Wojtyla cardinal *June 28, 1967*
- Modernizes the Curia *August 15, 1967*
- Creates an Office of Economics Affairs *1967*
- Announces the discovery of St. Peter's remains *June 26, 1968*
- Encyclical *Humanae Vitae July 29, 1968*
- Meeting with Mgr. Wojtyla *November 2, 1968*
- Names Mgr. Villot secretary of State *May 2, 1969*
- First pope to set foot in Africa *August 2, 1969*
- Alters the rules of the conclave *November 21, 1970*
- Beatifies Maximilian Kolbe *October 17, 1971*
- Grants an audience to Golda Meir *January 16, 1973*
- Receives the head of the Coptic Church *May 10, 1973*
- Anniversary of his papal consecration *June 21, 1974*
- Defines the rules of the conclave *October 1, 1975*
- Encyclical *Evangeli Nuntiandi December 8, 1975*
- Entrusts Mgr. Wojtyla with the Lent homilies *March 13, 1976*
- Suspends Mgr. Lefebvre *a divinis July 22, 1976*
- Meeting with Mgr. Lefebvre fails *September 11, 1976*
- Dies at Castel Gandolfo *August 6, 1978*

Paulos, Abouna (patriarch of Ethiopia)
- Received at the Vatican *June 11, 1993*

Pawela, Jan
- Karol's religious education teacher at Wadowice school
- Funeral at Wadowice *September 1, 1968*

Pax Association (Polish Catholic movement)
- Created by the Communist regime *February 3, 1947*
- Recruits patriotic priests *April 30, 1952*
- Movement's journal is inscribed in the Index *June 8, 1955*

Pecci, Giocchiano See Leo XIII

Peres, Shimon
- Granted an audience by John Paul II *February 19, 1985*
- Invites the pope to Israel *October 23, 1992*

Pertini, Sandro (president of Italy)
- Admires the pope's health *July 17, 1984*

Peru
- John Paul II meets Amazonian Indians *February 6, 1985*
- Pope's second visit *May 1988*

Pétain, Marshal Philippe
- Attends Jozef Pilsudski's funeral *May 17, 1935*

Peyrefitte, Alain
- Accompanies de Gaulle to Poland *September 8, 1967*

Philippines
- Visit of Cardinal Wojtyla *February 7, 1973*
- John Paul II beatifies Lorenzo Ruiz in Manila *February 22, 1981*
- Pope's visit for the World Youth Day (Manila) *January 14, 1995*

Pieracki, Bronislaw
- Minister of the Interior *1931*
- Receives Joseph Goebbels *June 13, 1934*
- Assassinated in Warsaw *June 15, 1934*

Pierre (l'Abbé) [Henri Grouès]
- Birth in Lyons *August 5, 1912*
- Founds the Chiffonniers d'Emmaüs *November 25, 1949*

Pilgrimages (places of) See Ars, Czestochowa, Fatima, Lourdes, Santiago de Compostela

Pilsudski, Marshal Jozef
- Birth *December 5, 1867*
- Creates a Polish Legion against the Russians *August 6, 1914*
- Named president of the Second Polish Republic *November 14, 1918*
- Elected president by the Diet *February 20, 1919*

- Defeats the Russians at Kiev *May 8, 1920*
- Beats the Bolsheviks in Warsaw *August 15, 1920*
- Resigns *December 9, 1922*
- Overthrows President Wojciechowski *May 12, 1926*
- Dies in Warsaw *May 12, 1935*
- Buried in Wawel Cathedral, Cracow *May 18, 1935*

Pius X (saint) [Giuseppe Sarto]
- Birth *June 2, 1835*
- Succeeds Leo XIII *August 4, 1903*
- Breaks diplomatic relations with France *July 7, 1904*
- Beatifies Joan of Arc *April 18, 1909*
- Death *August 20, 1914*
- Canonized by Pius XI *May 29, 1954*

Pius XI (Achille Ratti)
- Birth *May 31, 1857*
- Apostolic nuncio in Warsaw *July 3, 1919*
- Cardinal archbishop of Milan *June 30, 1921*
- Succeeds Benedict XV *February 6, 1922*
- Inaugurates Holy Year *January 3, 1925*
- Concordat with the Polish State *February 10, 1925*
- Starts proceedings for the beatification of Frédéric Ozanam *March 15, 1925*
- Canonizes Theresa of Lisieux *May 23, 1925*
- Canonizes Jean-Marie Vianney *May 1925*
- Beatifies Bernadette Soubirous *June 14, 1925*
- Publishes *Letter to Cardinal Bertram November 13, 1926*
- Condemns *Action Française December 19, 1926*
- Condemns anti-Semitism *March 25, 1928*
- Negotiates Lateran agreements with Mussolini *February 11, 1929*
- Answers those who reproach him *May 14, 1929*
- Proclaims the Constitution of the Vatican *June 7, 1929*
- Encyclical *Divini illius magistri December 31, 1929*
- Condemns the persecution of Christians in the USSR *February 8, 1930*
- Encyclical *Casti connubii December 31, 1930*
- Inaugurates Radio Vatican *February 12, 1931*
- Encyclical *Quadragesimo Anno May 15, 1931*
- Denounces Fascism *June 29, 1931*
- Grants Mussolini an audience *February 11, 1932*
- Condemns the persecution of Indians in Mexico *October 3, 1932*
- Concordat with Germany *July 9, 1933*
- Canonizes Bernadette Soubirous *December 8, 1933*
- Condemns Nazism *March 14, 1937*
- Denounces Communism *March 18, 1937*
- Violent speech against anti-Semitism *September 6, 1938*
- Death *February 10, 1939*

Pius XII (Eugenio Pacelli)
- Birth *March 2, 1876*
- Named secretary of state to the Vatican by Pius XI *February 10, 1930*
- Attends inauguration of Radio Vatican *February 12, 1931*
- Succeeds Pius XI *March 2, 1939*
- Encyclical *Summi Pontificatus* for world peace *October 20, 1939*
- Creates the Institute of Religious Works *July 27, 1942*
- Talks of war crimes *December 24, 1942*
- Encyclical *Mystici Corporis June 29, 1943*
- Canonizes Louis-Marie Grignion de Montfort *July 20, 1947*
- Names Mgr. Wyszynski primate of poland *November 12, 1948*
- Excommunicates Communists *July 13, 1949*
- Condemns artificial insemination *September 29, 1949*
- Proclaims the dogma of the Assumption *November 1, 1950*
- Encyclical *Orientales Ecclesia December 15, 1952*
- Condemns the worker-priests *September 15, 1953*
- Inaugurates Marian Year *December 8, 1953*
- Canonizes Pius X *May 29, 1954*
- Closes Marian Year *December 8, 1954*
- Blesses a copy of the painting of the Virgin of Czestochowa *August 26, 1957*
- Names Mgr. Wojtyla bishop of Cracow *July 4, 1958*
- Dies at Castel Gandolfo *October 9, 1958*
- Start of proceedings for his beatification *November 18, 1965*

Piwowarczyk, Jan
- Birth *January 29, 1889*
- Greets Karol Wojtyla at Cracow seminary *October 1942*
- Death *December 29, 1959*

Pla y Deniel, Enrique (archbishop of Salamanca)
- Supports General Franco *September 30, 1936*

Poland (See also Cracow and Warsaw)
- Battlefield between Russia, Germany and Austria *August 3, 1914*
- Advance of Russian troops *August 5, 1914*
- Creation of a Legion against the Russians *August 6, 1914*
- German victory over the Russians at Tannenberg *August 31, 1914*
- Germans occupy Warsaw *August 8, 1915*
- Humiliating peace at Brest-Litovsk *March 3, 1918*
- Regains independence *November 11, 1918*
- Jozef Pilsudski head of State *November 14, 1918*
- Versailles Treaty (Danzig) *June 28, 1919*
- Versailles Treaty comes into effect *January 10, 1920*
- Kiev is taken from the Russians *May 8, 1920*
- Russia declares war *May 28, 1920*
- Loses Kiev *June 12, 1920*
- Receives aid from France *July 21, 1920*
- Bolsheviks threaten Warsaw *August 4, 1920*
- "Miracle of the Vistula" *August 15, 1920*
- Armistice with Russia *October 6, 1920*
- Alliance treaty with France *February 1, 1921*
- Adopts a Constitution *March 17, 1921*
- Russian-Polish peace at Riga *March 18, 1921*
- Narutowicz succeeds Pilsudski who resigns *December 9, 1922*
- Assassination of President Narutowicz *December 16, 1922*
- Election of President Wojciechowski *December 20, 1922*
- Concordat with Pius XI *February 10, 1925*
- Marshal Pilsudski's coup *May 12, 1926*
- Ignacy Moscicki is president *June 2, 1926*
- Ashes of the poet Slowacki are brought back *June 26, 1927*
- Firedamp explosion in Silesia *July 10, 1930*
- Serious economic crisis *1930*
- Non-aggression pact with USSR *January 25, 1932*
- Non-aggression pact with Germany *January 26, 1934*
- Recognizes USSR *June 9, 1934*
- Visit of Joseph Goebbels *June 13, 1934*
- Minister Pieracki is assassinated *June 15, 1934*
- New Constitution *March 24, 1935*
- Death of Marshal Pilsudski *May 12, 1935*
- Creation of Camp of National Unity *February 21, 1937*
- Friendship treaty with Germany *November 5, 1937*
- Visit of French Prime Minister Delbos *December 1937*
- Social and economic situation worrying *January 1938*
- Mutual defense agreement with Great Britain *April 6, 1939*
- Hitler revokes the pact between Germany and Poland *April 28, 1939*
- Germany claims Danzig *July 30, 1939*
- German invasion *September 1, 1939*
- Germans occupy Cracow *September 6, 1939*
- Government flees to Romania *September 17, 1939*
- Soviet invasion *September 17, 1939*
- Warsaw surrenders *September 27, 1939*
- Setting up of government in exile in Paris *September 30, 1939*
- Forced labor for all Poles aged between 18 and 60 *October 26, 1939*
- Creation of first ghettoes for German Jews *December 1, 1939*
- Construction of Auschwitz camp *March 24, 1940*
- Government in exile is transferred to London *June 18, 1940*
- Discovery of Katyn mass grave *April 15, 1943*
- Tehran conference *November 28, 1943*
- Communist government in Lublin *July 22, 1944*
- Majdanek camp is freed by the Red Army *July 23, 1944*
- Warsaw ghetto uprising *August 1, 1944*
- "Black Sunday" raids *August 6, 1944*
- Adoption of a parliament *September 11, 1944*

– Pope meets Clinton in Missouri *January 26, 1999*

Upper Volta
– Visit of John Paul II *May 1980*

Uruguay
– Visit of John Paul II *March 31, 1987*
– Pope's second visit *May 1988*

USSR
– First see Russia
– Stalin controls the country *November 15, 1927*
– Pius XI condemns the persecution of Christians *February 8, 1930*
– The Church of the Redemption is blown up *December 5, 1931*
– Non-aggression pact with Poland *January 25, 1932*
– XVII Congress of the Communist party *January 26, 1934*
– Recognized by Poland *June 9, 1934*
– Pius XI condemns Communism *March 18, 1937*
– Non-aggression pact with Germany *August 23, 1939*
– Invades Poland *September 17, 1939*
– Invaded by the German troops *June 22, 1941*
– Counterattacks outside Moscow *December 6, 1941*
– Discovery of Katyn mass grave *April 15, 1943*
– Tehran conference *November 28, 1943*
– Communist government in Poland *July 22, 1944*
– Polish camp in Majdanek is freed *July 23, 1944*
– Treaty of alliance and mutual aid with France *December 10, 1944*
– Offensive in Poland *January 13, 1945*
– Warsaw is freed *January 17, 1945*
– Cracow is freed *January 18, 1945*
– Auschwitz camp is freed *January 27, 1945*
– Takeover of Poland at Yalta *February 11, 1945*
– End of Potsdam conference *August 2, 1945*
– Death of Stalin *March 5, 1953*
– Warsaw Pact *May 14, 1955*
– Threatens to intervene in Poland *October 20, 1956*
– Intervention in Budapest *November 4, 1956*
– Gagarin returns to earth *April 12, 1961*
– Brezhnev is secretary general of the party *October 14, 1964*
– Prague Spring suppressed *August 21, 1968*
– Helsinki conference *July 31, 1975*
– Politburo writes reports on John Paul II *November 4, 1978*
– Acts against the Vatican's policies *November 13, 1979*
– End of military exercises in Poland *April 23, 1981*
– Gorbachev is secretary general of the Communist party *March 11, 1985*
– Gorbachev visits Jaruzelski *April 1985*
– Gorbachev gives speech on religion in Uzbekistan *November 1986*
– Millennium of Russia's Christianity *June 5, 1988*
– Arrival of a delegation from the Vatican *June 13, 1988*
– Positive article on the Vatican in *Pravda January 27, 1989*
– Dissident Sakharov is received in the Vatican *February 6, 1989*
– Gorbachev is granted an audience at the Vatican *December 1, 1989*
– Death of Andrei Sakharov *December 14, 1989*
– Diplomatic relations with the Vatican *March 15, 1990*
– NKVD is found responsible for the Katyn massacre *April 13, 1990*
– Gorbachev receives the Nobel Prize for Peace *October 15, 1990*
– The Church is reorganized in three Republics *April 13, 1991*
– Catholics on Orthodox territory *June 3, 1991*
– Severe speech by the patriarch of Moscow *October 30, 1991*
– Creation of the CIS *December 8, 1991*
– Gorbachev resigns *December 25, 1991*
– Yeltsin is granted an audience at the Vatican *February 10, 1998*

Vaivods, Juiljans
– First Soviet cardinal *February 2, 1983*

Van Straaten, Werenfried
– Founds association Aid to the Church in Need *December 31, 1947*

Vasana Tara (head of the Thai Buddhists)
– Meets John Paul II in Bangkok *May 12, 1984*

Vatican (See also Castel Gandolfo)
● **Leo XIII Pontificate**
– Election of Cardinal Pecci *February 20, 1878*
– Encyclical *Rerum Novarum* (working conditions) *May 15, 1891*
– Death of Leo XIII *July 20, 1903*
● **Pius X Pontificate**
– Election of Cardinal Sarto *August 4, 1903*
– Break in relations with France *July 7, 1904*
– Joan of Arc is beatified *August 20, 1914*
– Death of Pius X *August 20, 1914*
● **Benedict XV Pontificate**
– Election of Cardinal Della Chiesa *September 3, 1914*
– First Code of Canon law *May 20, 1917*
– Joan of Arc is canonized *May 16, 1920*
– Relations with France are resumed *May 16, 1921*
– Death of Benedict XV *January 22, 1922*
● **Pius XI Pontificate**
– Election of Cardinal Ratti *February 6, 1922*
– Inauguration of Holy Year *January 3, 1925*
– Concordat with Poland *February 10, 1925*
– Start of beatification proceedings for Frédéric Ozanam *March 15, 1925*
– Theresa of Lisieux is canonized *May 23, 1925*
– Jean-Marie Vianney is canonized *May 1925*
– Beatification of Bernadette Soubirous *June 14, 1925*
– *Letter to Cardinal Bertram* is published *November 13, 1926*
– Condemns *Action Française December 29, 1926*
– Condemns anti-Semitism *March 25, 1928*
– Lateran agreements with Italy *February 11, 1929*
– Constitution of the Vatican State *June 7, 1929*
– Encyclical *Divini Illius Magistri* (Christian education) *December 31, 1929*
– Condemns persecution of Christians in the USSR *February 8, 1930*
– Mgr. Pacelli is appointed secretary of State *February 12, 1930*
– Monetary agreement with the Italian State *August 2, 1930*
– Encyclical *Casti Connubii* (Christian marriage) *December 31, 1930*
– Inauguration of Radio Vatican *February 12, 1931*
– Encyclical *Quadragesimo Anno* (Church social doctrine) *May 15, 1931*
– Encyclical *Non Abbiamo Bisogno* against Facism *June 29, 1931*
– Audience granted to Mussolini *February 11, 1932*
– Concordat with Germany *July 9, 1933*
– Bernadette Soubirous is canonized *December 8, 1933*
– Encyclical *Mit brennender Sorge* (With a Burning Doubt) *March 14, 1937*
– Encyclical *Divini Redemptoris* against Communism *March 18, 1937*
– Pope's diatribe against anti-Semitism *September 6, 1938*
– Death of Pius XI *February 10, 1939*
● **Pius XII Pontificate**
– Election of Cardinal Pacelli *March 2, 1939*
– Encyclical *Summi Pontificatus* for world peace *October 20, 1939*
– Creation of a Vatican bank *July 27, 1942*
– Pius XII pays tribute to war victims *December 24, 1942*
– Encyclical *Mystici Corporis* (Mystical Body of Christ) *June 29, 1943*
– Louis-Marie Grignion de Montfort is canonized *July 20, 1947*
– Assembly of the World Council of Churches in Amsterdam *August 23, 1948*
– Excommunication of Communists *July 13, 1949*
– Condemns artificial insemination *September 29, 1949*
– Against Israel joining UN *December 9, 1949*
– Proclaims the dogma of the Assumption *November 1, 1950*
– Encyclical *Orientales Ecclesia* (Churches of Eastern Europe) *December 15, 1952*
– Condemns worker-priests *September 15, 1953*
– Opens Marian Year *December 8, 1953*
– Pius X is canonized *May 29, 1954*
– Closes Marian Year *December 8, 1954*
– Inscribes journal of Pax movement in the Index *June 8, 1955*

– Death of Pius XII *October 9, 1958*
● **John XXIII Pontificate**
– Election of Cardinal Roncalli *October 28, 1958*
– Announces forthcoming synod *January 25, 1959*
– Creates Secretariat for the Promotion of Christian Unity *June 5, 1960*
– Fidel Castro is excommunicated *January 3, 1962*
– Inauguration of Vatican II *October 11, 1962*
– Encyclical *Pacem in Terris* (defense of peace) *April 11, 1963*
– Death of John XXIII *June 3, 1963*
● **Paul VI Pontificate**
– Election of Cardinal Montini *June 21, 1963*
– Pope's historic trip to the Holy Land *January 5, 1964*
– Secretariat for Non-Christians *May 19, 1964*
– Condemns the use of the pill *June 23, 1964*
– Third session of Vatican II *September 14, 1964*
– Mgr. Wojtyla is granted a private audience *November 30, 1964*
– Pope's speech at UN *October 5, 1965*
– Council's declaration on non-Christian religions *October 28, 1965*
– Beatification proceedings for Pius XII and John XXIII *November 18, 1965*
– Creation of the Congregation for the Doctrine of the Faith *December 7, 1965*
– Excommunication of 1054 is lifted *December 7, 1965*
– Closing of Vatican II *December 8, 1965*
– Creation of an Anglican-Catholic commission *March 24, 1966*
– Index of banned books is abolished *April 9, 1966*
– Millennium of Poland's Christianity *May 3, 1966*
– Wishes to rejuvenate the clergy *August 12, 1966*
– Encyclical *Populorum Progressio* (Development of Peoples) *March 26, 1967*
– Israel votes for free access to the Holy Places *June 27, 1967*
– Nomination of 27 cardinals *June 28, 1967*
– The Curia is modernized *August 15, 1967*
– Poland is absent from the synod of bishops *September 29, 1967*
– Creation of the Office of Economic Affairs *December 1967*
– Discovery of St. Peter's remains *June 26, 1968*
– Encyclical *Humanae Vitae* against contraception *July 29, 1968*
– Mgr. Villot is appointed secretary of State *May 2, 1969*
– Paul VI's speech in Uganda *August 2, 1969*
– Synod on collegial structure of the bishops *October 28, 1969*
– Recognizes legitimacy of Warsaw government *October 19, 1970*
– Conclave rules are modified *November 21, 1970*
– Synod on world justice and priesthood *September 30, 1971*
– Maximilian Kolbe is beatified *October 17, 1971*
– Mgr. Casaroli visits Warsaw *November 10, 1971*
– New rules for appointing bishops *March 25, 1972*
– Golda Meir is granted an audience *January 16, 1973*
– Sacred Congregation of the Clergy *March 27, 1973*
– Visit of the head of the Coptic Church *May 10, 1973*
– 7th centenary of St. Thomas of Aquinas' death *April 24, 1974*
– Dismayed at the passing of the Italian law on divorce *May 13, 1974*
– Anniversary of Paul VI's consecration *June 21, 1974*
– Synod on evangelism *September 27, 1974*
– Mgr. Lefebvre's manifesto against Vatican II *November 21, 1974*
– Constitution of the new conclave rules *October 1, 1975*
– Encyclical *Evangelii Nuntiandi* (Christian message) *December 2, 1975*
– Mgr. Lefebvre is suspended *a divinis July 22, 1976*
– Mgr. Lefebvre is granted an audience *September 11, 1976*
– Synod on catechism and the role of religious education *October 29, 1977*
– Death of Paul VI *August 6, 1978*
● **John Paul I Pontificate**
– Election of Cardinal Luciani *August 26, 1978*
– Mgr. Wojtyla is granted an audience *August 30, 1978*

- Metropolitan Nikodim has a stroke *September 5, 1978*
- Condemns Leninism *September 20, 1978*
- Death of John Paul I *September 29, 1978*
- Pope's funeral *October 4, 1978*
- Conclave for his succession *October 14, 1978*
- **John Paul II Pontificate**
- Election of Polish Cardinal Wojtyla *October 16, 1978*
- John Paul II's enthronement ceremony *October 22, 1978*
- Recommends wearing the habit *November 10, 1978*
- Death of Mgr. Villot *March 9, 1979*
- Encyclical *Redemptor Hominis* (The Redeemer of Man) *March 15, 1979*
- Mgr. Casaroli is appointed secretary of State *April 30, 1979*
- Fraternity and support to the Polish people *June 10, 1979*
- Nomination of 14 cardinals *June 30, 1979*
- Dialog with the Orthodox Church is resumed *December 1, 1979*
- The theologian Küng is condemned *December 18, 1979*
- Sedan chair is banished *1979*
- Dutch Catholic Church is called to order *January 1980*
- Letter to the bishops on the Eucharist *February 24, 1980*
- Warning to the Brazilian bishops *June 12, 1980*
- Queen Elizabeth II's official visit *October 17, 1980*
- Encyclical *Dives in Misericordia* (On the Mercy of God) *December 2, 1980*
- Visit of Lech Walesa *January 15, 1981*
- Historic beatification in Manila *February 22, 1981*
- Encyclical *Laborem exercens* (On Human Work) *September 14, 1981*
- Private visit of the primate of Poland *October 18, 1981*
- John Paul II's speech on Europe *November 12, 1981*
- Mgr. Ratzinger is in charge of doctrine *November 25, 1981*
- Nuclear research report *December 12, 1981*
- Calls for prayers for the Polish nation *December 13, 1981*
- A candle is lit in the name of solidarity *December 24, 1981*
- Pope pays tribute to the wisdom of Black Africa *February 19, 1982*
- No politics for prelates *March 8, 1982*
- Moves closer to the Anglican Church *May 28, 1982*
- Diplomatic relations with Sweden, Norway and Denmark *August 2, 1982*
- Yasser Arafat is granted an audience *September 15, 1982*
- Maximilian Kolbe is canonized *October 10, 1982*
- 4th centenary of Saint Theresa of Avila in Madrid *October 31, 1982*
- Calls for unity of the people of Europe *November 9, 1982*
- Opus Dei becomes the personal prelacy of the pope *November 28, 1982*
- Budgets are apportioned *December 31, 1982*
- New Code of Canon Law *January 25, 1983*
- Appointment of 18 cardinals *February 2, 1983*
- Publication of comic book on pope's life *March 23, 1983*
- Inauguration of the Holy Year of the Redemption *March 25, 1983*
- Shroud of Turin is given to the Holy See *March 25, 1983*
- Pope makes new visit to Poland *June 16, 1983*
- Beatification of Adam Chmielowski in Cracow *June 22, 1983*
- Meeting between pope and Jaruzelski *June 22, 1983*
- Meeting between pope and Lech Walesa *June 23, 1983*
- Painter Fra Angelico is beatified *July 8, 1983*
- Charter on family rights *November 24, 1983*
- Freemasons will no longer be excommunicated *November 26, 1983*
- Vatican staff strike *December 1, 1983*
- Inauguration of the underground rooms *1984*
- Diplomatic relations with the United States *January 10, 1984*

- Lateran agreements are revised *February 18, 1984*
- Aid to the Church in Need becomes public association *April 6, 1984*
- First mention of the State of Israel in *Redemptionis Anno April 20, 1984*
- 103 martyrs are canonized in Seoul *May 6, 1984*
- Convocation of two theoreticians of liberation theology *September 9, 1984*
- Mass in Latin is to be tolerated again *October 15, 1984*
- Inscribed in UNESCO's World Heritage Convention list *November 2, 1984*
- Shimon Peres is granted an audience *February 19, 1985*
- Critics within the Church *April 30, 1985*
- Gulf between society and the Church in the Netherlands *May 11, 1985*
- Carmelite convent issue in Auschwitz *May 1985*
- Encyclical *Slavorum Apostoli* for ecumenism *July 2, 1985*
- Calls for dialog between Christians and Muslims in Morocco *August 19, 1985*
- Announces opening of archives of Pius XI and Benedict XV *August 29, 1985*
- Extraordinary synod *November 24, 1985*
- 20th anniversary of Vatican II *December 8, 1985*
- Creation of World Youth Day *December 20, 1985*
- 20th World Day of Peace *January 1, 1986*
- Pope's position softens with regard to Brazilian episcopate *April 5, 1986*
- Special audience granted to the Albanian diaspora *April 27, 1986*
- Encyclical *Dominum et Vivificantem* (Holy Spirit) *May 30, 1986*
- Draws up a universal catechism *June 11, 1986*
- Theologian Curran is dismissed *August 1986*
- Pope's visit to the United States *September 10, 1986*
- Pope's high-security visit to France *October 4, 1986*
- World Day of Prayer for Peace in Assisi *October 27, 1986*
- Anglican Church defines pope's role *November 13, 1986*
- Jaruzelski is granted a special audience *January 13, 1987*
- Ali Agça's mother is granted an audience *February 20, 1987*
- Compromise concerning the Auschwitz issue *February 22, 1987*
- Says no to artificial insemination *March 13, 1987*
- Encyclical *Redemptoris Mater* (Mother of the Redeemer) *March 25, 1987*
- Calls for respect for human rights in Chile *April 3, 1987*
- Edith Stein is beatified in Cologne *May 1, 1987*
- Opening of Marian Year *June 7, 1987*
- Supports Solidarity *June 14, 1987*
- Visit of Kurt Waldheim *June 25, 1987*
- Marcel Callo is beatified *October 4, 1987*
- Mass in the presence of the patriarch of Constantinople *December 6, 1987*
- Michael Sabbah is the first Arab patriarch of Jerusalem *December 28, 1987*
- 21th World Day of Peace *January 1, 1988*
- Defends the Christian view of marriage *January 25, 1988*
- Encyclical *Sollicitudo Rei Socialis* (On Social Concerns) *February 19, 1988*
- Publishes the Holy See's accounts *March 3, 1988*
- Delegation for the millennium of Russia's Christianity *June 13, 1988*
- Beatification of 117 martyrs *June 19, 1988*
- Pope visits Mauthausen concentration camp *June 24, 1988*
- Nomination of 25 cardinals *June 28, 1988*
- Mgr. Lefebvre is excommunicated *July 2, 1988*
- End of Marian Year *August 15, 1988*
- Recognition given to the Zairean mass *September 1988*
- Papal letter addressed to women *September 30, 1988*
- Pope's speech in Strasbourg *October 11, 1988*
- Questioning of the Shroud of Turin's authenticity *October 13, 1988*

- Pope's strategic speech to the bishops *November 5, 1988*
- Pope receives Alexander Dubcek *November 19, 1988*
- Tensions with the German Church *January 25, 1989*
- Positive article in *Pravda January 27, 1989*
- 22nd World Day of Peace *January 31, 1989*
- Andrei Sakharov's historical visit *February 6, 1989*
- Diplomatic relations with Poland *June 17, 1989*
- World Youth Day in Santiago de Compostela *August 19, 1989*
- Gorbachev's official visit *December 1, 1989*
- Diplomatic relations with USSR *March 15, 1990*
- Diplomatic relations with Czechoslovakia *April 19, 1990*
- Calls for peace in the Gulf *August 24, 1990*
- Polemic in the Ivory Coast *September 10, 1990*
- First Code of Canon Law for Eastern Churches *October 18, 1990*
- Mgr. Casaroli retires *December 1, 1990*
- Catholics and Jews are united at Lateran University *December 6, 1990*
- Success of goods bearing the pope's image *1990*
- Encyclical *Redemptoris Missio* (value of missionary concept) *January 22, 1991*
- Priest census *February 24, 1991*
- Suspends beatification of Isabella the Catholic *March 26, 1991*
- Bishops' debate on sects *April 4, 1991*
- Encyclical *Centesimus Annus* (commemorates Rerum Novarum) *May 1, 1991*
- Catholics on Orthodox territory *June 3, 1991*
- Bitterness of the pope's visit to Poland *June 9, 1991*
- Consistory of cardinals *June 28, 1991*
- Document of the Congregation for the Doctrine of the Faith *June 1991*
- World Youth Day in Czestochowa (Poland) *August 14, 1991*
- Ecumenical prayor at St. Peter's *October 5, 1991*
- Recognizes Slovenia and Croatia *January 12, 1992*
- Ambassador appointed in Haiti *January 15, 1992*
- Mgr. Gaillot is granted an audience *January 22, 1992*
- Condemns slavery *January 22, 1992*
- New rules for the Roman Curia *March 7, 1992*
- 50th anniversary of the end of World War II *May 8, 1992*
- Creation of World Day for the Sick *May 13, 1992*
- Beatification of Sister Bakhita and Mgr. Escriva de Balaguer *May 17, 1992*
- Reminder of Rome's supreme power *June 15, 1992*
- Negotiates with Israel *July 29, 1992*
- Calls for peace in the Balkans *August 22, 1992*
- Mass in Santo Domingo for anniversary of America's discovery *October 12, 1992*
- Galileo is rehabilitated *October 31, 1992*
- Promulgation of new catechism *December 7, 1992*
- Recognizes the Czech and Slovak Republics *January 1, 1993*
- Prayer for peace in Assisi *January 9, 1993*
- Calls for chastity to fight AIDS *February 6, 1993*
- Controversial visit to Sudan *February 10, 1993*
- First World Day for the Sick *February 11, 1993*
- Pope's message of hope in Albania *April 25, 1993*
- Warning to the Italian Mafia *May 9, 1993*
- Abouna Paulos' visit *June 11, 1993*
- World Youth Day in Denver *August 14, 1993*
- Encyclical *Veritatis Splendor* (Catholic church morals) *October 5, 1993*
- Visit of Elias Hraoui *November 5, 1993*
- Speculations about the pope's health *November 11, 1993*
- Denies press rumors *December 1, 1993*
- Fundamental agreements with Israel *December 30, 1993*
- Priesthood crisis *1993*
- Pope denounces "the deification of the nation" *January 6, 1994*
- Creation of the Pontifical Academy for Life *February 11, 1994*
- Reacts against the ordination of women *March 31, 1994*
- Inauguration of the restored Sistine Chapel *April 8, 1994*

- Special Assembly of the synod of African bishops *April 10, 1994*
- Creation of a nuns' cloister *May 10, 1994*
- Rejects the ordination of women *May 22, 1994*
- Rumors of pope's death *September 4, 1994*
- Exchanges ambassadors with Israel *September 29, 1994*
- Refuses the Eucharist to divorced couples who marry again *October 14, 1994*
- World publication of *Crossing the Threshold of Hope October 20, 1994*
- Preparations for the Jubilee of the year 2000 *November 20, 1994*
- Record number of cardinals *November 26, 1994*
- Publication of *Letter to Children December 13, 1994*
- Dismissal of Mgr. Gaillot *January 13, 1995*
- Encyclical *Evangelicum Vitae* (The Gospel of Life) *March 30, 1995*
- Beatification of two Italian women *April 4, 1995*
- The pope is not expected to resign after his 75th birthday *May 18, 1995*
- Church asks forgiveness for the massacres of the wars of religion *May 21, 1995*
- Encyclical *Ut Unum Sint* (That They May Be One) *May 30, 1995*
- Publication of *Letter to Women July 10, 1995*
- Pope's exhortation *Ecclesia in Africa September 15, 1995*
- Apostolic constitution *Universi Dominici Gregis November 22, 1995*
- New health warning for the pope *December 25, 1995*
- Decline in respect for moral precepts of the Church *1995*
- Loss of influence on the behavior of individuals *1995*
- Peace in South America makes progress *February 11, 1996*
- Pope calls for television-free diet *February 21, 1996*
- Worries about the pope's health *March 25, 1996*
- The French deny their baptism *August 11, 1996*
- 15th centenary of Clovis' christening in Reims *September 22, 1996*
- Publication of *My Priestly Ordination November 1, 1996*
- Private audience with Fidel Castro *November 19, 1996*
- Visit of Benyamin Netanyahu and his wife *February 3, 1997*
- High-security visit to Sarajevo *April 13, 1997*
- Rumors of a foiled assassination attempt *May 9, 1997*
- Vocational crisis in Europe *May 1997*
- Pope's message to the young in Poznan *June 3, 1997*
- End of the World Youth Day in Paris *August 24, 1997*
- Tribute to Mother Teresa *September 13, 1997*
- Eucharistic Congress in Bologna *September 27, 1997*
- Ali Agça's brother is granted an audience *November 12, 1997*
- Pope challenges Castro *January 25, 1998*
- Debate on the Euro *January 1998*
- Boris Yeltsin is granted an audience *February 10, 1998*
- Private visit of Father Malinski *February 1998*
- Church of Rome asks the Jews for forgiveness *March 16, 1998*
- China absent from the bishops' synod *May 2, 1998*
- Head of the Swiss Guards is assassinated *May 4, 1998*
- The longest pontificate of the XXth century *May 22, 1998*
- Death of Mgr. Casaroli *June 9, 1998*
- Beatification of Croatian primate Mgr. Stepinac *October 3, 1998*
- Edith Stein is canonized *October 11, 1998*
- Opening of the legal archives *December 1998*
- Modernization of the ritual of exorcism *January 26, 1999*
- Launches laser disk *Abba Pater* with Sony *March 23, 1999*
- Opening of the Holy Doors at St. Peter's *December 24, 1999*
- John Paul II travels to Egypt *February 2000*
- The pope in Palestine, Jordan and Israel *March 2000*

Vatican II (council)
- John XXIII announces synod *January 25, 1959*
- Inauguration of Vatican II *October 11, 1962*
- Mgr. Wojtyla attracts notice with speech *October 28, 1964*
- Declaration about non-Christian religions *October 28, 1965*
- Closed by Paul VI *December 8, 1965*
- Synod for the 20th anniversary of Vatican II *December 8, 1985*

Venezuela
- Visit of John Paul II *January 1985*
- Pope says mass in Caracas *February 11, 1996*

Vianney, Jean-Marie (priest of Ars) See Jean-Marie Vianney (saint)

Villot, Jean-Marie
- Birth in France *December 1905*
- Appointed Vatican secretary of State by Paul VI *May 2, 1969*
- Considers Mgr. Wojtyla to be *papabile May 18, 1978*
- Mgr. Wojtyla is elected pope *October 16, 1978*
- John Paul II renews his post *October 25, 1978*
- Death *March 9, 1979*

W

Wadowice
- Karol and Emilia Wojtyla move to Cicha *1904*
- Birth of Edmund Wojtyla *August 27, 1906*
- Flight of the Wojtyla family (World War I) *November 1914*
- Birth and death of Olga Wojtyla *1914*
- The Wojtylas move to Rynek Square *1919*
- Birth of Karol Jozef Wojtyla *May 18, 1920*
- Karol's christening at the Church of Our Lady *June 20, 1920*
- Creation of the Society of Mary *1925*
- The Church recognizes the Society *June 20, 1926*
- Karol enters Marcin Wadowita School *September 15, 1926*
- Death of Emilia Wojtyla *April 13, 1929*
- Karol's first communion *May 25, 1929*
- Karol enters Marcin Wadowita High School *September 30, 1929*
- Karol becomes choirboy *December 31, 1931*
- Father Figlewicz leaves *August 1933*
- Karol joins the theater group *1934*
- Karol joins the Society of Mary *December 14, 1935*
- High School theater group is a success *March 1936*
- Karol is head of the Society of Mary *April 26, 1936*
- Football matches between Catholics and Jews *1936*
- Poetry recitation contest *January 1937*
- Karol is re-elected head of the Society *May 18, 1937*
- Anti-semitic protests *January 1938*
- Karol's speech *February 17, 1938*
- Visit of Mgr. Sapieha *May 6, 1938*
- Karol passes final exams *May 14, 1938*
- Germans destroy the synagogue *November 1939*
- Father Wojtyla says solemn mass *November 10, 1946*
- 20th anniversary of the 1938 Marcin Wadowita graduates *September 14, 1958*
- Father Wojtyla says mass for the High School's centenary *July 2, 1966*
- Father Pawela's funeral *January 9, 1968*
- Mgr. Wojtyla consecrates the church's new bells *May 18, 1970*
- Karol Wojtyla is elected to the Vatican *October 16, 1978*
- John Paul II visits his home town *June 7, 1979*
- Death of Father Zacher *February 13, 1987*
- Pope's letter to the Jewish community *May 9, 1989*
- Holy Father's private visit *August 13, 1991*

Wajda, Andrzej (film director)
- Birth at Suwalki *March 6, 1926*
- Wins Palme d'Or at Cannes film festival (*The Man of Iron*) *May 27, 1981*

Waldheim, Kurt (president of Austria)
- Controversial visit to the Vatican *June 25, 1987*

Walesa, Danuta
- Received at the Vatican by John Paul II with her husband *January 15, 1981*

Walesa, Lech
- Birth in Popowo *September 29, 1943*
- Head of the Gdansk strikers *August 14, 1980*
- Agreement with the Communist regime *August 31, 1980*
- President of the union "Solidarnosc" (Solidarity) *September 22, 1980*
- Received by John Paul II *January 15, 1981*
- Re-elected president of the Union *October 7, 1981*
- Under house arrest *December 13, 1981*
- End of house arrest *June 16, 1983*
- Meets John Paul II in Zakopane *June 23, 1983*
- Nobel Prize for Peace *October 5, 1983*
- Meets John Paul II in Gdansk *June 11, 1987*
- Recognized as leader of the opposition *April 17, 1989*
- Victory at the elections *June 18, 1989*
- President of Poland *December 9, 1990*
- Receives an official document on Katyn *October 14, 1992*
- Defeated at the presidential election *November 26, 1995*

Warsaw
- Taken by the Germans *August 8, 1915*
- Departure of German troops *November 11, 1918*
- Bolshevik threat *August 4, 1920*
- Russian defeat *August 15, 1920*
- President Narutowicz is assassinated *December 16, 1922*
- Marshal Pilsudski's coup *May 12, 1926*
- Minister Pieracki is assassinated *June 15, 1934*
- Death of Marshal Pilsudski *May 12, 1935*
- Occupied by German troops *September 23, 1939*
- Surrenders *September 27, 1939*
- German Jews are deported *December 1, 1939*
- 300,000 Jews are walled up in the ghetto *November 15, 1940*
- Ghetto uprising *August 1, 1944*
- End of uprising *October 2, 1944*
- Red Army offensive *January 13, 1945*
- Withdrawal of German troops *January 17, 1945*
- Lublin government transferred *January 18, 1945*
- Death of Primate, Cardinal Hlond *October 22, 1948*
- Mgr. Wyszynski is head of the Church *November 12, 1948*
- Mgr. Wyszynski is arrested *September 26, 1953*
- Warsaw Pact *May 14, 1955*
- Joy at Mgr. Wyszynski's return *October 28, 1956*
- Performance of Mickiewicz's play *The Forefather's Eve November 25, 1967*
- Student demonstration *January 30, 1968*
- Reconstruction of the Castle *January 20, 1971*
- Visit of Mgr. Casaroli *November 10, 1971*
- 30th anniversary of the ghetto uprising *April 19, 1973*
- 40th anniversary of Pilsudski's death *May 12, 1975*
- Protests against police violence *May 25, 1977*
- End of protest movement *June 17, 1977*
- Death of Mgr. Wyszynski *May 28, 1981*
- Polish primate's funeral *May 31, 1981*
- Death of Father Popieluszko *October 19, 1984*
- Father Popieluszko's funeral *November 3, 1984*
- Visit of John Paul II *June 14, 1987*

Wawel Cathedral (Cracow)
- Poet Slowacki's ashes are buried *June 27, 1927*
- Marshal Pilsudski's funeral *May 18, 1935*
- Father Wojtyla celebrates solemn mass *November 2, 1946*
- Mgr. Wojtyla is consecrated bishop *September 28, 1958*
- Mgr. Wojtyla is consecrated archbishop *March 8, 1964*
- Millennium of Poland's Christianity *May 7, 1966*
- Student Pyjas' funeral *May 15, 1977*
- John Paul II's service *June 9, 1997*

Weygand, General Maxime
- Military advisor to the Polish general staff *July 21, 1920*

Wiadrowska, Maria Anna (née Kaczorowska)
- Karol Wojtyla's godmother *June 20, 1920*
- Spends some time in Cracow with her godson *September 1938*
- Death *November 27, 1959*

- Teaches ethics at Lublin *October 1954*
- Obtains the Chair of Ethics *December 10, 1956*
- Appreciated by his students *January 31, 1957*
- Pays tribute to Kotlarczyk's work *April 7, 1957*
- **Wojtyla, Karol Jozef: bishop of Cracow**
- Named bishop by Pius XII *July 4, 1958*
- Prays at length in the chapel of a convent *July 1958*
- Meets up with his friends 20 years after graduating *September 14, 1958*
- Consecrated by Mgr. Baziak *September 28, 1958*
- Chooses *Totus tuus* as his motto (All for you) *October 1958*
- Still goes kayaking since his promotion *September 30, 1959*
- Death of his godmother *November 27, 1959*
- Writes *The Jeweller's Shop* 1960
- Publishes *Love and Responsibility December 1960*
- Suffers from anemia *December 31, 1960*
- Death of his half-aunt, Stefania *May 24, 1962*
- Vicar Capitular of Cracow *June 17, 1962*
- Accompanies Mgr. Wyszynski at inauguration of Vatican II *October 11, 1962*
- Death of his maternal aunt, Anna *December 7, 1962*
- Death of his maternal uncle, Robert *December 27, 1962*
- Praised by the clergy *February 1, 1963*
- Catches the scepter of the Virgin of Ludzmierz as it falls *August 15, 1963*
- Meets Wladyslaw Rubin in Rome *October 21, 1963*
- Trip to the Holy Land *December 15, 1963*
- **Wojtyla, Karol Jozef: archbishop of Cracow**
- Appointed archbishop by Paul VI *January 13, 1964*
- Consecrated in Wawel Cathedral *March 8, 1964*
- Makes noteworthy speech at Vatican II *October 28, 1964*
- Granted a private audience by Paul VI *November 30, 1964*
- Helps prepare *Gaudium et Spes* (Schema XIII) *January 31, 1965*
- Visits the ecumenical community of Taizé *September 1965*
- Interviewed on Radio Vatican *October 20, 1965*
- Calls for German-Polish forgiveness *November 18, 1965*
- Meets up with his friend Jurek in Rome *November 20, 1965*
- Account of his work in Vatican II *December 8, 1965*
- Insulted by the Communists *December 24, 1965*
- Hectic timetable *1965*
- Pope's trusted man in Poland *1965*
- Replaces Paul VI for Poland's millennium ceremonies *May 3, 1966*
- Celebrates the centenary of Wadowice High School *July 2, 1966*
- Government puts a stop to ceremonies *September 4, 1966*
- Consecrates Niegowic's new church *September 25, 1966*
- Signs petition in favor of the Rhapsodic Theater *April 11, 1967*
- **Wojtyla, Karol Jozef: cardinal**
- Named cardinal by Paul VI *June 28, 1967*
- Reacts against the closure of the Rhapsodic Theater *July 31, 1967*
- Turns down a meeting with General de Gaulle *September 8, 1967*
- Solidarity with Mgr. Wyszinski *September 29, 1967*
- Secret police report on him *December 1967*
- Attends Father Pawela's funeral *January 9, 1968*
- Takes possession of the Church of San Cesareo *February 18, 1968*
- Supports the Polish students' movement *March 22, 1968*
- His theses inspire the encyclical *Humanae Vitae July 29, 1968*
- Suggests to Paul VI beatifying Father Kolbe *November 2, 1968*
- Close to the people and to his collaborators *1968*
- Moves into the archbishop's palace in Cracow *January 10, 1969*
- Writes a book on the crisis of the Church *February 1969*
- Visits the synagogue in Kazimierz *February 28, 1969*

- Lays foundation stone of Nowa Huta church *May 18, 1969*
- Meets the Polish diaspora in North America *September 1969*
- Noteworthy speeches at the synod of bishops *October 28, 1969*
- Publishes *The Acting Person December 1969*
- Consecrates the new bells of Wadowice church *May 18, 1970*
- Pays tribute to an old sporting friend *December 20, 1970*
- On the secretariat of the bishop's synod *October 5, 1971*
- Attends the beatification of Maximilian Kolbe *October 17, 1971*
- Supports celibacy for priests *November 6, 1971*
- Celebrates midnight mass in Nowa Huta church *December 25, 1971*
- New year's message to the Catholic Poles *January 1, 1972*
- Cites Saint Stanislas as an example for the nation *April 9, 1972*
- Opens Cracow synod *May 8, 1972*
- Publishes *The Foundations of Renewal May 8, 1972*
- Celebrates a special mass in Auschwitz *October 15, 1972*
- Mgr. Luciani would like to see him become pope *November 1972*
- Shares the unleavened bread with his chamberlain *December 31, 1972*
- Goes to the Philippines *February 7, 1973*
- Stops in Papua New Guinea *February 8, 1973*
- Eucharistic Congress in Australia *February 9, 1973*
- Returns to Poland *March 9, 1973*
- Takes part in the Sacred Congregation of the Clergy *March 27, 1973*
- Impressed by Mrs. Tymieniecka *July 29, 1973*
- Visit to France *November 11, 1973*
- 7th centenary celebrations of the death of St. Thomas Aquinas *April 24, 1974*
- Attends Paul VI's enthronement anniversary *June 21, 1974*
- Discusses sexuality *June 30, 1974*
- Opposed to liberation theology *October 26, 1974*
- Takes part in a meeting of newspaper *Tygodnik Powszechny 1974*
- Creates the Institute of the Family *February 9, 1975*
- Supports premarital chastity *February 1976*
- Chosen by Paul VI to preach to the Curia *March 13, 1976*
- Gives a lecture at Harvard *July 27, 1976*
- Talks of religious freedom *August 8, 1976*
- American tour is a success *September 1, 1976*
- Presides over the synod in Rome *March 15, 1977*
- Consecrates the church of Nowa Huta *May 15, 1977*
- Condemns police repression in Poland *June 17, 1977*
- Made Doctor *honoris causa* of Mainz University *June 23, 1977*
- Presides over a Polish Catholics' meeting in Paris *July 1, 1977*
- Denounces the intolerance of atheism *October 29, 1977*
- Death of his friend Kotlarczyk *February 21, 1978*
- Celebrates his 58th birthday in Rome *May 18, 1978*
- Cheered by the miners at Piekary Slaskie *June 1978*
- Death of Paul VI *August 6, 1978*
- Considered to be *papabile August 24, 1978*
- Received by John Paul I *August 30, 1978*
- Meditates before the Shroud of Turin *September 1, 1978*
- Homily on papal duties *September 17, 1978*
- Impresses the German episcopate *September 25, 1978*
- Prays at Kalwaria sanctuary *September 27, 1978*
- 20th anniversary of his investiture as a bishop *September 28, 1978*
- Learns of John Paul I's death *September 29, 1978*
- Returns to Poland to rest *September 1978*
- Says mass for John Paul I *October 1, 1978*
- Favorite for the succession *October 13, 1978*
- Hitch-hikes to the conclave *October 14, 1978*
- **Wojtyla, Karol Jozef: pontificate (John Paul II)**
- Elected pope at the eighth ballot *October 16, 1978*

- Learns to "become a pope" *October 17, 1978*
- Enthronement ceremony *October 22, 1978*
- Receives Valéry Giscard d'Estaing *October 26, 1978*
- Cheered on the road to Castel Gandolfo *October 27, 1978*
- Pilgrimage to Mentorella sanctuary *October 29, 1978*
- Writes letter of thanks to Father Zacher *November 4, 1978*
- Urges the nuns and clergy of Rome to wear their habits *November 10, 1978*
- Embraces the Communist mayor of Rome *November 12, 1978*
- Chooses five Polish nuns to look after his everyday needs *November 30, 1978*
- Unhealthy rumors about his youth *December 9, 1978*
- Says he is "rusty" *1978*
- Mediator between Argentina and Chile *January 24, 1979*
- Visits Santo Domingo *January 25, 1979*
- Receives cold welcome in Mexico *January 26, 1979*
- Encyclical *Redemptor Hominis March 15, 1979*
- Names Mgr. Casaroli secretary of State *April 30, 1979*
- Message of fraternity to Poland *June 2, 1979*
- Stays in Czestochowa sanctuary *June 4, 1979*
- Goes to Wadowice *June 7, 1979*
- Prays on his parents' grave *June 9, 1979*
- End of his trip to Poland *June 10, 1979*
- Father Dziwisz remains his private secretary *June 18, 1979*
- Names 14 cardinals *June 30, 1979*
- Speech at the UN *October 1, 1979*
- Declares he wants to go to Israel *October 5, 1979*
- Bluntly addressed about ordination of women priests *October 7, 1979*
- Death threat by a Turkish terrorist *November 26, 1979*
- Revives dialog with the Orthodox Church *December 1, 1979*
- Approves condemnation of the theologian Küng *December 18, 1979*
- The pope's typical day *1979*
- Travels around in a "popemobile" *1979*
- Meets young delinquents *January 6, 1980*
- Calls the Dutch Church to order *January 31, 1980*
- Letter to the bishops about the Eucharist *February 24, 1980*
- Attends performance of *The Jeweller's Shop February 28, 1980*
- African tour *May 2, 1980*
- Historic trip to France *May 30, 1980*
- Speech at UNESCO *June 2, 1980*
- Warning to the Brazilian bishops *June 30, 1980*
- Supports the Polish strikers *August 20, 1980*
- Gift from the American "Polonia" *August 1980*
- Receives Queen Elizabeth II *October 17, 1980*
- Encyclical *Dives in Misericordia December 2, 1980*
- Game of bowls in Rome *December 9, 1980*
- Informed of a Soviet threat to Poland *December 1980*
- Receives a Christmas tree from Poland *December 1980*
- Receives Lech Walesa *January 15, 1981*
- Warned of a plot against him *January 1981*
- Names Mgr. Lustiger archbishop of Paris *February 2, 1981*
- Arrives in Pakistan *February 16, 1981*
- Beatifies Lorenzo Ruiz in Manila *February 22, 1981*
- Gives speech in nine languages in Hiroshima *February 25, 1981*
- Victim of an assassination attempt in Rome *May 13, 1981*
- Doctors cautious about his state of health *May 14, 1981*
- Learns of the legalization of abortion in Italy *May 15, 1981*
- Forgives his assailant, Ali Agça *May 17, 1981*
- Comes out of intensive care *May 18, 1981*
- First proper meal since assassination attempt *May 20, 1981*
- Affected by Mgr. Wyszynski's death *May 28, 1981*
- Hospitalized again *June 20, 1981*
- Comes out of hospital *August 14, 1981*
- Encyclical *Laborem Exercens September 14, 1981*

- Must lose weight *September 1981*
- Meeting with the primate of Poland, Mgr. Glemp *October 18, 1981*
- Speech on Europe *November 12, 1981*
- Informed of the Soviet-Polish situation *November 30, 1981*
- Calls for prayers for Poland *December 13, 1981*
- Solidarity towards "those nations in suffering" *December 24, 1981*
- Pays tribute to the wisdom of Black Africa *February 19, 1982*
- Opposed to the clergy's involvement in political matters *March 8, 1982*
- Supports the Solvay workers *March 19, 1982*
- Escapes an assassination attempt in Portugal *May 12, 1982*
- Meets Sister Maria Lucia *May 13, 1982*
- Speech to the workers in Porto *May 15, 1982*
- Moves toward the Anglican Church *May 28, 1982*
- Calls for peace in the Falklands *June 13, 1982*
- Grants an audience to Yasser Arafat *September 15, 1982*
- Canonizes Maximilian Kolbe *October 10, 1982*
- In Spain for the 4th centenary of Saint Theresa of Avila *October 31, 1982*
- Message to the people of Europe in Santiago de Compestela *November 9, 1982*
- Opus Dei becomes the personal prelacy of the pope *November 28, 1982*
- 50th anniversary of his brother Edmund's death *December 5, 1982*
- New Code of Canon Law *January 25, 1983*
- Names 18 cardinals *February 2, 1983*
- Difficult visit to Nicaragua *March 4, 1983*
- Meets Maya Indians in Guatemala *March 7, 1983*
- Allows publication of a comic book on his life *March 23, 1983*
- Opens the Holy Year of the Redemption *March 25, 1983*
- Receives the Holy Shroud of Turin as a gift *March 25, 1983*
- Leaves an *ex-voto* to the Black Virgin *June 19, 1983*
- Beatifies Adam Chmielowski in Cracow *June 22, 1983*
- Made doctor *honoris causa* of Jagiellonian University *June 22, 1983*
- Meeting with Jaruzelski *June 22, 1983*
- Private meeting with Walesa *June 23, 1983*
- Furious with the *Osservatore Romano June 24, 1983*
- Beatifies the painter Fra Angelico *July 8, 1983*
- Pilgrimage to Lourdes sanctuary *August 14, 1983*
- Death of Father Figlewicz *September 23, 1983*
- Publishes charter on family rights *November 24, 1983*
- Vatican staff strike *December 1, 1983*
- First pope to pray in a Protestant church *December 11, 1983*
- Visits Ali Agça in jail *December 27, 1983*
- Resumes diplomatic relations with the United States *January 10, 1984*
- Prays on Gandhi's grave *February 1, 1984*
- Sends Father Popielusko a breviary *February 11, 1984*
- Devotion to the Virgin of Fatima *March 25, 1984*
- Aid to the Church in Need is made a public association *April 6, 1984*
- Apostolic Letter to Jerusalem *April 20, 1984*
- Canonizes 103 martyrs in Seoul *May 6, 1984*
- Speech on ethics and politics in Thailand *May 12, 1984*
- Received by the World Council of Churches in Geneva *June 12, 1984*
- Skis in the Dolomites *July 17, 1984*
- Condemns the "Marxist infiltration in the Church" *August 6, 1984*
- Message of tolerance in Canada *September 20, 1984*
- Reconciles Argentina and Chile *October 18, 1984*
- Shocked by Father Popielusko's murder *October 30, 1984*
- Inaugurates the Vatican's underground rooms *December 1984*
- Convokes a synod on Vatican II *January 25, 1985*

- Denounces extreme ideologies in Ecuador *January 31, 1985*
- Meets Amazonian Indians in Peru *February 6, 1985*
- Grants an audience to Shimon Peres *February 19, 1985*
- First international youth gathering *March 30, 1985*
- Angry outbursts in the Netherlands *May 11, 1985*
- Presides over a ceremony for peace in Ypres *May 17, 1985*
- Celebrates his 65th birthday in Malines (Belgium) *May 18, 1985*
- Encyclical *Slavorum Apostoli* (for ecumenism) *July 2, 1985*
- Calls for dialog between Christians and Muslims in Morocco *August 19, 1985*
- Opens the secret archives of Pius XI and Benedict XV *August 29, 1985*
- Closure of the extraordinary synod *December 8, 1985*
- Institutes World Youth Day *December 20, 1985*
- Guided through Calcutta by Mother Teresa *February 4, 1986*
- Prays on Saint Thomas' grave in Madras *February 5, 1986*
- Conciliatory message to the episcopate of Brazil *April 5, 1986*
- First pope to enter a synagogue *April 13, 1986*
- Receives the representatives of the Albanian diaspora *April 27, 1986*
- Encyclical *Dominum et Vivificantem May 30, 1986*
- Charges council to draw up a universal catechism *June 11, 1986*
- Restores body and soul on Mont Blanc *September 7, 1986*
- Greeted by Reagan in Miami *September 10, 1986*
- High-security visit to France *October 4, 1986*
- Visits Ars sanctuary *October 6, 1986*
- Presides over the World Day of Prayer for Peace in Assisi *October 27, 1986*
- Grants an audience to General Jaruzelski *January 13, 1987*
- Message on World Day of Peace *January 1987*
- Death of Father Zacher *February 13, 1987*
- Grants an audience to Ali Agça's mother *February 20, 1987*
- Skis in the Abruzzi (Italy) *February 1987*
- Opposed to artificial insemination *March 13, 1987*
- Encyclical on the role of the Virgin in the Church *March 25, 1987*
- Addresses youths in Chile *April 2, 1987*
- Speech in Santiago on human rights *April 3, 1987*
- In Buenos Aires for the second World Youth Day *April 12, 1987*
- Beatifies Edith Stein in Cologne *May 1, 1987*
- Speech in Augsburg, Lutheran sanctuary *May 3, 1987*
- Opens Marian Year *June 7, 1987*
- Receives triumphant welcome in Poland *June 8, 1987*
- Meets Lech Walesa in Gdansk *June 11, 1987*
- Prays on Father Popielusko's grave *June 14, 1987*
- Receives Kurt Waldheim *June 25, 1987*
- Holidays in the Dolomites *July 8, 1987*
- Embraces a child suffering from AIDS *September 17, 1987*
- Beatifies Marcel Callo *October 4, 1987*
- Receives the patriarch of Constantinople *December 3, 1987*
- Names Michael Sabbah patriarch of Jerusalem *December 28, 1987*
- Defends the Christian view of marriage *January 25, 1988*
- Message for 21st World Day of Peace *January 1988*
- Encyclical *Sollicitudo Rei Socialis February 19, 1988*
- Receives letter of criticism from Mgr. Lefebvre *June 2, 1988*
- Calls Mgr. Lefebvre to order *June 9, 1988*
- Beatifies 117 martyrs *June 19, 1988*
- Homily at Mauthausen camp *June 24, 1988*
- Names 25 cardinals *June 28, 1988*
- Excommunicates Mgr. Lefebvre *July 2, 1988*
- Holidays in the Cadore mountains *July 13, 1988*
- Attends performance of play by the Comédie Française *July 27, 1988*

- Closes Marian Year *August 15, 1988*
- Apostolic *Letter to Women September 30, 1988*
- Speech on Europe in Strasbourg *October 11, 1988*
- Explains the strategy of the Church in Europe *November 5, 1988*
- Receives Alexander Dubcek *November 19, 1988*
- Message for the World Day of Peace *January 1989*
- Receives Andrei Sakharov *February 6, 1989*
- Letter to his friend Jurek *May 9, 1989*
- Calls for ecumenical unity in Scandinavia *June 10, 1989*
- In Santiago de Compostela for the 4th World Youth Day *August 19, 1989*
- Calls for the reconciliation of Koreans *October 8, 1989*
- Denounces the philosophers of the Enlightenment *November 25, 1989*
- Receives Gorbachev *December 1, 1989*
- Confidence on Gorbachev *January 25, 1990*
- Plants a tree in the Cumura leprosy *January 28, 1990*
- Declares: "It is God who has vanquished in the East" *April 21, 1990*
- Speech in Prague on Europe's Christian identity *April 21, 1990*
- Calls for peace in the Gulf region *August 24, 1990*
- Witness to Africa's poverty *September 2, 1990*
- Consecrates Yamoussoukro Cathedral *September 10, 1990*
- Codifies the laws of the Eastern Churches *October 18, 1990*
- Names Mgr. Sodano Vatican secretary of State *December 1, 1990*
- First pope to quote the Talmud *December 6, 1990*
- *The Jeweller's Shop* is adapted for the cinema *December 1990*
- Encyclical *Redemptoris Missio January 22, 1991*
- Encyclical *Centesimus Annus May 1, 1991*
- Gives thanks to the Virgin of Fatima *May 13, 1991*
- Answers the Orthodox Church's accusations *June 3, 1991*
- Bitterness of his trip to Poland *June 9, 1991*
- Addresses the consistory of cardinals *June 28, 1991*
- Private visit to Cracow and Wadowice *August 13, 1991*
- In Czestochowa for the 6th World Youth Day *August 14, 1991*
- Prays with Lutheran archbishops *October 5, 1991*
- Opposed to the Gulf war *October 15, 1991*
- Denounces the exploitation of Brazilian children *October 20, 1991*
- Calls Mgr. Gaillot to order *January 22, 1992*
- Visits the slave island of Gorée *January 22, 1992*
- Institutes World Day for the Sick *May 13, 1992*
- Beatifies Sister Bakhita and Mgr. Escriva de Balaguer *May 17, 1992*
- Undergoes operation for a tumor of the colon *July 15, 1992*
- Leaves hospital *July 27, 1992*
- Calls for peace in the Balkans *August 22, 1992*
- Mass in Santo Domingo *October 12, 1992*
- Invited to visit Israel *October 23, 1992*
- Promulgates a new catechism *December 7, 1992*
- Inherits his aunts' house in Cracow *1992*
- Prays for peace in Assisi *January 9, 1993*
- Calls for chastity in order to combat AIDS *February 6, 1993*
- Insists on respect for tolerance in Sudan *February 10, 1993*
- Does not fear critics *March 10, 1993*
- Ends a 10-year dispute in Auschwitz *April 14, 1993*
- Encourages democracy in Albania *April 25, 1993*
- Gives warning to the Mafia *May 9, 1993*
- Receives Abouna Paulos *June 11, 1993*
- In Denver for the 8th World Youth Day *August 14, 1993*
- Climbs the Hill of Crosses in Lithuania *September 7, 1993*
- Surprises the faithful in Riga *September 9, 1993*
- Encyclical *Veritas Splendor October 5, 1993*
- Grants an interview to a number of newspapers *November 2, 1993*
- Grants an audience to Elias Hraoui *November 5, 1993*
- Dislocates his right shoulder *November 11, 1993*

- Rumors about his health *December 1, 1993*
- Denounces the "deification of the nation" *January 6, 1994*
- Mass in the restored Sistine Chapel *April 8, 1994*
- Falls while skiing *April 1994*
- Breaks his hip bone *April 28, 1994*
- Has a hip replacement for his right leg *April 29, 1994*
- Creates a nuns' cloister in the Vatican *May 10, 1994*
- Rejects the ordination of women priests *May 22, 1994*
- Continues to accomplish his tasks *May 1994*
- Taken ill during mass *August 26, 1994*
- Undergoes physical therapy in Castel Gandolfo *August 1994*
- Learns of his own death! *September 4, 1994*
- Furious at UN project *September 5, 1994*
- Trip to Sarajevo cancelled *September 6, 1994*
- Too weak to kiss the Croatian ground *September 10, 1994*
- Receives Schamouel Hadas *September 29, 1994*
- Publishes *Crossing the Threshold of Hope* *October 20, 1994*
- Prepares Jubilee for the year 2000 *November 10, 1994*
- Names 30 cardinals *November 26, 1994*
- Publishes *Letter to Children December 13, 1994*
- Dismisses Mgr. Gaillot *January 13, 1995*
- Receives cold welcome in Colombo *January 20, 1995*
- Encyclical *Evangelicum Vitae March 30, 1995*
- Beatifies two Italian women *April 4, 1995*
- Denounces "the worship of the cult of the nation" *May 8, 1995*
- Answers rumors about his resignation *May 18, 1995*
- Canonizes martyr Jan Sarkander *May 21, 1995*
- Ignored by the faithful in Prague *May 30, 1995*
- Encyclical *Ut Unum Sint May 30, 1995*
- Pays tribute to Baudouin I, king of Belgium *June 3, 1995*
- Publishes *Letter to Women July 10, 1995*
- Signs the exhortation *Ecclesia in Africa* in Yaoundé *September 15, 1995*
- Reaffirms the rules of the conclave *November 22, 1995*
- Interrupts his Christmas speech *December 25, 1995*
- Calls Sarajevo "the Jerusalem of Europe" *January 1996*
- Pleased about progress toward peace in South America *February 11, 1996*
- Calls for television-free diet *February 21, 1996*
- Has a sudden fever *March 15, 1996*
- Resumes his activities *March 25, 1996*
- Visits the Colle di Val d'Elsa and Sienna *March 30, 1996*
- Calls Islam to "a respect for the differences" *April 14, 1996*
- Tribute to Raoul Follereau *April 27, 1996*
- Denounces Western materialism in Berlin *June 22, 1996*
- Learns of the assassination of the archbishop of Oran *August 1, 1996*
- Goes to the Vendée (France) *September 19, 1996*
- Speech in Brittany on the family *September 20, 1996*
- Undergoes appendicitis operation *October 6, 1996*
- Leaves hospital *October 15, 1996*
- Publishes *My Priestly Ordination November 1, 1996*
- Grants Fidel Castro a private audience *November 19, 1996*
- Receives Benyamin Netanyahu *February 3, 1997*
- Risky trip to Sarajevo *April 13, 1997*
- Calls for restoring the sovereignty of Lebanon *May 11, 1997*
- 7th visit to Poland *May 31, 1997*

- Addresses the young in Poznan *June 3, 1997*
- Celebrates St. Adalbert's millennium *June 3, 1997*
- Grants himself a day's rest *June 5, 1997*
- Canonizes Queen Edwige in Cracow *June 8, 1997*
- Prays at his family's grave *June 9, 1997*
- In Paris for the 12th World Youth Day *August 21, 1997*
- Beatifies Frédéric Ozanam *August 22, 1997*
- Closes the World Youth Day at Longchamp (France) *August 24, 1997*
- Pays tribute to Mother Teresa *September 13, 1997*
- Grants an audience to Ali Agça's brother *November 12, 1997*
- Leaves an *ex-voto* to the Virgin of Fatima *December 1997*
- Historic trip to Cuba *January 25, 1998*
- Receives Boris Yeltsin *February 10, 1998*
- Called to order by his secretary *February 1998*
- Asks the Jews for forgiveness *March 16, 1998*
- Names Stanislaw Dziwisz bishop *March 19, 1998*
- Speech in Nigeria *March 23, 1998*
- *Our God's Father* is adapted for the cinema *March 27, 1998*
- Ritual kissing of the feet at Santa Maria Maggiore *April 10, 1998*
- Condolences to the parents of Commandant Estermann *May 4, 1998*
- Reaches longest pontificate of the 20th century *May 22, 1998*
- Prays before the Holy Shroud of Turin *May 24, 1998*
- Beatifies the Croatian primate Mgr. Stepinac *October 3, 1998*
- 13th encyclical: *Fides et Ratio October 15, 1998*
- Canonizes Edith Stein *October 11, 1998*
- Opens the legal archives of the Vatican *December 1998*
- Receives a Jewish delegation *January 13, 1999*
- Trip to Missouri and Mexico *January 22 to January 28, 1999*
- Meets Iranian head of State Mohammad Khatami in Rome *March 11, 1999*
- Launching of laser disc *Abba Pater March 23, 1999*
- Calls for peace in Kosovo *April 4, 1999*
- Canonizes Marcellin Champagnat *April 18, 1999*
- In Bucharest for biggest Othodox/Catholic meeting *May 7 to May 9, 1999*
- Longest trip in Poland *June 5 to June 17, 1999*
- Presides over the opening of the Holy Doors at St. Peter's *December 24, 1999*
- Impassioned plea for tolerance and respect at the foot of Mount Sinai (Egypt) *February 2000*
- Pilgrimage in Palestine, Jordan and Israel *March 2000*

Wojtyla, Maciej (Karol's paternal grandfather)
- Birth in Lipnik *January 1, 1852 (or February 1, 1852)*
- Marries Anna Przeczek *September 3, 1878*
- Birth of his son Karol *July 18, 1879*
- Birth of his grandson Edmund *August 27, 1906*
- Birth of his grandson Karol Jozef *May 18, 1920*
- Death in Lipnik *September 23, 1923*

Wojtyla, Olga
- Dies soon after her birth *January 1914*

Wojtyla, Stefania Adelayda (Karol's half-aunt)
- Birth *December 16, 1891*
- Death in Cracow *May 24, 1962*

World Youth Day (national meeting once a year and international every other year)
- Created by John Paul II *December 20, 1985*
- Held in Buenos Aires *April 12, 1987*
- Held at Santiago de Compostela *August 19, 1989*
- Held at Czestochowa *August 14, 1991*
- Held in Denver *August 14, 1993*
- Held in Manila *January 14, 1995*

- Held in Paris *August 18, 1997*

Wrezinski, Joseph
- Founder of ATD Fourth World *1957*
- Homage paid by John Paul II *August 21, 1997*

Wyporek, Stanislaw (Father Wojtyla's secretary)
- Kidnapped and beaten up by the secret police *December 1954*

Wyszynski, Stefan
- Birth in Zuzela *August 3, 1901*
- Named primate of Poland by Pius XII *November 12, 1948*
- Confronted with Polish repression *February 1949*
- Manages to avoid all schism within the Polish Church *January 27, 1951*
- Under house arrest in Silesia *September 26, 1953*
- Disowned by bishops *September 28, 1953*
- Message to the pilgrims of Czestochowa *August 26, 1956*
- Returns to Warsaw *October 28, 1956*
- Names Father Wojtyla bishop of Cracow *July 4, 1958*
- Attends opening of Vatican II with Mgr. Wojtyla *October 11, 1962*
- Calls for German-Polish forgiveness *November 18, 1965*
- Stopped from going to Rome *June 29, 1967*
- Meets Prime Minister Jaroszewicz *March 3, 1971*
- Attends beatification of Maximilian Kolbe *October 17, 1971*
- New Year message to the Catholics *January 1, 1972*
- Involves the Church in the political debate *January 1974*
- Receives birthday gift from the Communist regime *August 3, 1976*
- Delivers Epiphany sermon *January 6, 1978*
- Reconciliation trip to West Germany *September 25, 1978*
- Attends John Paul II's enthronement ceremony *October 22, 1978*
- Dying, he receives the pope's blessing *May 25, 1981*
- Death in Warsaw *May 28, 1981*
- Funeral *May 31, 1981*

YZ

Yeltsin, Boris
- Received at the Vatican *February 10, 1998*

Young Christian Workers (JOC)
- Founded by Abbot Cardijn *July 20, 1924*
- First world congress at Laeken *August 25, 1935*
- Death of Mgr. Cardijn *July 24, 1967*

Zacher, Edward (Wadowice priest)
- Takes Karol Wojtyla as choirboy *1931*
- Receives Mgr. Sapieha *May 6, 1938*
- Greets Mgr. Wojtyla *November 10, 1946*
- Karol is elected pope *October 16, 1978*
- Wishes "Charles" a happy patron saint's day *November 4, 1978*
- Death in Wadowice *February 13, 1987*

Zaire
- Visit of John Paul II *May 1980*
- Pope's second visit *August 1985*
- The Vatican recognizes Zairean mass *September 1988*

Zak, Franciszek
- Baptizes Karol in Wadowice *June 20, 1920*

Zambia
- Visit of John Paul II *April 1989*

Zanussi, Krzysztof
- Adapts Karol Wojtyla's *Our God's Brother* for the cinema *March 27, 1998*

Zimbabwe
- Visit of John Paul II *September 1988*

Picture credits

While every effort has been made to trace the copyright of the photographs and illustrations used in this publication, there may be an instance where an error has been made in the picture credits. If this is the case, we apologize for the mistake and ask the copyright holder to contact the publisher so that it can be rectified.
The position of a picture is indicated by letters : b = bottom, t = top, r = right, l = left, m = middle.

Front cover – r: Corbis – l: Sipa/Rex
Back cover – tl: AKG London – ml: Sipa/Rex – bl: Profile/Rex – tr and br: Sipa/Rex
1 – Corbis UK Ltd: AFP
3 – Corbis UK Ltd: AFP
5 – Hulton Getty
6 – Keystone
10 – b: W. Laski/Sipa Press – t: Viviane Rivière/Sipa Press
11 – br: W. Laski/Sipa Press – t and bl: L'Illustration/Sygma
12 – t: Sipa Press – b: DR/Adam Boniecki
13 – t: DR/JLSA – b: W. Laski/Sipa Press
14 – L'Illustration/Sygma
15 – L'Illustration/Sygma
16 – t: DR/JLSA – b: L'Illustration/Sygma
17 – t: DR/JLSA – b: Viviane Rivière/Sipa Press
18 – t: L'Illustration/Sygma – b: DR/Adam Boniecki
19 – t and b: L'Illustration/Sygma
20 – W. Laski/Sipa Press
21 – Viviane Rivière/Sipa Press
22 – W. Laski/Sipa Press
23 – L'Illustration/Sygma
24 – Adam Bujak
25 – t: L'Illustration/Sygma – bl: Adam Bujak – br: Viviane Rivière/Sipa Press
26 – W. Laski/Sipa Press
27 – t: DR/JLSA – bl: DR/Adam Boniecki – br: Keystone/Sygma
28 – Keystone
29 – t and b: DR/JLSA
30 – L'Illustration/Sygma
31 – DR/Adam Boniecki
32 – t and b: L'Illustration/Sygma
33 – t: L'Illustration/Sygma – br: Adam Bujak – bl: Keystone
34 – t: Adam Bujak – bl: DR/JLSA – br: Viviane Rivière/Sipa Press
35 – t and b: DR/JLSA
36 – t: Viviane Rivière/Sipa Press – b: Adam Bujak
37 – t: L'Illustration/Sygma – b: Editions Chronique
38 – t: DR/JLSA – b: Adam Bujak
39 – t, bl, and br: Adam Bujak
40 – t: DR/JLSA – b: Keystone
41 – W. Laski/Sipa Press
42 – t: Adam Bujak – b: Keystone
43 – b: W. Laski/Sipa Press – t: Viviane Rivière/Sipa Press
44 – t: Bildarchiv (T) – b: Editions Chronique

45 – t and bl: Konrad Pollesch – mr: DR/JLSA
46 – W. Laski/Sipa Press
47 – t and m: DR/JLSA – bl: DR/Adam Boniecki – br: Interpress
48 – t: L'Illustration/Sygma – b: Adam Bujak
49 – t: DR/JLSA – b: W. Laski/Sipa Press
50 – t and b: DR/JLSA
51 – t: L'Illustration/Sygma – b: DR/JLSA
52 – t: DR/JLSA – b: Adam Bujak
53 – t: DR/JLSA – b: Konrad Pollesch
54 – t: DR/JLSA – b: W. Laski/Sipa Press
55 – L'Illustration/Sygma
56 – tr: W. Laski/Sipa Press – l and br: Adam Bujak
57 – Adam Bujak
58 – t: Keystone – b: Adam Bujak
59 – t: Keystone (T) – b: Adam Bujak
60 – b: W. Laski/Sipa Press – t: Photoreport/Sipa Press
61 – t: Adam Bujak – b: DR/JLSA
62 – t: DR – b: Keystone
63 – Jan Babecki
64 – t: DR – b: Adam Bujak
65 – t: Adam Bujak – b: Keystone
66 – t and br: Keystone – bl: Jan Babecki
67 – DR/Adam Boniecki
68 – t: Keystone – b: Adam Bujak
69 – t: James Andanson/Sygma – b: Keystone
70 – Adam Bujak
71 – Adam Bujak
72 – t and b: Adam Bujak
73 – tl and tr: DR/JLSA – b: Adam Bujak
74 – t: W. Laski/Sipa Press – b: Keystone (T)
75 – Adam Bujak
76 – t: Adam Bujak – b: DR
77 – t: DR/Tygodnik Powszechny – b: DR/JLSA
78 – t: Adam Bujak – bl and br: W. Laski/Sipa Press
79 – t: W. Laski/Sipa Press – b: Keystone
80 – t and b: DR/JLSA
81 – t and b: Adam Bujak
82 – t and br: Sipa Press – bl: East News/Sipa Press
83 – t: Keystone – b: DR/Adam Boniecki
84 – DR/Tygodnik Powszechny
85 – t: Alain Keler/Sygma – b: W. Laski/Sipa Press
86 – Adam Bujak
87 – t: Adam Bujak – b: DR/JLSA
88 – t and b: Keystone
89 – tl and bl: Adam Bujak – r: DR/Adam Boniecki
90 – b: W. Laski/Sipa Press – t: Boccon-Gibod/Sipa Press
91 – b: Fabian/Sygma – tl and tr: Alain Keler/Sygma
92 – t: James Andanson/Sygma – b: Boccon-Gibod/Sipa Press
93 – t and b: Alain Keler/Sygma
94 – b: Fabian/Sygma – t: Boccon-Gibod/Sipa Press
95 – t: Boccon-Gibod/Sipa Press – b: Howe/Sipa Press
96 – t: Sygma – b: Fabian/Sygma
97 – t: L'Illustration/Sygma – bl: W. Laski/Sipa Press – br: Guadrini/Sipa Press

98 – t: Keystone – b: Henri Bureau/Sygma
99 – t and bl: Boccon-Gibod-Setboun/Sipa Press – br: Fabian/Sygma
100 – t: L'Illustration/Sygma – br: Giniès/Sipa Press – bl: Sipa Press
101 – t: W. Laski/Sipa Press – b: Setboun/Sipa Press
102 – t: Boccon-Gibod/Sipa Press – b: Sygma
103 – t: L'Illustration/Sygma – b: Keystone
104 – t: Zihnioglu/Sipa Press – b: Fabian/Sygma
105 – t: Zihnioglu/Sipa Press – b: Keystone
106 – b: Fabian/Sygma – t: Boccon-Gibod/Sipa Press
107 – t: Peltier/Sipa Press – b: W. Laski/Sipa Press
108 – Fabian/Sygma
109 – mr and bl: P. Robert/Sipa Press – t: Torregano/Sipa Press
110 – t: Sygma – b: W. Laski/Keystone
111 – t and bl: Keystone – br: Sihnioglu/Sipa Press
112 – t: Sygma – b: Durand-Aubert/Sygma
113 – t: La Penna/Sipa Press – b: Komenich/Sipa Press
114 – t: Keystone/Sygma – b: Matteini/Sipa Press
115 – b: Petillot/Sipa Press – t: Alain Noguès/Sygma
116 – t: Alain Keler/Sygma – b: Sipa Press
117 – t: Wallis/Sipa Press (T) – b: B. Bisson/Sygma
118 – t: Kipa – b: B. Bisson/Sygma
119 – t: Nicolas/Sipa Press – b: B. Bisson/Sygma
120 – Giansanti-Fabian/Sygma
121 – t: A. Gyori/Sygma – b: W. Laski/Sipa Press
122 – t: Sipa Press – b: DR/Tygodnik Powszechny
123 – b: DR/Tygodnik Powszechny – t: Franco Origlia/Sygma
124 – t: Witt/Sipa Press – b: Terpini Ilya/Sipa Press
125 – t: G. Wampler/Sygma – b: G. de Keerle/Sygma
126 – t and b: Franco Origlia/Sygma
127 – t and b: Galazka/Sipa Press
128 – t: Pizzoli-Origlia/Sygma – b: Franco Origlia/Sygma
129 – t and m: Franco Origlia/Sygma – b: Sygma
130 – t: G. Giansanti/Sygma – b: Franco Origlia/Sygma
131 – t: R. Bossu/Sygma – b: Viviane Rivière/Sipa Press
132 – Sygma (T)
133 – t: DR/JLSA – bl: Malanca/Sipa Press – br: Sama/Sipa Press
134 – t: Sygma – b: Franco Origlia/Sygma
135 – t: Sygma – b: Galazka/Sipa Press
136 – t: Jorge Nunez/Sipa Press – b: Galazka/Sipa Press
137 – t: Laski/Sipa Press – b: Pool Vatican/Sygma
138 – Corbis UK Ltd: Reuters Newmedia Inc.
139 – Corbis UK Ltd: AFP
140 – t, m, and b: Mary Evans Picture Library
141 – t: Bridgeman Art Library: Private Collection – m: Mary Evans Picture Library: Sarah Lorimar Collection – b: Rex Features